Northern Voices
Inuit Writing in English

NORTHERN VOICES

Inuit Writing in English

EDITED BY PENNY PETRONE

University of Toronto Press

Toronto Buffalo London

© University of Toronto Press 1988
Toronto Buffalo London
Printed in Canada

ISBN 0-8020-5772-1

Printed on acid-free paper

Canadian Cataloguing in Publication Data

Main entry under title:

Northern voices : Inuit writing in English

Bibliography: p.
Includes index.
ISBN 0-8020-5772-1

1. Inuit literature – Canada – Translations into
English.*   2. English literature – Translations
from Inuktitut.*   3. Canadian literature (English) –
Inuit authors.*   4. Inuit – Canada – History –
Sources.*   I. Petrone, Penny.

PS8235.I65N67   1988   C897'.1   C88-094169-3
PR9194.5.E84N67   1988

The Gladys and Merrill Muttart Foundation helped
defray the costs of field research for this book. Further
assistance with the writing was provided by the Ontario
Arts Council under its writers' grant program.

This book has been published with the help of financial
assistance from Multiculturalism Canada and from the
Canada Council and the Ontario Arts Council under
their block grant programs.

Contents

Preface

They used to be called Eskimos by Europeans, but now some prefer to be called Inuit, *the people*. Isolated from the rest of the world and from each other, they once believed that they were the only *true* human beings anywhere. Their very presence for century after century in the vast and harsh land that is Canada's north was a marvel of survival.

In recent years modern technology, as well as government interest and activity, has ended their isolation and made survival easier. Almost all of Canada's 28,000 Inuit now live in permanent settlements scattered throughout the Northwest Territories, Yukon, Labrador, and northern Quebec. They share a relatively common culture as well as one basic language, called Inuktitut. Six regional dialects are spoken across the Canadian Arctic in Labrador, Baffin Island, northern Quebec, Keewatin, central Arctic, and western Arctic. There are eight main cultural groupings: the Labrador, Ungava, Baffin Island, the four principal groups of the central Arctic – the Iglulik, the Netsilik, the Caribou, the Copper – and the western Arctic Inuit. Within these broad groups there are also a number of subgroups, identified with a place and named accordingly, for example, the Aivilingmiut or 'people of the walrus,' a branch of the Iglulik.

Their material culture – stone carvings, prints, and weaving – are known all over the world. But Inuit intellectual culture is not as well known despite the fact that for a thousand years and more, in a long history that has no certain beginning, Canada's Inuit have been transmitting the wisdom and truth of their ancestors in stories and songs.

This book presents this literature as it has survived in historical writings and in modern memory. It traces the evolution in Canada of

Inuit writing in English from an oral literature of a non-western culture, through transitional stages of varying degrees of acculturation, to its modern expression.

Traditionally there was no written language. 'We were stupid. We should have thought of writing on sealskins,' said Peter Pitseolak in *Peter Pitseolak's Escape from Death*. Writing systems for Inuktitut were introduced by Christian missionaries after European contact, and literacy began its spread. But the development of literacy throughout Canada's Arctic varied markedly by region in time and orthography.

Although explorers from different countries – Britain, France, Norway, Denmark, Germany, and the United States – kept arriving in different parts of the Arctic at different times, over a period of 400 years, encounters were brief and sporadic and made no substantial impact on Inuit literacy. British and American whalers, who spent winters on their shore-based whaling stations off the east coast of Baffin Island, around Hudson Bay, and the Beaufort Sea, and hired Inuit as pilots, sledge-drivers, harpooners, and seamstresses throughout the latter half of the nineteenth and the early twentieth century, were responsible for profound change in Inuit lifestyles with their day-to-day contact, but their influence on Inuit literacy was minimal. The Hudson's Bay Company first established posts on the shores of Hudson Bay and James Bay in the later seventeenth century. It did not expand its operations in much of the Arctic until into the twentieth century, and its primary concern was always trade.

Literacy was made possible only by the systematic efforts of the missionaries who provided education for the Inuit until after World War II.

The Moravian missionaries, who established permanent missions among the Inuit of Greenland as early as 1721, in 1771 began setting up stations along the coast of Labrador where they taught the fundamentals of Christianity, as well as how to read and write the Labrador dialect in a Moravian orthography. Literacy in the rest of the Arctic was introduced by the Protestant missionaries sent by the Church of England's Church Missionary Society and Roman Catholic missionaries from the Oblates of Mary Immaculate. They began introducing Roman orthographies to write Inuktitut in the Mackenzie region in the second half of the nineteenth century. Almost all early reading material published in Inuktitut was religious in nature.

In the eastern Canadian Arctic (except Labrador) the development of writing systems was different. The Reverend Edmund James Peck, who in 1894 established the first permanent mission station on Baffin Island, began using a system adapted from James Evans's Cree syllabics mainly to spread the Gospel. The Inuit quickly became skilful in the use of syllabics, learning from missionaries, native lay ministers, parents, or other Inuit, and the syllabic orthography soon spread across the Arctic.

Although the Inuit first began writing their own language in the various orthographies as early as the eighteenth century in Labrador, and as late as the first quarter of the twentieth century elsewhere, writing in English has been a recent development. Soon after World War II, the Canadian government began a new and serious involvement in the north by establishing centralized communities, replacing mission schools with new residential schools, and creating a formal education system. Since the early 1960s the intensity and quality of education have increased with an ever-growing number of young people writing in English. More recently, however, there has been a revival of interest in the preservation and use of Inuktitut as well as attempts to standardize the various regional dialects and orthographies. And in 1988 almost all material is published bilingually (English and Inuktitut) or trilingually (English, Inuktitut, and French).

In this book selections have been arranged to give historical perspective and continuity. The first chapter celebrates the oral tradition of a pre-literate society and is organized according to the eight cultural groupings. The principal source for this literature is the *Report of the Fifth Thule Expedition, 1921–24* by the celebrated Danish explorer, Knud Rasmussen, who made an unrivalled four-year sledge journey across Arctic North America, studying the Inuit who lived between southern Baffin Island and the Coronation Gulf. He thus documented for the white world the existence of an integrated Inuit culture from Greenland to the Pacific. Other important sources include the German Franz Boas, the first anthropologist to do field work in Canada, who studied the Inuit around Cumberland Sound, Baffin Island, during the winter of 1883–4, and Diamond Jenness, Canada's most distinguished pioneer anthropologist and a member of the Canadian Arctic Expedition of 1913–18.

Chapter 2 presents the comments and observations made by some of the first Inuit to come into contact with the white newcomers, the first Inuit reactions to European and American values and institutions, as documented in official reports, oral interviews, letters, and diaries. These are the earliest examples of Inuit speaking and writing in English. Chapter 3 enters into the first Inuit attempts at European forms in the world of the autobiography, narrative, memoir, reminiscence, letter, and novel. This transitional literature represents a break with oral tradition and is typical of newly literate people everywhere. Chapter 4 provides diverse samples of contemporary Inuit writing in English from essays and speeches to fiction and poetry and other genres of imaginative literature. The chronological context is not always precise. The line between what can be considered personal narrative and early contact literature, moreover, is at times oblique, and I have had to be arbitrary in my decisions. I have also included four selections by polar Inuit and one by an Alaskan Inuk in the interests of circumpolar unity, since the Inuit used to be a migratory people, moving about freely in the Arctic.

This book includes all types of writing, such as letters, diary entries, speeches, essays, history, autobiography, and reports. Its scope is as wide as possible in content, form, regional coverage, and authorship. Selections have been chosen primarily for their intrinsic literary merit. But because they are unique and universal at the same time, they offer new insights into the way of life and thought of the Inuit people. And because these selections differ in aesthetics, structure, and style, they open new ways of looking at a people's literature.

In the growth of an Inuit literary tradition in English, the intermediate stage between the pre-literate past and literate present – between the oral in Inuktitut and the written in English – is, perforce, one of translation. Hence, many of the selections in this collection are in English translation, either directly from the Inuktitut or indirectly from the Danish and German. Many have been translated by native speakers who speak both Inuktitut and English.

But translation of any language poses difficulties. And the orthographical diversity of Inuit dialects in addition to the archaic expressions make transcription difficult and translation even more difficult. The holophrastic nature of Inuktitut, moreover, as well as the great differences of syntax and sentence structure between a non-western and western language, not to mention the linguistic competence of the translator, add to the problem. One can only guess, therefore, what subtleties of thought and style have been lost through translation. Despite these drawbacks, the selected pieces, most of which have been translated by native speakers, retain their vigour and effect. They are distinctively the Inuit's own, in their emotions, attitudes, sensitivities and visions, subject matter, idiom, and allusions. They provide the link between the cultural past and its expression in the present.

Except for correcting obvious printing errors, I have not altered any text. Each piece appears with its own stylistic devices and peculiarities of spelling, grammar, syntax, and punctuation, preserved to show development in the use of language. Brief introductions to each item give background and contextual purposes. A glossary of Inuktitut words and their English translations as well as a few pertinent notes are also provided. I have tried to resist critical interpretation or comments to allow the Inuit authors to speak for themselves.

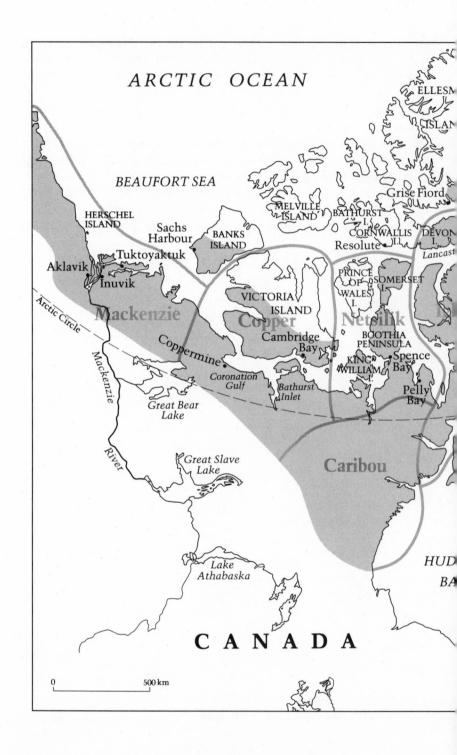

KALAALLIT
NUNAAT

Nettilling
Fiord

Pangnirtung

Kekerten

CUMBERLAND SOUND

Blacklead

Cape
Mercy

BAFFIN
ISLAND

0   40 km

le

Cape
York

BAFFIN
BAY

FIN ISLAND

South Baffin

Iqaluit

ATLANTIC

OCEAN

Ungava   Labrador

1 'There Was Might in Their Tongues'

ORAL TRADITIONS

... in the time of long, long ago. They did not understand how to hide words in written signs like you do; they could only speak, the men that lived before us.

Augustine Courtauld, *From the Ends of the Earth*
(London: Oxford University Press 1958) 384

It is not always that we want a point in our stories, if only they are amussing [sic]. It is only the white men that want a reason and an explanation of everything; and so our old men say that we should treat white man as children who always want their own way. If not, they become angry, and scold.

Rasmussen, *Intellectual Culture of the Copper Eskimos* 124

These stories were made when all unbelievable things could happen.

Rasmussen, *Intellectual Culture of the Iglulik Eskimos* 257

Inuit oral literature may be distinguished by two distinct forms: narrative and song. Narrative encompassed myths or sacred stories of origin and creation; legends, which told of fantastic events popularly regarded as historical; folk-tales, which included beast fables; and oral history, which reported events believed to be true within a tradition of eyewitnesses. Oral song incorporated traditional songs and poetry, both ritual and secular.

Although the ancient narratives differed from one geographical group to another as to details, regional variations were remarkably similar in subject and theme, considering the 4,000 miles of frozen coastline from Tuktoyaktuk in the west to Labrador in the east. When Danish Arctic explorer Knud Rasmussen asked the Iglulik woman, Orulo, to account for the variations, she replied, 'all this that we are talking about now happened in a time so far back that there was no time at all. We Eskimos do not concern our selves with solving all riddles' (*Intellectual Culture of the Iglulik Eskimos* 69).

Much of this ancient folklore has been lost over the years and much of what has survived is fragmented. Although oral narrative was literature in performance that to a large extent defined its form and content, the extant corpus, even on the printed page, is testimony to a rich, precious birthright that is still a great source of spiritual energy and physical strength.

A variety of representative narratives are presented in this chapter, from the ancient Iglulik myth of the origin of the sun and moon – in their human life they were doomed to eternal separation because as sister and brother they had committed incest – to a legend about a local landscape feature around Nain in Labrador. All are of great interest because they take us into a world where the basic assumptions about the universe and mankind's place in it are alien concepts to non-Inuit thought.

'Among the arts of the Eskimo, poetry and music are by far the most prominent,' wrote anthropologist Franz Boas in 1888 (*The Central Eskimo* 240). The Inuit were outstanding song-makers and poets. Oral song was part of every Inuk's way of life. That delight in the genius of a language that could create over a score of words to differentiate the various kinds of snow or the successive stages of a deer's growth made every man a poet. Singing was as vital to life as breathing. The eminent Netsilik shaman-poet Orpingalik explained to Knud Rasmussen that 'all my being is song and I sing

as I draw breath' [*Intellectual Culture of the Netsilik Eskimos* 16].
Although a measure of skill in composition was expected of everyone, and although outstanding poets like Orpingalik, Aua, and
Ivaluartjuk were admired, they were not set apart, socially or eco-
nomically, by virtue of their skill.

Orpingalik stressed the element of improvisation and spontaneity
when he said, 'the words we need will come themselves ... shoot
up of themselves' (ibid 321), but the problems of composition were a
constant preoccupation in many poems. Considered by Rasmussen
as one of his best singers, Ivaluartjuk lamented that 'songs/Call for
strength/And I seek after words' [*Intellectual Culture of the Iglulik
Eskimos* 19]. And Orpingalik himself gave his poetry all the deliber-
ation and self-conscious attention that were typical of many traditional poems.

In ancient times the *word* was sacrosanct. It embodied the very
essence of being. And it carried the power to make things happen.
Through this sacred power, the Inuit sought to shape and control the
cosmic forces that govern human life.

The shaman, who was priest, physician, and prophet, possessed
this special power with words. He was not only required to master
the difficult shaman's language, much of which was so ancient that
its exact meaning has been lost, but also expected to have a large
repertoire of magic songs, prayers, and words. The shaman's faith in
his magic words was so enormous that he actually believed they
had the power to stop the bleeding from a wound: 'This is blood/
That flowed from a piece of wood' (ibid 167). Going into a self-
induced trance he would compose words characterized by the special
metaphorical shaman's language to summon his helping spirits to
bring good fortune and work miracles.

In addition to the magic songs, secular music including dancing
songs and lullabies celebrated the experience of daily life, such as
hunting and fishing. Often woven into the texture of such practical
matters was a concern with old age and death, the difficulties of
composition, and the importance of a man's reputation and his self-
esteem.

The spirit of rivalry, which characterized Inuit games and sports,
was also found in Inuit song. Song contests were held regularly,
and song duels were used for amusement and judicial purposes.
When used to resolve grudges and disputes, these songs of derision,
which relied on cryptic allusion and ironic understatement for their

4

good-natured humour or vitriolic ridicule, functioned as a court of justice.

Traditional Inuit poetry was intense and direct. In a society where there were no luxuries, it is not surprising that the poetic imagination was straightforward and sparse with the sophisticated economy of the Japanese *haiku*. The power of the emotion is isolated in a few words, in sharp and vivid images. The American anthropologist, Edmund Carpenter, expressed his amazement at the poetic genius of the Inuit, when he wrote 'that within this prison of ice and wind they are able to draw from themselves images, powerful enough to deny their nothingness' (*Anerca*).

IGLULIK

O   **Ivaluartjuk** (fl. 1921), Iglulik story-teller and singer, was regarded by Rasmussen, who met him at Lyon Inlet, as one of his best informants. Ivaluartjuk recalled the miseries of winter and summer, as symbolized in *cold* and *mosquitoes*, and reflected self-consciously on the process of poetic composition. (It is interesting to note that Vilhjalmur Stefansson, the great Canadian Arctic explorer, considered the mosquitoes far more serious than winter darkness, cold, or violent winds.)

Cold and Mosquitoes

Cold and mosquitoes,
These two pests
Come never together.
I lay me down on the ice,
Lay me down on the snow and ice,
Till my teeth fall chattering.
It is I,
Aja – aja – ja.

Memories are they,
From those days,
From those days,

Mosquitoes swarming
From those days,
The cold is bitter,
The mind grows dizzy
As I stretch my limbs
Out on the ice.
It is I,
Aja – aja – ja.

Ai! but songs
Call for strength
And I seek after words,
I, aja – aja – ja.

Ai! I seek and spy
Something to sing of,
The caribou with the spreading antlers!

And strongly I threw
The spear with my throwing stick (sic!).
And my weapon fixed the bull
In the hollow of the groin
And it quivered with the wound
Till it dropped
And was still.

Ai! but songs
Call for strength,
And I seek after words.
It is I,
Aja, aja – haja – haja.

Rasmussen, *Intellectual Culture of the Iglulik Eskimos* 18-19

○ **Aua** (c. 1870–), an Iglulik shaman and Ivaluartjuk's older half-brother, was one of Rasmussen's important informants. Here are three of his magic songs. The first was to guide a new-born infant's first sledge journey. The second was to make heavy things light, and the third was to stop bleeding.

6

A Magic Prayer

I arise from rest with movements swift
As the beat of a raven's wings
I arise
To meet the day
Wa – wa.
My face is turned from the dark of night
To gaze at the dawn of day,
Now whitening in the sky.

Words Which Make Heavy Things Light
(to be uttered beside a heavily laden sledge)

I will walk with leg muscles
which are strong
as the sinews of the shins of the little caribou calf.
I will walk with leg muscles
which are strong
as the sinews of the shins of the little hare.
I will take care not to go towards the dark.
I will go towards the day.

Words to Stop Bleeding

This is blood from the little sparrow's mother.
Wipe it away!
This is blood
That flowed from a piece of wood.
Wipe it away!

Rasmussen, *Intellectual Culture of the Iglulik Eskimos* 47, 166, 167

Aua unabashedly sang a glorious song of praise to his own hunting prowess.

A Walrus Hunt

I could not sleep
For the sea was so smooth
Near at hand.

So I rowed out
And up came a walrus
Close by my kayak.
It was too near to throw.
So I thrust my harpoon into its side
And the bladder-float danced across the waves.
But in a moment it was up again,
Setting its flippers angrily
Like elbows on the surface of the water
And trying to rip up the bladder.
All in vain it wasted its strength,
For the skin of an unborn lemming
Was sewn inside as an amulet to guard.
Then snorting viciously it sought to gather strength,
But I rowed up
And ended the struggle.
Hear that, O men from strange creeks and fiords
That were always so ready to praise yourselves;
Now you can fill your lungs with song
Of another man's bold hunting.

Rasmussen, *Across Arctic America* 151

O   **Tûglik** (Tutlik) (fl. 1921) was an Iglulik woman whom Rasmussen met at Lyon Inlet. She 'drew forth a couple of little girls, little bundles of skins with ruddy cheeks, and placed them one opposite the other. Then, as soon as she started the song, which was sung at a breathless rate which left her gasping, the little girls joined in, crouching down and hopping with bent knees in time to the music.'

An Old Dance Song

Aja – ja – japape!
Aja – ja – japape!
Bring out your hair ornaments!
We are but girls
Who will keep together.
Aja – ja – japape!
Aja – ja – japape!

Hard times, dearth times
Plague us every one,
Stomachs are shrunken,
Dishes are empty.
Aja – ja – japape!
Aja – ja – japape!

Joy bewitches
All about us,
Skin boats rise up
Out of their moorings,
The fastenings go with them,
Earth itself hovers
Loose in the air.
Aja – ja – japape!
Aja – ja – japape!

Mark you there yonder?
There come the men
Dragging beautiful seals
To our homes.
Aja – ja – japape!
Aja – ja – japape!

Now is abundance
With us once more,
Days of feasting
To hold us together
Aja – ja – japape!
Aja – ja – japape!

Know you the smell
Of pots on the boil?
And lumps of blubber
Slapped down by the side bench?
Aja – ja – japape!
Hu – hue! Joyfully
Greet we those
Who brought us plenty!

Rasmussen, *Intellectual Culture of the Iglulik Eskimos* 41-2

○ It is interesting to compare the following two legends narrated approximately fifty-four years apart. The first was told to Rasmussen by **Naukatjik**, an Iglulik.

Women Become Dangerous When They Have No Husbands

In the days when there were many people living at Nuvuk (near Wager Bay), there were also two brothers living there, both married. They were bold and skilful hunters, and it was therefore not long before their neighbours grew envious of them. Once when they were out hunting caribou, both of them were murdered, and all the animals they had killed were stolen. After the killing of the brothers, the various men now lay with the wives of the murdered men. This the women did not like, and therefore one day they spoke to each other and said:

'Next time a man comes in here to lie with us, we will laugh him to scorn; one of us can pretend she is willing to receive him, but then the other shall come up and catch hold of him and make water in his mouth.'

The night came, and when a man came along as usual to visit them, one of the women called out to her fellow:

'Ah, here he is!' And then the other woman came up, and they caught hold of the man, and one of them sat astride his head and made water in his mouth, and they kept on like that, until the man was suffocated. Then quietly they prepared to leave the place in the middle of the night, while the others were asleep, and fled away. They fled across the ice, and in the morning, when the neighbours found out what had happened, they set out in pursuit. The two women took with them their husband's mother, and when they perceived that they were being followed, they said to her:

'You know a lot of magic songs; sing a magic song that will break up the ice behind us, so that our pursuers cannot reach us.'

'Yes, I know a little magic song, I will try it,' said the old woman.

She then drew a line on the ice behind the uprights of their sledge, and recited the magic song, and at once the ice broke away behind the sledge, and the one in pursuit of them was so near that the leader of the team fell into the water, but the three women escaped, being carried out to sea. They came to Southampton Island, and here they lived all alone, and there were no other men there save their little sons, that they carried in their amauts. But now it was not long before these women began to long for men so greatly that they lay with their own children, and these little boys did not grow up because the women took all the strength out of them, and they stayed small. The women were therefore obliged to go out hunting themselves, and this they did by taking with them their sons, who were still carried in the amauts, but had the understanding of grown men, to show them how to manage. And thus they captured whales, walrus, seal and other animals.

But the shamans, from whom nothing is hidden, discovered them, and did not approve of the life they were living. But the women, who were skilled in shamanism themselves, found out that others were seeking to do them harm, and so they sang this song to their husbands:

'My husband I carry in my amaut,
love him and kiss him,
and hide him away now,
because he is hunted by one
who is not a real human being.
My husband I carry in my amaut,
love him and kiss him,
Ajaja – ajaja.

Walrus I hunt
With my husband in the amaut.
following his wise counsel,
loving him and kissing him.
and hiding him now
that he is hunted by one
who is not a real human being,
a shaman that seeks to kill him.
Ajaja – ajaja.'

It is said that a real man once came to these women who had no grown-up husband of their own. The stranger met one of the women, and she took him in to her house at once and he lay with her, and when he got up to go, the woman said to him:

'Take this tent pole by way of thanks, for that you lay with me. Lay with me who am lonely, having no husband to lie with me.'

And the man took the tent pole home with him, that had been given him as a gift.

And another time, it is said, a white man landed on the island where lived the women without husbands. The women ran to meet him as he came, and so eager were they to embrace him, so eager to have him lie with them, that they suffocated him.

Thus women become dangerous when they have no husbands to lie with them.

Rasmussen, *Intellectual Culture of the Iglulik Eskimos* 300–1

O **William Okomâluk** (1894–1956), the second son of Itudsiayuar, 'king of the Igloolik Eskimos,' was the 'best huntsman of the Igloolik tribe.' He had the distinction of being an excellent story-teller and 'of being the first Igloolik Eskimo to fly in an airplane' (Schulte, *Flying Priest* 14, 48, 57).

The Sadlermiut of his story were the ancient inhabitants of Southampton Island, who, according to one account, were completely wiped out by an epidemic of some disease in the winter of 1902–3 after a visit by a Scottish whaler, the *Active*. It is said that the Sadlermiut retained a significant amount of Dorset culture within their own tradition. Aivilik Inuit, related to the Caribou Inuit, now live on Southampton Island.

Origin of the Sadlermiut

Walinarmiut [on the west coast of Baffin Island] hunters were away on an island. Their companions returned and said to the wives of the others: 'Your husbands killed lots of caribou, many bears and things to make "komaksiut" [louse-catcher].

But the men did not return: they had been killed.

An old woman then said to the others: 'Our husbands have been killed: they will never return ... '

A young man had taken one of them as a wife by force: the widows killed him during the night.

A litter of young pups lay under the platform; the women whipped them with the 'k'annerk' of a bearded seal attached to the end of a line and so changed them into full grown dogs. They then hitched them up to a sleigh and left. The only male with them was a youth.

As day was breaking; the boy was struck with fear but his grandmother said to him: 'Don't be afraid: if they follow us, I will cut the ice-pack in two.'

In the morning, the other Eskimos discovered the body of the one who had been killed and several of them left in pursuit of the fugitives.

Seeing their pursuers approaching, the women headed away from the land. As the old woman was dozing, the young boy cried out: 'Where is she who was to cut the ice-pack? ... Hey! ... There it goes.' And sure enough, *the old woman having drawn a line on the ice with an outstretched finger*, the pan on which the fugitives were broke loose from the main ice-pack.

The lead dog of the pursuers was so close it is said, that he fell into the water. The men started to shoot arrows. But a sudden fog came up and hid the fugitives from view and none of them were hurt ...

Far off, at Sadlerk, the women landed. They became the Sadlermiut. As for the youth, the women took him for a husband and he stopped growing.

Even though they had no hunters, the women did not suffer from hunger. One of them had a kayak and, during the summer, she found food for all. One day, she cried: 'A big ugjuk, a big bearded seal that the men would try hard to get.' She ran and shoved the kayak into the water and went to kill the bearded seal.

Soon there were male children and they promised one another their sons as fiancés ...

A woman carrying a baby on her back exclaimed one day:

'He whom I am carrying on my back is hungry; give him some frozen meat.' In fact, it was her husband she was carrying in her 'amaut.'

It is said the children often asked: 'Where is Walinark? They say it is our country.'

The women who had fled gradually died off. When the last of these was gone, their children were already adults. They wanted to return to Walinark, but as they didn't know the way, they couldn't and thus they became the Sadlermiut ...

There: that is all I know.

'Three Igloolik Legends,' *Eskimo*, 38 (December 1955): 22–4

O   The tale of the origin of the sun and moon is one of the great Inuit myths. It is told in many variations across the Arctic. This is the Iglulik version.

Origin of the Sun and Moon

An old woman lived with her two grandchildren, a boy and a girl, in an igloo. The boy, Aningât, became blind. They lived alone, and almost without food. One day a bear came to the house and began to gnaw at the frame of the window. The old woman took the bow of her grandson, and aimed for him while the boy drew the bow and loosened the arrow. The bear was struck, but the old woman pretended that the boy had only hit the window frame. She built a small house for Aningât where he was to live on his own. She killed a dog and gave its meat to the boy while she and the girl, Seqineq, ate the delicious bear's meat. But the girl often hid some of the meat in her sleeve and brought it to her brother.

One day Aningât asked his sister if there was a loon at the nearby lakes, and when she affirmed this he asked her to take him there. Seqineq did so, and at his request she built a row of stone landmarks so that he would be able to find his way home. In the meantime, the young man stood by the lake and waited until he heard the sound of a kayak. A voice invited him to sit in it. He sat down and was rowed out to the sea. Then he was taken down under the water several times, and each time he reappeared his sight improved. Finally he became thoroughly dizzy, but by that time he could even see the little blades of grass far off.

14

The stranger (apparently a loon in human appearance) and Aningât rowed back to the land. The loon flew away and Aningât returned to the igloo of his grandmother. He saw the skin of the bear stretched out and asked his grandmother where it came from. She told him that it had been left behind by some people who had passed by.

It was spring by that time and the white whales were moving along the edge of the ice. Aningât often went hunting them with his sister, who helped him by holding the end of the harpoon line. One day the old woman decided to come with them. She took the line and went to the edge of the ice. She cried to her grandson to harpoon a young whale, but instead he struck one of the very largest and the old woman was drawn into the water. And as soon as she had got her head above water, she sang to her grandchild:

'Grandchild, grandchild,
Why do you leash me like a dog?
Have you forgotten that it was always I
Who with never so much as a grimace
Cleaned up dirt and wet after you?
Have you forgotten that it was I?'

Her grandchild answered:

'Grandmother, grandmother,
Why did you give me nothing?
Why was I given nothing of the meat
From the bear that I shot,
The first bear I ever shot?'

His grandmother sang again:

'Grandchild, grandchild,
If only I could reach
Up to that little hillock on dry land!'

and with that she disappeared under the water.

Thus the brother and the sister were left alone. When winter came they left the igloo and went into the world because they were ashamed of having killed their grandmother. First they came to an impish people with long claws. Aningât began to build an igloo. He became thirsty, and asked his sister to fetch him some water. She went to an igloo and asked for some. The people inside the snow house told her to pull her clothes up over her hips and to enter the igloo backwards. When she did so they assaulted her with their long claws, but Aningât ran in to help her, and killed all of them.

Then they settled among people who had no openings in the lower halves of their bodies. Thus they were unable to defecate, and Aningât could never lie with his wife. Therefore he cut a slit in her lap such as women usually have.

Seqineq became pregnant and her mother-in-law prepared herself to cut open her lap to deliver the child. Seqineq, however, brought forth a healthy child by herself. It had all the normal openings in the lower half of its body. All the women then began to open their laps with meatforks. Those who hit the wrong spot died, the others survived.

While Seqineq lay in the birth hut there was often singing and dancing in the feasting house. Aningât used to visit his sister in order to have intercourse with her, but he always took care to put out the lamp so that she would not be able to recognise him. One day she took a bit of soot from the lamp and blackened the face of her unknown lover. She followed him to the feasting house and there she heard people crying: 'Look, Aningât has soot on his face!'

Seqineq was so ashamed that she fetched a knife from her igloo, entered the feasting house, cut off of her breasts, and threw it in front of her brother. She cried: 'You are so fond of my body; eat that too!' Then she grasped a torch and ran out of the igloo. Aningât took another torch and pursued her and so they ran around the igloo. Aningât fell over a snowblock and his torch went out. While they were still running around the igloo they suddenly began to rise into the sky, and they became sun and moon, circling around the dome of heaven. Seqineq with her burning torch was the sun, while Aningât became the moon, with little light and no warmth.

Etudes/Inuit/Studies, 7, 1 (1983) 145–6

O   The story of the abused orphan boy is one of those well-loved Inuit tales that has survived generations of story-tellers.

The Revenge of the Orphan Boy

A boy and his sister during a seal hunt on the sea ice were cut off from their people. No one was able to help them as their ice pan floated away. Their parents and elder brother gave them up for dead. But this was not so – after many days the wind blew the ice pan near the shore of a strange land where people lived. Each was adopted by a different family and that is how they came to live among strangers.

From these strangers they received no kindness. The girl had to braid sinews for holding up trousers, and the boy, Kaujjar-juk, was made to work crushing blubber. He was not allowed to sleep in the house and had to sleep in the porch with only the dogs to keep him from freezing. The dogs were kind to him. It was as though he was one of them. One dog served him as a mattress, another as a pillow and a dog lay on either side of him to keep him warm at night.

As for the people, they would often have drum dances and great feasts in the gathering house. The boy was never invited. Instead he had to carry the large urine tubs and empty them; he was so small that he could hardly lift them and often he was splashed from head to foot. The older men and boys delighted in picking him up by the nostrils. It was very painful and caused his nostrils to grow to a very large size, although the rest of his body grew hardly at all. This is no wonder because all he had to eat was tough walrus hide and scraps of fish that even dogs would not eat.

Except for two old women who occasionally took pity on him and gave him bits of food, there was no one to sympathize with him at all. Often he longed for his mother, father and brother. He did not complain because his parents and his older brother (who, it is said, was a conjuror) had often told him to be patient in all suffering. His sister received no pity either, though her fingers were worn to the bone from braiding. But at least she was allowed to eat in the house and her food was better.

One night in a winter hunting camp, when all were asleep, Kaujjarjuk heard a voice calling from outside the igloo; 'Kaujjarjuk! Kaujjarjuk! come out!' But he was frightened and did not move from his place among the dogs. 'I will not go out, I am afraid, I will not go out and see. You, dog, you who are my pillow, you go out and see who it is.' So the dog went out and when he came back he said, 'I see nothing, go back to sleep.'

Again in a little while the voice came; 'Kaujjarjuk, Kaujjarjuk, come out,' but again he answered 'I am afraid.' Then the old dog who was his mattress went out to look. He too came back and said, 'There is no one there.' And again the third time the voice called. This time the dogs paid no attention, so Kaujjarjuk went out himself and there in the moonlight, he recognized his elder brother.

'Come with me,' said the elder brother. Together they walked inland until they came to a high mountain that no one had ever climbed before. They climbed higher and higher until finally they came to the top. Kaujjarjuk was very frightened. 'Have no fear, little brother, I have come to teach you strength and with the magic of my words you shall be a strong man. You must do exactly as I say and tell no one that I am staying in the camp. In the daytime I shall be invisible to everyone but you.'

'What must I do?' answered Kaujjarjuk eagerly.

'First, lift that big rock,' commanded his elder brother.

'But I cannot,' said Kaujjarjuk, trying with all his might. It was a large rock and frozen fast.

'Try harder,' commanded his brother.

'I cannot,' protested Kaujjarjuk.

The elder brother carried a short whip and with it he began to beat Kaujjarjuk. When he stopped beating him he said 'Try again' and Kaujjarjuk tried again. Many times they repeated this, until Kaujjarjuk finally found strength in the fear of the whip and lifted the frozen rock.

'That will do for tonight,' said his brother. 'Tomorrow night I shall come and call on you again.'

And so it was repeated night after night and each day Kaujjarjuk grew stronger and stronger but he told no one of his strength and continued to take all the abuse the people heaped upon him. On the last night they met, Kaujjarjuk was able to lift the largest boulder on the mountain and his brother was pleased. 'You are strong enough now. Tomorrow, hide yourself well because three large polar bears are coming to the camp.'

It was as foretold – early the next morning three hungry bears arrived searching for food. All the men were excited and they ran out and put bait in various places but the bears just sniffed the bait, tasted it and vomited. Then all the women began to scream and sing, 'They will not eat that bait. Where is Kaujjarjuk, where is that miserable fellow, go find him, he will make bait for the bears.' They searched everywhere but he could not be found.

All the people gathered about, watching the bears. They did not see Kaujjarjuk as he ran from his hiding place and right to the headman who had made his life miserable. He picked this man up and threw him through the air to the waiting bears. Then, one by one, he picked up all the men in the village and threw them to the bears who killed them. Then he threw all the women to the bears except four. As he threw each person to their death he mentioned some injustice that they had done to him. All this time Kaujjarjuk was singing the magic words his brother had taught him and he escaped unharmed, even though some of the men shot arrows at him. The harpoons they threw at him also fell useless onto the snow.

Thus all the people who had ill-treated the orphan were now killed and the bears went away.

Now, the two women who had treated him well he gave to his brother and they became his brother's wives. But two women that treated him ill he took for wives to himself, because only he could punish them. Thus only four women were not killed.

The two wives of his brother behaved well and were well treated and because he was a conjuror they had everything they needed to make life happy. But the other two, the wives of Kaujjarjuk, did everything they could to make him happy but they could not escape his vengence. He would say 'bring me meat,' and they would both come running with the meat, but the one who came last would be whipped; or again, 'are my braiding sticks clean?' and the one who brought them first was spared and the other was beaten. It is said that both were beaten to death. Thus was the revenge of Kaujjarjuk, the orphan who was ill-treated by strangers.

'The Revenge of the Orphan Boy,' trans. Leah Idlout d'Argencourt, *North*, 14, 4 (July/ August 1967) 57–8

○ **Felix Kopak** (1918–), hunter and carver, was born in the Repulse Bay area. After working in the nickel mines in the 1950s
at Rankin Inlet, he lived in Chesterfield Inlet. In 1988 he was
living in Repulse Bay. He still remembers being a little boy
when Knud Rasmussen visited Repulse Bay. Kopak told this
amusing story to the Reverend Rogatien Papion.

The Crow and the Two Eider Ducks

A crow had two eider ducks as mates. When spring came, the
ducks decided to go north. As the crow wanted to follow
them, his two mates said: 'You should rather stay here,
because we're going to fly over the sea and this will be very
tiresome for you.'

But the crow answered: 'We shall surely reach land in one
day.'

'As you wish,' said the eider ducks. And away they all went.

The crow at first kept ahead of the others, but during the
day he was passed and left behind. That night, overtaking his
two mates who had settled on the water, he said: 'Women!
Place yourselves side by side.' The two ducks drew nearer together and the crow perched on their backs. When he was
rested, he flew away ... And again, when he felt tired, he
perched on their backs ...

As there were strong waves (and the crow had to cling to
the ducks to keep in balance) the two soon had lost all their
back feathers.

The other ducks who were going with them told the two
mates: 'Next time he tells you to draw closer together, do so,
but just as he comes to rest on your back, pull apart.'

They did as they were told. When the crow ordered them to
come close together, they obeyed, but just as he was about
to perch on them, they pulled apart and the crow fell into the
water. So he cried:

'My in-laws! I'm sinking!'

– Up to where, son-in-law?

– Up to here, up to my leg-calf.

Then he cried out again:

– My in-laws! I'm sinking!

20

– Up to where, son-in-law?
– Up to here, up to my legs! My in-laws! I'm sinking!
– Up to where, son?
– Up to here, up to my waist! My in-laws! I'm sinking!
– Up to where son?
– Up to here, up to my neck. My in-laws! I'm sinking!
– Up to where son?
– Up to here, up to my throat ... and he sank in a gurgle.

'The Crow and the Two Eider Ducks,' *Eskimo*, 30 (June 1955) 16–17

○ **Uvavnuk** (fl. 1923) was an Iglulik woman who suddenly one night became a powerful shaman. Uvavnuk was struck by a meteor whose spirit entered into her and made her clairvoyant. Overwhelmed with joy, she burst into ecstatic song, a song which would always put her into a trance.

Ecstasy

The great sea
Moves me!
The great sea
Sets me adrift!
It moves me
Like algae on stones
In running brook water.
The vault of heaven
Moves me!
The mighty weather
Storms through my soul.
It tears me with it
And I tremble with joy.

Freuchen, ed., *Peter Freuchen's Book of the Eskimos* 278–9

○ **Inugpasugjuk** (fl. 1922) was an immigrant Netsilingmio living on Depot Island who told this story to Knud Rasmussen.
Pregnant women were strictly forbidden to touch anything taken from a seal. In this story the Moon Spirit, the only known good spirit among the Iglulik, rescued a woman who, because she broke a rule of taboo, would have been a danger to her people.

Tutukatuk, Who Was Carried off by the Moon for Breach of Taboo

There was once a young woman whose name was Tutukatuk. She was about to have her first child, and although she was with child, she one day played with the pieces of a game made from bones of a seal ...

One evening when the moon was shining, a sledge was heard approaching. The sledge stopped outside the house, and a man came up to the window and shouted: 'Come outside, Tutukatuk, and bring your pieces with you.'

Tutukatuk went out, taking the pieces with her, and placed herself on the sledge and drove off with the stranger.

'Now you must not open your eyes,' he said. 'If you do, you will fall off the sledge.'

Suddenly they rose up in the air, for this was none other than the Moon Spirit who had come down to fetch Tutukatuk, and they dashed off now through space at a terrific speed, the sledge bounding every time they passed a star. Across the clear sky the sledge moved evenly, without much shaking, but rapidly. After a long journey, they halted. Now at last Tutukatuk opened her eyes and saw a great number of people playing ball, and the players stopped their game and came forward to greet them. The Moon Spirit said: 'It is a live human being I have with me.'

Then the others, who were all dead, went away again, and the Moon Spirit led Tutukatuk into his house and set her on the bench. On the floor over at the other side of the house lay a shoulder bone with no meat on. The Moon Spirit lifted it up and said: 'Just look down through the opening here, and you can see all the dwellings of men.' Some lay far apart, others close together, and looking down on them from the sky, it was as if they had no roofs, for one could see right into the houses. The Moon Spirit opened the peephole every morning, and then Tutukatuk could see that some of the people were asleep, others awake ...

When the time came for Tutukatuk to bring forth her child, the Moon Spirit brought her back to earth, but before doing so, he said to her: 'You must not eat any food procured by human hands. If you do, you will die (for breaking the rules of taboo). But I will bring you food, and you will find it on the drying place above your lamp.'

Tutukatuk came home to her own place and gave birth to her child, and all that she needed in the way of food she found on the drying place above her lamp. The lamp itself was filled with oil from there, and joints of caribou meat were ready for her when she felt hungry and wanted something to eat.

The child was born and grew big, and at last Tutukatuk's husband said to her: 'Your child is grown big now. There is no need for you to be so careful about what you eat. Why do you never eat any of the meat I bring home?'

But it was in vain that her husband urged her to eat of the meat he brought home from his hunting; she would not do so, and at last the man grew angry. Then his wife dared not refuse to eat of the meat he brought home. As soon as she had eaten of it, the child fell ill and was on the point of death, merely because the woman had broken the taboo which the Moon Spirit had decreed for her. So dangerous a thing is it to break one's taboo. But the visit to the Moon Spirit made such an impression on Tutukatuk that she always in future observed the taboo prescribed for women.

Rasmussen, *Intellectual Culture of the Iglulik Eskimos* 85–6

NETSILIK

O **Orpingalik** (fl. 1921) was a shaman and poet of high esteem among his people, the Netsilik. 'Of all the Netsilingmiut,' whom the Danish explorer, Knud Rasmussen, met during his Arctic expedition of 1921–4, he considered Orpingalik 'the most poetically gifted man.' Here Orpingalik explains to Rasmussen 'how a song is born in the human mind.'

The Genesis of Song

... Songs are thoughts, sung out with the breath when people are moved by great forces and ordinary speech no longer suffices.

Man is moved just like the ice floe sailing here and there

out in the current. His thoughts are driven by a flowing force when he feels joy, when he feels fear, when he feels sorrow. Thoughts can wash over him like a flood, making his breath come in gasps and his heart throb. Something, like an abatement in the weather, will keep him thawed up. And then it will happen that we, who always think we are small, will feel still smaller. And we will fear to use words. But it will happen that the words we need will come of themselves. When the words we want to use shoot up of themselves – we get a new song.

Rasmussen, *The Netsilik Eskimos* 321

Orpingalik composed this poem while he was recovering from a severe illness. As he struggled to regain his strength, he reflected on his helplessness and reminisced about the past when he was a great hunter.

My Breath

I will sing a song,
A song that is strong.
    Unaya – unaya.
Sick I have lain since autumn.
Helpless I lay, as were I
My own child.

Sad, I would that my woman
Were away to another house
To a husband
Who can be her refuge,
Safe and secure as winter ice.
    Unaya – unaya.

Sad, I would that my woman
Were gone to a better protector
Now that I lack strength
To rise from my couch.
    Unaya – unaya.

Dost thou know thyself?

So little thou knowest of thyself.
Feeble I lie here on my bench
And only my memories are strong!
    Unaya – unaya.

Beasts of the hunt! Big game!
Oft the fleeing quarry I chased!
Let me live it again and remember,
Forgetting my weakness.
    Unaya – unaya.

Let me recall the great white
Polar bear,
High up its back body,
Snout in the snow, it came!
He really believed
He alone was a male
And ran towards me.
    Unaya – unaya.

It threw me down
Again and again,
Then breathless departed
And lay down to rest,
Hid by a mound on a floe.
Heedless it was, and unknowing
That I was to be its fate.
Deluding itself
That he alone was a male,
And unthinking
That I too was a man!
    Unaya – unaya.

I shall ne'er forget that great blubber-beast,
A fjord seal,
I killed from the sea ice
Early, long before dawn,
While my companions at home
Still lay like the dead,
Faint from failure and hunger,

Sleeping.
With meat and with swelling blubber
I returned so quickly
As if merely running over ice
To view a breathing hole there.
And yet it was
An old and cunning male seal.
But before he had even breathed
My harpoon head was fast
Mortally deep in his neck.

That was the manner of me then.
Now I lie feeble on my bench
Unable even a little blubber to get
For my wife's stone lamp.
The time, the time will not pass,
While dawn gives place to dawn
And spring is upon the village.
    Unaya – unaya.

But how long shall I lie here?
How long?
And how long must she go a-begging
For fat for her lamp,
For skins for clothing
And meat for a meal?
A helpless thing – a defenceless woman.
    Unaya – unaya.

Knowest thou thyself?
So little thou knowest of thyself!
While dawn gives place to dawn,
And spring is upon the village.
    Unaya – unaya.

Rasmussen, *The Netsilik Eskimos* 321–3

As a shaman, Orpingalik possessed many magical skills. Here
he coaxes the caribou – who have the magical power to hear
and understand the human word – to come to him.

Caribou Magic

Wild caribou, land louse, long-legs,
With the great ears,
And the rough hairs on your neck,
Flee not from me.
Here I bring skins for soles,
Here I bring moss for wicks,
Just come gladly
Hither to me, hither to me.

Rasmussen, *The Netsilik Eskimos* 15

Although songs of derision for judicial purposes were very popular in Greenland and Alaska, they were not as strong in Arctic
Canada. This song of derision was sung at Pelly Bay by Orpingalik against his old song fellow, Takutjartak, and was told
to the anthropologist, Asen Balikci, by Orpingalik's daughter
Karmatziar in 1960. Song duelists usually began with a great
show of modesty and used animal characteristics to ridicule
their opponents. Although song duelling is no longer done in
Canada today, political satire often exploits its two-part respon-
sive form.

A Song of Derision

There
How shall I go to compose this important song
How shall I invent it to help me
I am wholly ignorant
There
Those who have great facility to invent songs
Those who dance with elegance
Those who know the beautiful old chants
I will get inspiration from them
There
Where one gets caribou skins
To these places I will walk and my thoughts will
    follow me
Early in the morning I get up

27

There
Between Oadlerk and Areark lakes I was hunting
There was Takutjartak like a great wolverine
There
Among the tall grass looking for mice to feed himself
I made a noise
You run away
There
With your two eyes you looked at me
Fascinated, astounded
A good large arrow I threw
At your fat ass
It was very annoying for you
You run away fast
There

Balikci, *The Netsilik Eskimo* 143–4

○ **Uvlunuaq** (fl. 1921) was the wife of Orpingalik and herself a
skilled poet. In 1921, when this song was recorded, their son,
Igsivalitaq, had killed a hunting companion in a fit of rage some
years before and was then living as an outlaw up in the hills
near Pelly Bay, in fear of being found by the Royal Canadian
Mounted Police. The sorrowful mother found relief in her sad
drum song.

A Mother's Lament

Eyaya – eya.
I recognize
A bit of a song
And take it to me like a fellow being.
Eyaya – eya.

Should I be ashamed
At the child I once carried
With me in my back-pouch,
Because I heard of his flight
From the haunts of man?
Eyaya – eya.

Truly I am ashamed:
But only because he had not
A mother who was blameless as the blue sky,
Wise and without foolishness.
Now people's talk will educate him
And gossip complete the education.
I should perhaps be ashamed,
I, who bore a child
Who was not to be my refuge;
Instead, I envy those
Who have a crowd of friends behind them,
Waving on the ice,
When after festive leave-taking they journey out.
Oh, I remember a winter,
We left the island 'The squinting eye';
The weather was mild,
And the feet sank, gently creaking, into the thawing snow.
I was then as a tame animal among men;
But when the message came
Of the killing and the flight,
Then I staggered,
Like one unable to get a foothold.

Rasmussen, *The Netsilik Eskimos* 16–17

○   **Qaqortingneq** (fl. 1923), from Pelly Bay, was one of Rasmussen's
best informants about the Netsilik. He was 'a first-rate map
drawer with a thorough knowledge of the whole land territory
of the Netsilik.' He related the origin and customs of the Itqilît
people (Indians).

The Origin of the Indians

... We counted the Tunrit a foreign people, yet they spoke our
language, lived with us and had the same habits and customs
as we had; the Itqilît are quite different. Human beings they
are, no doubt, but not at all like us, and they speak in a
tongue that we do not understand; and their customs are not
ours. Yet we are distant relations of theirs, so to speak. You
have heard the story of the girl who rejected all men and at

last, to punish her for her haughtiness, was married to her father's dog. When she had made her dog-young tear her father to pieces and then repented of it, she wanted to send her young ones away, and so she put them, the most horrible among them, those that where [sic] half man and half dog, on a kamik sole and made them sail over to the mainland; she made magic over them and, as they drifted away, shouted that they were always to be at enmity with people. That is how the Itqilît became wicked people, and there has always been enmity between them and the Inuit. The words of our forefathers could be sharp and fateful; there was might in their tongues.

We know that the Itqilît live far inland, right up there where the big forests ... are said to grow, and the people who used to go up to Akilineq to trade in the old days have sometimes seen them and told of their cruelty. We Netsilingmuit have never seen them; they have never been in our country; they were nearest us that time when two Itqilît were seen at a place near Utkuhikjalik, but there were only two of them; the Inuit were more numerous, and so the Itqilît hurriedly went their way.

The old people have also told us that the Itqilît were half dog and half man, but we do not believe that their bodies were different to ours. We believe that their character as dog-men lies not in their bodies, but in their minds and manners.

We call them Itqilît (those with many louse eggs) because they are full of lice. They are quick runners and clever hunters, but when they bring down a caribou they do not carry the meat as we do. People say that they carry it in their teeth like a dog does. In fact they have many dog-habits. If an Itqilîq is taken by surprise, he will show his teeth and growl like a dog. When they are out hunting they try to smell as dogs do. Inuit who have lain concealed and watched Itqilîk hunters that were looking for game, have seen them sniff the air and the ground just like dogs trying to get the scent. People say that like shy dogs they hate the smell of the Inuit.

They live in tents that are very like the pointed tents (conical) that many of us still use. They like to make a big fire and then sit round it, warming themselves. Otherwise their village life is not at all like ours, for their women have different impulses to ours; it is said that they only care to lie with men at certain periods, just like dogs. When an Itqilîk woman gets into the state when she wants to mate with men, she flings out her hair and runs about the village, and then the men fight for her just as dogs do.

This is all that our forefathers have told us about the Itqilît. I myself know nothing for my own part; I only repeat what I have heard.

Rasmussen, *The Netsilik Eskimos* 121–2

Qaqortingneq told Rasmussen what he knew of the ill-fated British naval expedition of exploration led by Sir John Franklin in 1845–7 in search of the Northwest Passage. Some months after their meeting, Rasmussen visited one of the sites which Qaqortingneq had mentioned and found a number of human bones that undoubtedly were the mortal remains of members of the Franklin expedition.

Inuit oral history has been passed down with a high degree of accuracy, and was often relied upon by baffled non-Inuit seeking information.

The Fate of the Franklin Expedition

Two brothers were out hunting seal to the northwest of Qeqertaq (King William's Land). It was in the spring, at the time when the snow melts about the breathing holes of the seal. They caught sight of something far out on the ice; a great black mass of something, that could not be any animal they knew. They studied it and made out at last that it was a great ship. Running home at once, they told their fellows, and on the following day all went out to see. They saw no men about the ship; it was deserted; and they therefore decided to take from it all they could for themselves. But none of them had ever before met with white men, and they had no knowledge as to the use of all the things they found.

One man, seeing a boat that hung out over the side of the ship, cried: 'Here is a fine big trough that will do for meat! I will have this!' He had never seen a boat before, and did not know what it was. And he cut the ropes that held it up, and the boat crashed down endways on to the ice and was smashed.

They found guns, also, on the ship, and not knowing what

31

was the right use of these things, they broke away the barrels and used the metal for harpoon heads. So ignorant were they indeed, in the matter of guns and belonging to guns, that on finding some percussion caps, such as were used in those days, they took them for tiny thimbles, and really believed that there were dwarfs among the white folk, little people who could use percussion caps for thimbles.

At first they were afraid to go down into the lower part of the ship, but after a while they grew bolder, and ventured also into the houses underneath. Here they found many dead men, lying in the sleeping places there; all dead. And at last they went down also into a great dark space in the middle of the ship. It was quite dark down there and they could not see. But they soon found tools and set to work and cut a window in the side. But here those foolish ones, knowing nothing of the white men's things, but a hole in the side of the ship below the water line so that the water came pouring in and the ship sank. It sank to the bottom with all the costly things; nearly all that they had found was lost again at once.

But in the same year, later on in the spring, three men were on their way from Qeqertaq to the southward, going to hunt caribou calves. And they found a boat with the dead bodies of six men. There were knives and guns in the boat, and much food also, so the men must have died of disease.

There are many places in our country here where bones of white men may still be found. I myself have been to Qavdlu-narsiorfik [a spit of land on Adelaide Peninsula, nearly opposite the site where Norwegian explorer Roald Amundsen wintered in 1904] we used to go there to dig for lead and bits of iron. And then there is Kangerarfigdluk, quite close here, a little way along the coast to the west.

And that is all I know about your white men who once came to our land, and perished; whom our fathers met but could not help to live.

Rasmussen, *Across Arctic America* 239–40

COPPER

O   **Uloqsaq** (1886–), 'the most famous shaman among the western Copper Eskimos,' and **Ikpakhuaq**, a man of great note and influence, gave their version of the origin of the clouds to Diamond Jenness when he was studying the Copper Inuit as part of the Canadian Arctic Expedition of 1913–18.

The Origin of the Clouds

The earth was once very warm; there were then no clouds, no snow, no ice, no fog. The sun said, 'I know the people all over the earth.' In the evening, when the moon went down, it said, 'Now the people are going to have their eyes protruding from their heads because of the darkness.'

During those days animals talked like men. A female brown bear captured an Eskimo named *Upaum* and carried him off to her den for her young cubs to eat ... 'Here's something for you to suck,' she said to them. She lay down to sleep, leaving the two cubs to keep watch. *Upaum* pretended to be dead and lay with his eyes closed. After a time, when all was quiet, he opened them very cautiously, but the cubs saw him ... '*Upaum* is opening his eyes,' they called to their mother. The old bear sprang up, but seeing *Upaum* lying quite motionless with his eyes closed, she lay down to sleep again. After a time the cubs went off to get some wood. *Upaum* said to himself, ' ... *Upaum*, open your eyes and do something.' Then he rose, seized a billet of wood and smote the mother bear over the head. The blow was not fatal, but it left the animal stunned for a few minutes, during which time *Upaum* made his escape. Presently he heard the bear following him, so he climbed to the top of some willows and remained there while the bear was vainly searching for him on the ground. 'As long as it is light,' he thought to himself, 'I can hold on to these willows without getting tired.' After a time he descended and ran away, but the bear found his tracks and followed. Then he stooped down and drew an imaginary line along the ground. Immediately a great stream of water gushed forth, which swelled into a mighty river flowing between him and his enemy – the modern ... or Coppermine River ... 'How did you cross this river?' called out the bear; and the man replied ... 'I drank it and snuffled it up and emptied it.' The bear tried to do the same, and drank and drank until it burst. The warm stream that mounted up from its body became the clouds.

Canadian Arctic Expedition, *Report*, XIII 79A

○ **Netsit** (fl. 1923), poet and story-teller, belonged to the Copper group of Inuit. He dreamt this song which tells of the joys and tribulations of human life.

Dead Man's Song
(Dreamed by one who is alive.)

I am filled with joy
When the day peacefully dawns
Up over the heavens,
　ayi, yai ya.
I am filled with joy
When the sun slowly rises
Up over the heavens,
　ayi, yai ya.
But else I choke with fear
At greedy maggot throngs;
They eat their way in
At the hollow of my collarbone
And in my eyes,
　ayi, yai ya.
Here I lie, recollecting
How stifled with fear I was
When they buried me
In a snow hut out on the lake,
　ayi, yai ya.
A block of snow was pushed to,
Incomprehensible it was
How my soul should make its way
And fly to the game land up there,
　ayi, yai ya.
That door-block worried me,
And ever greater grew my fear
When the fresh-water ice split in the cold,
And the frost-crack thunderously grew
Up over the heavens,
　ayi, yai ya.
Glorious was life
In winter.
But did winter bring me joy?

No! Ever was I so anxious
For sole-skins and skins for kamiks.
Would there be enough for us all?
Yes, I was ever anxious,
　ayi, yai ya.
Glorious was life
In summer.
But did summer bring me joy?
No! Ever was I so anxious
For skins and rugs for the platform,
Yes, I was ever anxious,
　ayi, yai ya.
Glorious was life
When standing at one's fishing hole
On the ice.
But did standing at the fishing hole bring me joy?
No! Ever was I so anxious
For my tiny little fish-hook
If it should not get a bite,
　ayi, yai ya.
Glorious was life
When dancing in the dance-house.
But did dancing in the dance-house bring me joy?
No! Ever was I so anxious,
That I could not recall
The song I was to sing.
Yes, I was ever anxious,
　ayi, yai ya.
Glorious was life ...
Now I am filled with joy
For every time a dawn
Makes white the sky of night,
For every time the sun goes up
Over the heavens,
　ayi, yai ya.

Rasmussen, *Intellectual Culture of the Copper Eskimos* 136–8

○　**Itireitok** (c. 1910–45) was from Bathurst Island. She died of
influenza at Burnside. In early December 1940, full winter in
the high Arctic, she left Burnside with a group of people going

to trade their furs at Cambridge Bay, and they battled fierce winds and difficult terrain across the barren lands. When they finally caught sight of the sea, near Cambridge Bay, Itireitok began this joyful chant.

A Sea Chant

Namunme, sumunme ... Down to the sea I went
Where seals breathe through the ice.
Surprised, I heard:
Hai-ee-ya, hai-ee-ya, hai-ee-ya! Ee-ai, ee-ai, ee-ai!
The song of the sea
And the wail of the young ice:
Hai-ee-ai, hai-ee-ai, hai-ee-ai! Ee-ai, ee-ai, ee-ai!

de Coccola and King, *Ayorama* 56

CARIBOU

O   A Caribou hunter finds the body of his son near the High Hill and sings this sad song.

The Death of a Son

A man was leaving,
He was leaving alone,
He was walking in the cold,
He was walking in the wind,
He was going to the High Hill.
In the snow he saw something,
It was not a hare,
It was not a grouse,
It was something cold.
From the hands protruding from the snow,
From the feet protruding from the snow,
The hands had been chewed by the foxes,
The feet had been chewed by the wolves,
The father looked,
He looked without speaking.
He brushed the snow off the clothes,

He blew on the eyes,
He blew on the mouth;
He pressed his heart
His heart against the other's heart.
But the son remained cold,
Remained hard as a rock,
Still as ice,
And for three nights
The father could think no longer,
He lost his way,
He forgot the road,
He had no light,
No more light in his head.
Now the father sings,
He sings under the tent,
He sings with the Eskimo,
And together they all sing
They sing for the son.

Zavatti, 'La Poesia degli Eschimesi' 102–3 (editor's translation)

O   **Kibbârjuk** (fl. 1922) was the first wife of the prominent Caribou
shaman, Igjugârjuk. Although she was displaced by a second
wife, she still exercised great influence. She told Rasmussen
this funny animal story.

The Owl Woos the Snow-bunting

A little snow-bunting ... is weeping because it has lost its
husband. Then there came an owl and sang:
   Pray do not weep
   For that worthless husband,
   One that had only
   Weapons of grass to throw,
   And willow twigs.
   I alone
   Will be your husband.
The snow-bunting answered:
   Who would have you for a husband?
   You with the huge feathers all over your body,
   You with that great big beak,

37

And those thick legs,
And that high forehead,
And that bulge at the back of your head,
And that short neck.
But the owl was angry at these words, and struck the snow-bunting on the back. And when the snow-bunting complained of the pain in its back, the owl cried:
... Look at that woman there, who can feel pains in her back in spite of having such a sharp tongue.
   Here ends this story.

Rasmussen, *Intellectual Culture of the Caribou Eskimos* 86

The Old Man's Song

I have grown old,
I have lived much,
Many things I understand,
But four riddles I cannot solve.
Ha-ya-ya-ya.

The sun's origin,
The moon's nature,
The minds of women,
And why people have so many lice.
Ha-ya-ya-ya.

Freuchen, ed., *Peter Freuchen's Book of the Eskimos* 275

○   When an Inuit child was in its amautik, the carrying hood of its mother's parka, a dialogue often developed. In this piece the child was 'mother's sister.' The namesake was addressed with the same title of relationship as the deceased relative. The soul or personality of the ancestor also came with the name.

Mother and Child

See her up there, the innocent coquette –
No man yet has touched her,
No man yet has stamped her –
She is not my child's mother,
She is not my child's brother –

But she is mother's sister
Crook-backed (as she was)
Stammering
Restless in all her movements –
From early morning wishing but to fall in with menfolk,
She tries to outwit them, the little creature –
See how she raps with her hands,
Hear how she whimpers –
Hey! How she can run!

Carpenter, 'Eskimo Poetry' 111

WESTERN ARCTIC, BAILLIE ISLAND

O   Whaling rituals were very important to the Inuit of the western
     Arctic. The people from Baillie Island used to chant this song
     whenever they harpooned a whale.

A Whaling Chant

You that we are towing along
Ah, ya ah e ya
Big whale, big whale,
Stir up the sea with your tail
E ya ah e ya
Give us fair weather today
So we arrive safe and sound on shore.
E ya ah e ya
Tug – tug along hard
E ya ah e ya
Row – Row!
After the whale was harpooned and was being towed to the land
the ancients would intone these magic words.

Magic Words to a Whale

Drag along, drag along the skin bag;
Whale – lose your strength.

I, Nuligak (1975) 65, 66

○   When Vilhjalmur Stefansson left his winter base on Langton
    Bay at Cape Parry to penetrate into the unknown frozen east
    towards Coronation Gulf on 21 April 1910 during his second
    expedition, his three Inuit companions were not enthusiastic.
    They had heard grotesque tales from the Baillie Island Inuit
    about the area's inhabitants.

The People of the Caribou Antler

These people bear the name of the caribou antler ... because of
a peculiar custom they have. When a woman becomes of mar-
riageable age her coming-out is announced several days in
advance. At the appointed time she is made to take her place
in an open space out-of-doors, and all the men who want wives
form around her in a circle, each armed with the antler of a
large bull caribou. The word is given, and they all rush at her,
each trying to hook her toward him with the antler. Often
the woman is killed in the scrimmage, but if some one suc-
ceeds in getting her alive from the others he takes her for a
wife. As strength and the skill which experience gives are the
main requirements for success, some of the Nagyuktogmiut
have a great many wives, while most of them have none. Because so many women are killed in this way there are twice as
many men as women among them. We know many stories,
of which this is one, to show what queer people these Eastern-
ers are. They also kill all strangers.

Stefansson, *My Life with the Eskimo* 162–3

○   Words carry the power to make things happen. Through this
    sacred power of utterance the Inuit sought to exert control over
    natural phenomena. Repetition has an hypnotic effect. This
    weather incantation sung by a Coppermine River man, achieves
    an hypnotic state of consciousness.

An Incantation for Good Weather

They have gone, it is said, the people who travel in
    kayaks,
They have gone, it is said, the people who travel in
    kayaks,

Kayaks, people,
Kayaks, people,
To the lands farthest north,
To the lands last of all,
Lands, these,
In front of all lands, these,
Return equipment, eating utensils
Having on top those, packs, packs.
Let me land, let me land,
Let me land, let me land, let me land,
The spirit yonder following it.
Let me land, let me land,
Let me land, let me land, let me land.

Roberts and Jenness, *Songs of the Copper Eskimo* 487

O   The joy of the dance was captured in this Herschel Island song, sung by **Unalina** and **Cukaiyoq**, two women from the Mackenzie River region.

The Joy of the Dance

My arms they wave high in the air.
My hands they flutter behind my back; they wave above
   my head like the wings of a bird.
Let me move my feet, let me dance, let me shrug my
   shoulders, let me shake my body.
My arms let me fold them; let me crouch down;
Let me hold my hands under my chin.

Roberts and Jenness, *Songs of the Copper Eskimo* 497

BAFFIN ISLAND

O   Animal songs were very common among the Inuit. This piece from Baffin Island was one part of a traditional song duel where the duck ridicules his opponent, the ptarmigan. The singer goes through all the action of this bit of burlesque.

*The Song of the Pintailed Duck in Competition with the
Ptarmigan*

His head is like a swollen thumb joint,
His beak is like a thumb nail.
His lower beak is like a shovel, and his tongue is like a
   spoon.
They come together (the Ptarmigans) in the winter;
They walk together, and make a soft sleeping place
By covering the hard rocks with dung.
But their breasts freeze hard down to this,
They flap their wings,
And try to fly away ...
Bilby, *Among Unknown Eskimo* 250

O   The myth of the sea-goddess Sedna, mother and guardian of the
     great sea mammals, who dwells at the bottom of the sea, had
     deep religious significance for the coastal Inuit who hunt at sea.
     This version was recorded by the German anthropologist, Franz
     Boas, from the Inuit who lived in the vicinity of Cumberland
     Sound in Baffin Island.

Sedna and the Fulmar

Once upon a time there lived on a solitary shore an Inung
[Inuk] with his daughter Sedna. His wife had been dead for
some time and the two led a quiet life. Sedna grew up to be a
handsome girl and the youths came from all around to sue
for her hand, but none of them could touch her proud heart.
Finally, at the breaking up of the ice in the spring a fulmar
flew from over the ice and wooed Sedna with enticing song.
'Come to me,' it said; 'come into the land of the birds, where
there is never hunger, where my tent is made of the most
beautiful skins. You shall rest on soft bearskins. My fellows,
the fulmars, shall bring you all your heart may desire; their
feathers shall clothe you; your lamp shall always be filled with
oil, your pot with meat.' Sedna could not long resist such
wooing and they went together over the vast sea. When at last
they reached the country of the fulmar, after a long and hard
journey, Sedna discovered that her spouse had shamefully de-

42

ceived her. Her new home was not built of beautiful pelts, but was covered with wretched fishskins, full of holes, that gave free entrance to wind and snow. Instead of soft reindeer skins her bed was made of hard walrus hides and she had to live on miserable fish, which the birds brought her. Too soon she discovered that she had thrown away her opportunities when in her foolish pride she had rejected the Inuit youth. In her woe she sang: 'Aja. O father, if you knew how wretched I am you would come to me and we would hurry away in your boat over the waters. The birds look unkindly upon me the stranger; cold winds roar about my bed; they give me but miserable food. O come and take me back home. Aja.'

When a year had passed and the sea was again stirred by warmer winds, the father left his country to visit Sedna. His daughter greeted him joyfully and besought him to take her back home. The father hearing of the outrages wrought upon his daughter determined upon revenge. He killed the fulmar, took Sedna into his boat, and they quickly left the country which had brought so much sorrow to Sedna. When the other fulmars came home and found their companion dead and his wife gone, they all flew away in search of the fugitives. They were very sad over the death of their poor murdered comrade and continue to mourn and cry until this day.

Having flown a short distance they discerned the boat and stirred up a heavy storm. The sea rose in immense waves that threatened the pair with destruction. In this mortal peril the father determined to offer Sedna to the birds and flung her overboard. She clung to the edge of the boat with a death grip. The cruel father then took a knife and cut off the first joints of her fingers. Falling into the sea they were transformed into whales, the nails turning into whalebone. Sedna holding on to the boat more tightly, the second finger joints fell under the sharp knife and swam away as seals (pagomys foetidus); when the father cut off the stumps of the fingers they became ground seals (phoca barbata). Meantime the storm subsided, for the fulmars thought Sedna was drowned. The father then allowed her to come into the boat again. But from that time she cherished a deadly hatred against him and swore bitter revenge. After they got ashore, she called her dogs and let them gnaw off the feet and hands of her father while he was asleep. Upon this he cursed himself, his daughter, and the dogs which had maimed him; whereupon the earth opened and swallowed the hut, the father, the daughter, and the dogs. They have since lived in the land of Adlivun, of which Sedna is the mistress.

Boas, *The Central Eskimo* 175–7

○   The legend of Kiviung is a well-known tale of the epic hero who, in his many wanderings, suffers hardships to become learned and wise.

Kiviung

An old woman lived with her grandson in a small hut. As she had no husband and no son to take care of her and the boy, they were very poor, the boy's clothing being made of skins of birds which they caught in snares. When the boy would come out of the hut and join his playfellows, the men would laugh at him and tear his outer garment. Only one man, whose name was Kiviung, was kind to the young boy; but he could not protect him from the others. Often the lad came to his grandmother crying and weeping, and she always consoled him and each time made him a new garment. She entreated the men to stop teasing the boy and tearing his clothing, but they would not listen to her prayer. At last she got angry and swore she would take revenge upon his abusers, and she could easily do so, as she was a great angakoq.

She commanded her grandson to step into a puddle which was on the floor of the hut, telling him what would happen and how he should behave. As soon as he stood in the water the earth opened and he sank out of sight, but the next moment he rose near the beach as a yearling seal with a beautiful skin and swam about lustily.

The men had barely seen the seal when they took to their kayaks, eager to secure the pretty animal. But the transformed boy quickly swam away, as his grandmother had told him, and the men continued in pursuit. Whenever he rose to breathe he took care to come up behind the kayaks, where the men could not get at him with their harpoons; there, however, he splashed and dabbled in order to attract their attention and lure them on. But before any one could turn his kayak he had dived again and swam away. The men were so interested in the pursuit that they did not observe that they were being led far from the coast and that the land was now altogether invisible.

Suddenly a gale arose; the sea foamed and roared and the waves destroyed or upset their frail vessels. After all seemed to be drowned the seal was again transformed into the lad, who went home without wetting his feet. There was nobody now to tear his clothing, all his abusers being dead.

Only Kiviung, who was a great angakoq and had never abused the boy, had escaped the wind and waves. Bravely he strove against the wild sea, but the storm did not abate. After he had drifted for many days on the wide sea, a dark mass loomed up through the mist. His hope revived and he worked hard to reach the supposed land. The nearer he came, however, the more agitated did the sea become, and he saw that he had mistaken a wild, black sea, with raging whirlpools, for land. Barely escaping he drifted again for many days, but the storm did not abate and he did not see any land. Again he saw a dark mass looming up through the mist, but he was once more deceived, for it was another whirlpool which made the sea rise in gigantic waves.

At last the storm moderated, the sea subsided, and at a great distance he saw land. Gradually he came nearer and following the coast he at length spied a stone house in which a light was burning. He landed and entered the house. Nobody was inside but an old woman whose name was Arnaitiang. She received him kindly and at his request pulled off his boots, slippers and stockings and dried them on the frame hanging over the lamp. Then she went out to light a fire and cook a good meal.

When the stockings were dry, Kiviung tried to take them from the frame in order to put them on, but as soon as he extended his hand to touch them the frame rose out of his reach. Having tried several times in vain, he called Arnaitiang and asked her to give him back the stockings. She answered: 'Take them yourself; there they are; there they are' and went out again. The fact is she was a very bad woman and wanted to eat Kiviung.

Then he tried once more to take hold of his stockings, but with no better result. He called again for Arnaitiang and asked her to give him the boots and stockings, whereupon she said: 'Sit down where I sat when you entered my house; then you can get them.' After that she left him again. Kiviung tried it once more, but the frame rose as before and he could not reach it.

Now he understood that Arnaitiang meditated mischief; so he summoned his tornaq, a huge white bear, who arose roaring from under the floor of the house. At first Arnaitiang did not hear him, but as Kiviung kept on conjuring the spirit came nearer and nearer to the surface, and when she heard his loud roar she rushed in trembling with fear and gave Kiviung what he had asked for. 'Here are your boots,' she cried; 'here are your slippers; here are your stockings. I'll help you put them on.' But Kiviung would not stay any longer with this horrid witch and did not even dare to put on his boots, but took them from Arnaitiang and rushed out of the door. He had barely escaped when it clapped violently together and just caught the tail of his jacket, which was torn off. He hastened to his kayak without once stopping to look behind and paddled away. He had only gone a short distance before Arnaitiang, who had recovered from her fear, came out swinging her glittering woman's knife and threatening to kill him. He was nearly frightened to death and almost upset his kayak. However, he managed to balance it again and cried in answer, lifting up his spear: 'I shall kill you with my spear.' When Arnaitiang heard these words she fell down terror stricken and broke her knife. Kiviung then observed that it was made of a thin slab of fresh water ice.

He traveled on for many days and nights, following the shore. At last he came to a hut, and again a lamp was burning inside. As his clothing was wet and he was hungry, he landed and entered the house. There he found a woman who lived all alone with her daughter. Her son-in-law was a log of driftwood which had four boughs. Every day about the time of low water they carried it to the beach and when the tide came in it swam away. When night came again it returned with eight large seals, two being fastened to every bough. Thus the timber provided its wife, her mother, and Kiviung with an abundance of food. One day, however, after they had launched it as they had always done, it left and never returned.

After a short interval Kiviung married the young widow.

Now he went sealing every day himself and was very success-ful. As he thought of leaving some day, he was anxious to get a good stock of mittens (that his hands might keep dry during the long journey?). Every night after returning from hunting he pretended to have lost his mittens. In reality he had concealed them in the hood of his jacket.

After awhile the old woman became jealous of her daughter, for the new husband of the latter was a splendid hunter and she wished to marry him herself. One day when he was away hunting, she murdered her daughter, and in order to deceive him she removed her daughter's skin and crept into it, thus changing her shape into that of the young woman. When Kiv-iung returned, she went to meet him, as it had been her daughter's custom, and without exciting any suspicion. But when he entered the hut and saw the bones of his wife he at once became aware of the cruel deed and of the deception that had been practiced and fled away.

He traveled on for many days and nights, always following the shore. At last he again came to a hut where a lamp was burning. As his clothing was wet and he was hungry, he landed and went up to the house. Before entering it occurred to him that it would be best to find out first who was inside. He therefore climbed up to the window and looked through the peep hole. On the bed sat an old woman, whose name was Aissivang (spider). When she saw the dark figure before the window she believed it was a cloud passing the sun, and as the light was insufficient to enable her to go on with her work she got angry. With her knife she cut away her eyebrows, ate them, and did not mind the dripping blood, but sewed on. When Kiviung saw this he thought that she must be a very bad woman, and turned away.

Still he traveled on days and nights. At last he came to a land which seemed familiar to him and soon he recognized his own country. He was very glad when he saw some boats com-ing to meet him. They had been on a whaling excursion and were towing a great carcass to the village. In the bow of one of them stood a stout young man who had killed the whale. He was Kiviung's son, whom he had left a small boy and who was now grown up and had become a great hunter. His wife had taken a new husband, but now she returned to Kiviung.

Boas, *The Central Eskimo* 213–16

UNGAVA

○ In this incantation a shaman tries to cure an illness through the power of his magical words. The Reverend G.F. Le Gallais of the Colonial and Continental Church Society recorded the words which he obtained from a Hudson's Bay Company employee in Ungava Bay who had witnessed the ritual.

A Healing Chant

Spirit I see,
Annérsok of brute,
Form not I know,
Know not his name,
Like never seen here,
Seen here by Angekok,
Form now he hideth,
Form he now changeth,
Name I can call him,
Again Spirit changeth,
He is not our Kumuc,
Kumuc our Kattangut,
Angekok weary,
Torngak departed.

Unknown Ungava 7

LABRADOR

○ **Rose Pamack** (1944–) was born in Nain, Labrador, and attended Moravian and Grenfell mission schools in Labrador and Newfoundland. In 1974 she graduated from the Teacher Education Program at Memorial University of Newfoundland and taught for a few years. From 1977 to 1983 she worked as a translator for Tunngassuk, a special program of the Labrador Inuit Associaton that collected poems, stories, songs, and legends from Labrador Innus. In 1988 she was employed by the Okalakatiget Society, an Inuit training centre for media services in Nain. She retells the legend of Tikisiak, a landscape feature around Nain.

Tikisiak

Looking across the harbour from Nain, you can see a polar bear, or rather a rock in the shape of a polar bear. This polar bear is only visible on certain days and there is a very old story about it.

On a typical summer day a long time ago when Nain was just a tiny village, the hunters left on their kajaks for the day's hunting. There was no one left in the village except the women, the children, and the old people.

It was a typical summer day in Nain. The old people sat and watched the children at play. The children amused themselves in various childhood pursuits; skimming flat rocks across the surface of the water to see how far each rock would go and to see how many times it would bounce before it sank; chasing and catching young sculpine amongst the seaweed in the little ponds left by the ebbing tide; little girls playing house with unwilling husky puppies as their babies. There was an air of relaxation and contentment. Suddenly the air was pierced by a loud cry of alarm, 'Tikigaattaulikqugut; We are being attacked!'

Children were handed into tents by anxious mothers with orders that they keep still and quiet. Huskies paced uneasily emitting that unique low half-growl half-bark that is their [signal that] danger is lurking. Fear gripped each Inuk heart.

Across the harbour with slow and steady steps walked a huge polar bear. It was approaching the village of helpless and defenceless women, each step a toll of death and mutilation.

All waited for the moment of confrontation. The women readied their ulus with the slim hope that by sheer numbers they could defeat and kill this predator without too much loss of life. They would fight to the death to protect their children.

Mikigaak, an old grandfather, also made preparations. He took his drum that he had fashioned from the bladder-thin tissue of a seal's bladder, the same drum he had used at the feast to celebrate a successful hunt. He took the drum and began beating it gently, the gentle, regular beating of life.

The drum hypnotized the villagers. The mothers laid down their ulus, the babies fell asleep, the children ceased their whimpering, the dogs stopped their pacing.

The only sound to be heard was the measured steps of the white intruder and the answering beat of the old man's drum fashioned from a seal's bladder.

Alone Mikigaak stood at the edge of the village with the most powerful tool of his ancestors, the ancient lore of milleniums ago when his ancestors learnt the core of survival.

He chanted to Tunggak, the Supreme Spirit of the high mountains far to the north. What he said I cannot reveal to you because those people, the Angakkuk, those people with the power to communicate with the spirit, have their own language. The chanting ceased.

The polar bear froze in his tracks. There he stood in mid-step, immobilized. He had been turned to stone. Then slowly he crumbled and shattered, till all there was left was a pile of quartz fragments.

To this day, if you go to Nain, you can still see the polar bears across the harbour from Nain. It is Nain's landmark! The old people of Nain used to say it would appear on those days that strangers would arrive. When it appeared, everyone waited expectantly for visitors. It can only be seen from a distance and it is only seen on certain days. If you go across to hunt for it as each generation of unbelieving young Inuit do, you will not find it.

O   As a translator for Tunngassuk, Pamack translated over one hundred traditional songs found in old Moravian song books. 'Winter's Exodus' is one of them.

Winter's Exodus

Winter, let's get divorced!
Your parting, truly,
holds little sorrow.
I don't care
if you distance,
far, far away.
If you don't leave,
the spring thaw shall destroy you.
You, winter,
let's be parted!
Inuktitut (May 1982) 71

EASTERN ARCTIC

O Myths of creation and origin were strikingly similar across Arctic Canada. Two short variants from the eastern Arctic and a longer one from the west told of the creation of man and the origin of light.

Creation

When the raven became aware of himself,
light came into the world,
and grass tussocks turned into men.
Eastern Eskimo
Houston, *Songs of the Dream People* 80

O **Inernerunashuaq**, also known as **Unaleq** (fl. 1922), had emigrated from Pelly Bay to the area around Lyon Inlet around 1900. As a shaman he enjoyed a considerable reputation. He gave Rasmussen this creation story.

The Creation of Man

It is said that once upon a time the world fell to pieces, and every living thing was destroyed. There came mighty downpours of rain from the heavens, and the earth itself was destroyed. Afterwards, two men appeared on earth. They came from hummocks of earth; they were born so. They were already fully grown when they emerged from the ground. They lived together as man and wife, and soon one of them was with child. Then the one who had been husband sang a magic song: ...

A human being here
A penis here.
May its opening be wide
And roomy.
Opening, opening, opening!

When these words were sung, the man's penis split with a

loud noise and he became a woman, and gave birth to a child. From these three mankind grew to be many.

Rasmussen, *Intellectual Culture of the Iglulik Eskimos* 252

MACKENZIE

The Raven and the Red Fox

In the early days here on earth there was no light, no day. It was always dark. All the light which should have illuminated the earth had been stolen and was hidden in two urine bladders, one having a dazzling light, much stronger than what was confined in the other.

The two urine bladders were stolen and carried away by a man who lived far away from all others together with his wife.

It so happened that a large raven determined to find the light and bring it back to the earth and the people on it, so it turned itself into human form and set out. It was a great shaman, so that it soon arrived at the place where the two urine bladders were hidden, and there it concealed itself.

It soon discovered that the man kept a very careful guard over the stolen light, and that it was impossible to steal the bladders from him in any ordinary way. So the wise raven thought out a ruse. It would make a little child – for people find it hardest of all to refuse anything to a child, and this child, which the woman in the house would be made to deliver, should be part of the raven itself; in this fashion the child should help, without the man who possessed the light of the world suspecting anything.

This the raven did one evening by causing the woman to feel the urge to make water, and she went outside to do so.

The moment she began to make water, the raven by magic made a small catkin enter her womb.

On going into the house again she said to her husband:

'It was strange. While I was out making water something hurt me. It was like something coming into me.'

That same night she could feel that she was with child – a

child which grew so rapidly that it was born after only a few nights.

The child grew up quickly, and the people in the house loved it because it thrived so unusually well, and it was allowed to have its way in everything.

Now it happened that nothing in the house attracted the child so much as the two urine bladders in which the light of the world was kept, and every evening it cried for them; the father, who could not refuse the child anything, allowed it to play with one of the bladders on the floor, but only the less bright one; the larger one he would not give it, no matter how much the child cried for it.

So of an evening the child would play with the shining bladder on the floor, bouncing it up and down like a ball.

The cunning raven knew that one evening the bladder would roll down into the passage, and therefore it summoned a red fox, which every evening stood in the darkness of the passage, just below the inside entrance.

Then finally one evening, when the parents least suspected it, the child suddenly knocked the bladder down into the passage, where the fox snapped it at once and leapt away with it.

At the same moment the child which the raven had created turned into a raven itself, and uttering the raven's call: qaɔq, qaɔq, qaɔq, flew out through the passage and started after the fleeing fox.

With all its might the fox ran across the land, with the raven hovering above it; every time the fox became tired it passed the light-bladder on to the raven, who flew with it until he too became tired and passed it back to the fox.

Behind them came the man who had stolen the light. He pursued them, and, being a great shaman himself, was able to keep close up to them.

In the end both fox and raven grew tired of stumbling about in the dark. They ran and flew all they could without being able to see. So the fox bit the bladder with his sharp teeth, and the raven pecked it with its sharp bill; the bladder burst and light welled out over the country and filled the sky, so that the man who had carried it off could never more get hold of it.

Thus day came, and thus light came to the people of the world.

It was the less bright of the two urine bladders that the raven succeeded in recovering for mankind. Had it been the larger one, the light would have been so tremendous and powerful that there would always have been daylight on earth.

Now there was light enough for daytime only, which is the reason why night alternates with day all over the world.

Rasmussen, *The Mackenzie Eskimos*, x, 2, 71–3

Attuiock

Orpingalik

Minik Wallace

Eric Anoee conducting a Bible class
at Maguse Lake, Keewatin, 1956

Ipirvik

Taqulittuq

Inuluapik

Mikak

Kallihirua

Hans Hendrik and family

Ada Blackjack Johnson

2 'What Great Creatures Are These'

EARLY CONTACT LITERATURE

Are you one of those white men who forbid the Eskimo to
enter their tents?

Rasmussen, *Across Arctic America* 191

They see his ship and think it from some fairyland filled with crackers and coffee

'Esquimau hunts Pole,' *New York Tribune*, 22 June 1909

Tell me, stranger, are you a man whom a woman can make smile?

Rasmussen, *Intellectual Culture of the Copper Eskimos* 128

To people who believed themselves the only true human beings in the world, the first strangers who came to their land were, surely, sub-human, inferior beings from other galaxies, from the sun or moon perhaps. 'Qallunaat,' the men of heavy eyebrows, the Inuit called these strangers who kept arriving at different places at different times by ship or overland.

At first, encounters were brief and sporadic. The Inuit were fearful and cautious. The newcomers were strange curiosities, indeed. And then, gradually lured by the amazing wonders the Europeans brought with them, the Inuit become dependent, and new desires became actual needs. Further encounters – more frequent and sustained – with whalers, missionaries, and fur traders led eventually to fraternization.

The first missionaries to the Inuit, the Moravian Brethren who arrived in Nain, Labrador, in 1771, introduced a strange, new religion. Conversion to this peculiar ideology demanded renunciation of traditional religious practices, and it was not until 1776 that the first convert, Kingminguse, was baptized. The missionaries reported the minutiae of the difficulties and successes of their work, and verbatim testimony of Christian piety, such as that given by Kingminguse, was religiously recorded.

If the Inuit thought the intruders were peculiar, the latter, in turn, were fascinated by 'these strange children of the snows' and were anxious to display them in their native countries. Thus, ever since 1576 when Martin Frobisher, in search of the Northwest Passage, captured an Eskimo hunter from Baffin Island to take back to England, Inuit have been taken abroad, initially as unwilling captives and later as willing candidates for promotional, education, or religious reasons. The culture shock, however, was too great. Whether it was Attuiock, a Labrador Inuk taken to London in 1772 by Captain George Cartwright, who wanted to impress him with the power and riches of his country, or Ugarng, a Baffin Island Inuk, who was taken to New York nearly a century later, probably by whalers, the Inuit were homesick and wanted only to return home.

By the middle of the nineteenth century, the exhibiting of exotic peoples from the remote corners of the world at great world expositions was developing into a regular business. Many Inuit, principally from southern Labrador, because the Moravian missionaries to the north were always opposed to the Inuit leaving the country, were exhibited in Europe or the United States. Pomiuk and Zecharias, for example, were exhibited at the World's Columbian Exposition held in Chicago in 1893 and then abandoned and left destitute by their exploiters.

Conversely, with increased interaction, the newcomers to Canada became dependent on the Inuit as models of survival. The search for the elusive Northwest Passage to the riches of the Orient continued to bring voyages; the missing Franklin expedition of 1845–7 itself brought a concentrated impetus to exploration of the Arctic in the next ten years. In the paths of the explorers followed whalers, fur traders, missionaries, the Royal Canadian Mounted Police, government officials, and scientists. Whether the pursuit was whales, furs, souls, scientific data, or the law, the Inuit – as hunters, guides, dog drivers, seamstresses, pilots, interpreters, or informants – were indispensable to the success of the white mission. Many of their names have been lost to history. But buried in a few records that survive is the testimony of a few Inuit from this early contact period.

Their comments and observations in English are few and rudimentary. And their English is halting and idiosyncratic. But they are the first recorded reactions of the Inuit to the white intruders. In these selections, except for the eight-year-old Karpik and the young wife of Eketcheak, the Inuit demonstrated courtesy and dignity. There is a lack of sentimentality to be sure: the Inuit saw themselves modestly, continuing the practice of the self-depreciation of their forebears. The dominant impression is one of selfless courage, of a strength and modesty greater than ordinary.

This chapter begins with a testimony by the Moravian Brethren's first convert to Christianity in 1776, translated from Inuktitut, and ends a century and a half later, in 1923, with diary extracts written in English by an unsung Inuk heroine.

O   **Karpik** (1756–69), an orphan, was captured along with Mikak near Chateau Bay, Labrador, in 1767 and taken to England in 1768. On Governor Hugh Palliser's special direction, Karpik was given to the care of Jens Haven who in the summer of 1769 placed him in the school of the United Brethren at Fulneck in Yorkshire to be instructed for mission work in Labrador, but that fall the young lad caught smallpox and died.

Karpik's Conversation with Jens Haven, 1769

When Karpik asked Haven for a hat and coat embroidered with gold and Haven remonstrated as to the uselessness of such finery and exhorted the boy to learn to know the Lord, Karpik responded:

Poor clothes ... will not teach me that: my countrymen, who are clad meanly enough, die, and know nothing of the God in heaven, of whom you say so much. The king wears fine clothes, and why then should not I? I can still become acquainted with God, and love him ...

When Haven told Karpik that he had no money to buy fine clothes, Karpik retorted:

Then go to the King ... and get some money from him.

Missions in Labrador 59–60

O **Mikak** (c. 1740–95) was one of a group of Inuit encamped near Chateau Bay in southern Labrador, who in 1765 met a group of Moravian Brethren, including Jens Haven, sent on an exploratory expedition to contact the Labrador Inuit. In 1768, at the instigation of Newfoundland Governor Hugh Palliser, she was taken to England where she created a great sensation. She was presented to Augusta, Dowager Princess of Wales and mother of King George III, who gave her a finely ornamented white dress trimmed with gold. Her portrait was painted by the distinguished artist, John Russell. And she again met Jens Haven, who, on behalf of the Moravian missionaries, was in London to petition the British government for permission to establish a mission station among the Inuit. Mikak strongly supported Haven's plan and promoted it among the influential and powerful of London.

Mikak returned to Labrador in 1769, and when Haven arrived in Byron Bay, she had not forgotten him. On 19 July 1770, on board the *Jersey Packet*, she extended her invitation for the missionaries to stay.

Mikak to Jens Haven, 1770

You will see ... how well we will behave, if you will only come. We will love you as our countrymen, and trade with you justly, and treat you kindly.

The Moravians in Labrador 73

Although she was largely instrumental in the peaceful establishment of the Moravian mission station at Nain in Labrador, Mikak disappointed the missionaries by refusing to live at the station and by visiting European traders nearby. It was not until shortly before her death that, full of remorse, she returned to the mission station.

Mikak to the Moravian Missionaries, 1795

Ah, I have behaved very bad, and am grieved on that account, but what shall I do! I cannot find Jesus again!

Periodical Accounts, II, 171

○ **Attuiock** (fl. 1772), shaman, was one of a family of five Inuit whom Captain George Cartwright, a former army officer and a trader and entrepreneur on the Labrador coast from 1770 to 1786, took back with him to London, England, in 1772. In London Attuiock created considerable interest, meeting with King George III and members of the Royal Society, including naturalist Joseph Banks and James Boswell. The cultivated land was a surprise to him: 'the land is all made,' Attuiock observed. But the wonders and riches of the great city did not impress him.

Attuiock's Impressions of London, 1772

'Oh! I am tired; here are too many houses; too much smoke; too much people; Labrador is very good; seals are plentiful there; I wish I was back again.'

Cartwright, A Journal of Transactions, I, 269

○ **Kingminguse** (baptized Peter) (fl. 1776–92), a young shaman from a band in the vicinity of Nain, Labrador, became the Moravian Brethren's first convert to Christianity on 19 February

1776. The event created considerable excitement among the local Inuit. At first Kingminguse proved a model convert, but he later returned to his traditional ways.

Candidates for baptism were asked to renounce 'their heathenish customs'; Kingminguse is eloquent in his renunciation.

Kingminguse's Renunciation

I have been a Angakok, and used to believe what had been told me by my predecessors; but now I believe it no longer, and will abandon all evil customs for the future, and will follow the Lord Jesus only, even if I should be persecuted for it by my countrymen. I was an ignorant man, but when the Brethren came here and told us of the Lord of Heaven and earth, who, out of love to us, became a man and shed His blood for us, I rejoiced greatly at hearing of it. I received this word into my heart, and I will quit every other thing. I am alone like an orphan, and have no brothers or sisters, and therefore am the more happy that ye will receive me as your brother. As yet I know but little of Jesus, but I fain would know Him better in my heart, and all my confidence is in Him, as I verily believe that in Him alone one is happy, and when the body dies the soul will find rest and be forever in that place where it will be continually happy.

Davey, *The Fall of Torngak* 167–8

Kingminguse's baptism influenced other conversions, but **Aula** who witnessed the baptismal ceremony had more pressing concerns:

I believe very much, but at present I want a knife.

Davey, *The Fall of Torngak* 169

Eketcheak and Wife's Responses to Captain George Cartwright's Proposal, 1786

O **Eketcheak** (fl. 1786) was a Labrador Inuk. When Captain George Cartwright asked Eketcheak for his young wife, he replied:

You are very welcome to her, but I am afraid she will not please you, as her temper is very bad, and she is so idle, that

61

she will do no work; nor can she use a needle: but my other wife is the best tempered creature in the world; an excellent sempstress [sic], is industry itself, and she has two children; all of which are much at your service; or, if you please, you shall have them both; and, when I return next year, if you do not like either one or the other, I will take them back again ...

When Cartwright replied that 'he would be contented with the bad one,' Eketcheak answered:

You shall have her ... but before we proceed any farther in this business, I wish you would mention it to her relations, and obtain their consent ...

Although her relatives eagerly consented to the alliance, the young girl responded contemptuously. And Cartwright's courtship ended in failure.

You are an old fellow, and I will have nothing to say to you.

Cartwright, *A Journal of Transactions*, III, 189–90

First Meeting, 1818

O   When a group of polar Eskimos, who had never before seen white men, met the British Arctic explorer John Ross, in 1818, the meeting was one of fear and distrust. Pointing to his ships, they asked eagerly:

What great creatures are these? Do they come from the sun or the moon? Do they give us light by night or by day?

When John Sackheuse, the Eskimo interpreter [from south Greenland] said that he was a man and pointing to the south said that he came from a distant country in that direction, they answered:

That cannot be, there is nothing but ice there.

And when Sackheuse explained that the ships were houses made of wood, the Inuit were filled with disbelief.

No, they are alive, we have seen them move their wings.

Even when a group followed John Ross and William Edward Parry to the *Isabella* they still believed it to be a living creature and addressed her:

Who are you? What are you? Where do you come from? Is it from the sun or the moon?

Smith, *Arctic Expeditions* 91, 93–4

O **Inuluapik** or **Eenoolooapik** (1820–47) was born at Qimisuk on the west coast of Cumberland Sound. In 1839 Captain William Penny, a whaler from Aberdeen, Scotland, and master of the *Neptune*, took Inuluapik who had drawn a wonderful map of the Cumberland Sound area for Penny back to Aberdeen. But the climate did not agree with the lad who was constantly annoyed with 'too much cough.' And so the following year Inuluapik returned home on the *Bon Accord*, another Aberdeen whaler. On board the whaler, Inuluapik dictated this letter to a benefactor, Mr Hogarth of Aberdeen, from Cumberland Sound on 20 August 1840. Inuluapik died of consumption in the summer of 1847. His sister Taqulittuq or Hannah later accompanied Charles Francis Hall to the United States, Hudson Bay, King William Island, and Greenland.

Inuluapik's Letter to Mr Hogarth, 1840

Mr. Hogarth – Eenoolooapik has arrived in Tenudiackbeek, and intends to remain at Keimovksook.
   The Innuit say that for many suns the whales were very numerous, but before the ship came they had all disappeared. They also say that the whales will return when the sun becomes low.
   Captain Penny has been very kind to me and to many Innuits, who all thank him. Next to him you were the kindest to me when I was with you.

Eenoolooapik

McDonald, *A Narrative*, insert between 102 and 103

O **Qalasirssuaq, Kallihirua,** or **Erasmus York** (c. 1832–56), guide, was born in the Thule Region of northwest Greenland. In 1850, he joined Captain Erasmus Ommanney's ship, the *Assistance,* that was part of the Franklin search expedition of 1850–1 at Cape York, Greenland. In 1851 he went with the expedition to England and gave testimony to the British Admiralty. In the same year he was placed in St Augustine's College at Canterbury, a college for the education of missionary clergy of the Church of England. There he was considered 'a youth of intelligence and quick observation' who conducted himself 'well and properly in all respects.' In 1855 he left England to further his religious training at Queen's College in St John's, Newfoundland, before beginning missionary work among the Inuit of Labrador, but he died at the college shortly after his arrival.

In the first of the two letters which follow, written 'to a friend,' his description of the state of his health is very 'simple and affecting.' In the second letter, written to Mr Blunsom, a benefactor, there is no mention of his illness, although he was to die six months later.

Kallihirua's Letter, 1853

E. York, St. Augustine's College, April, 1853

My dear Sir,

I am very glad to tell, How do you do, Sir? I been England, long time none very well. Long time none very well. Very bad weather. I know very well, very bad cough. I very sorry, very bad weather, dreadful. Country very difference. Another day cold. Another day wet, I miserable.

Another summer come. Very glad. Great many trees. Many wood. Summer beautiful, country Canterbury.

Kallihirua's Letter, 1856

St. John's College, Newfoundland,
January 7, 1856.

I received your kind letter by the December mail, and am very sorry to hear of your illness. The weather here is very cold; I feel it more than at Cape York. I have begun to skate, and find it a pleasant amusement. There is a lake a little distance from the College, called, 'Quidi, Vidi,' on which we practise. The Bishop is very kind and good to me. College here is not so large and fine a place as St. Augustine's nor are there so many students. I hope that all my kind friends at Canterbury are quite well. Please remember me kindly to Mr. and Mrs. Gipps, and all at St. Augustine's. With kind love to yourself.

I remain, yours affectionately,
Kalli.

Murray, *Kalli* 31, 52–3

O   **Ugarng** (c. 1810–), Ipirvik's uncle, was born near Newton's Fiord in Frobisher Bay. As a prominent and successful hunter, he was frequently employed by the whalers who came to Cumberland Sound. According to Charles Francis Hall, Ugarng 'was a remarkably intelligent man and a very good mechanic.' When he visited the United States in 1854–5, the vast crowds on the streets of New York overwhelmed him.

Ugarng's Impressions of New York

'G-d-! too much horse – too much house – too much white people. Women? Ah! women great many – good!'

Hall, *Life with the Esquimaux* 82

O   Of all the Inuit who assisted the white man, the most remarkable were the couple **Ipirvik** (**Ebierbing**) and **Taqulittuq** (**Tookoolito**), known in English as Joe (or Eskimo Joe) and Hannah. In 1860 they met the American Arctic explorer, Charles Francis Hall, and their attachment to him was a special one of genuine affection and steadfast loyalty.

Taqulittuq (c. 1839–76), seamstress and interpreter, was born near Cumberland Sound in Baffin Island. Ipirvik (c. 1837 – c. 1881), hunter, guide, sledge-driver, and interpreter, was also born in the same vicinity. About 1853, they were taken to England by a British whaler and dined with Queen Victoria and Prince Albert. (Taqulittuq later told Hall that Buckingham Palace was 'a fine place, I assure you, sir.') Around 1855 the couple returned to Cumberland Sound where Ipirvik worked with the whale fisheries. After meeting Hall in the autumn of 1860, however, the couple devoted their time and energies to the

65

American explorer teaching him the importance and skills of Arctic living and survival.

Taqulittuq's gracious manner and accomplishments never failed to amaze Hall. Although it had been some years since her return to Baffin Island from England, she had preserved a few European customs. She liked to wear her Victorian dresses and bonnets on special occasions. And on their second meeting in her skin tent, she invited Hall to tea asking him the strength he preferred.

During Hall's three Arctic expeditions of 1860–2, 1864–9, and 1871, Ipirvik and Taqulittuq were his companions and mentors, following him into regions considered taboo, and into regions inhabited by peoples regarded as unfriendly and dangerous, such as the Pelly Bay Inuit. During his two visits to the United States in 1862–4 and 1869–71, they helped him raise funds for his expeditions by making guest appearances in their native dress and speaking at public lectures. (In February 1870 they were received by President Grant at the White House.)

When not travelling with Hall on his many lecture tours, they spent much time with the family of whaling master Sidney O. Budington of Groton, Connecticut, with whom Hall sailed to and from the Arctic. Taqulittuq and Mrs Budington soon became good friends. And Taqulittuq, said to be 'full of frolicsome and comical ways,' became a celebrity with the Budingtons' circle of friends.

The couple's courageous and patient part during Hall's third expedition (1871) – known as the *Polaris* expedition after the steamer captained by Budington – is one of the most heroic in the annals of Arctic exploration. On 15 October 1872, nearly a year after Hall had died of suspicious causes (in 1968 an autopsy of his remains revealed 'an intake of considerable amounts of arsenic by C.F. Hall in the last two weeks of his life'), a panic cry arose that the *Polaris* was sinking during a storm in Smith Sound. During the night, boats were lowered and supplies were thrown onto the ice floe to which the ship was anchored. But a sudden violent gale tore the *Polaris* from its moorings, and the next day, nineteen people stranded on the ice floe saw that the *Polaris* with the captain and the rest of the crew had been swept away. Six months later on 30 April, twenty survivors (a baby boy, Charlie Polaris, had been born on the ice floe to the wife of Hans Hendrik) were rescued by the New-foundland sealer *Tigress*, a little to the north of Belle Isle.

It is doubtful that anyone would have survived the 190-day ordeal without the Inuit's help. Through the darkness and cold of an Arctic winter, the ice floe kept growing smaller and smaller as it drifted south, and death from starvation was a constant threat. Even the hair from the seals was eaten. As Ipirvik said to Captain George Tyson who took command of the expedition after Hall's death: 'Anything is good, that don't poison you.'

All who had served on the *Polaris* were immediately called to Washington where the government launched an investigation. As soon as they could leave Washington, Ipirvik, Taqulittuq, and Punna, their adopted daughter, returned to Groton where Hall had bought a house for them. Ipirvik worked as a carpenter in Connecticut, and Taqulittuq sewed furs and other articles of clothing. Punna went to school where she was reported to be 'one of the most brilliant pupils in her class.' On 18 March 1875, at nine, Punna died of pneumonia, and on 31 December 1876, Taqulittuq died of tuberculosis.

Shortly after his daughter's death in 1875 Ipirvik left for England to assist a new British attempt to sail the Northwest Passage and joined the *Pandora* expedition led by Captain Allen Young. When the expedition failed because of heavy ice, Ipirvik returned to the United States to discover that Taqulittuq had died. He remained in Groton briefly and then joined the Franklin search expedition under Lieutenant Frederick Schwatka funded by the American government in 1878–80. At that time Ipirvik decided to remain with his people rather than go back to the United States.

Taqulittuq's Complaint to Hall about the Whalers

I feel very sorry to say that many of the whaling people are very bad, making the Inuits bad too; they swear very much, and make our people swear. I wish they would not do so. *Americans swear a great deal – more and worse than the English*. I wish no one would swear. It is a very bad practice, I believe.

Hall, *Life with the Esquimaux* 138

The Inuit have a tradition of a deluge which they attribute to an unusually high tide. When Hall asked Taqulittuq why, she taught him a lesson in geology.

Taqulittuq's Object Lesson in Geology

Did you never see little stones, like clams and such things as live in the sea, away up on the mountains?
Hall, *Life with the Esquimaux* 525

While at Depot Island in the Arctic, Taqulittuq wrote to her friend, Mrs Budington.

Taqulittuq's Letter, 1864

July 10, 1864

Dear Mother Budington.
how are you, I Been I sick. And. three or four day. I like to come see my Pretty mother.
Think time. I like to go now and see you in igloo or house. never mind mother. few years more. Come see you again I hope. I can tell we die some time. Man give to me two apples to eat make better in four days. Can not eat so sick. home sick. Better now I sewing and knit everyday. Go in boat to King William Land. ice and snow and rock. never mind. do all for the best. go any where. Sometime hot sometime cold. I like warm Summer best. I must try to be good. take good care off father [Hall] and Joe when he sick.
Joe lame back and leg. Some time he cant Rest in night. I sorry for him. I think of him every day.
He no use cry and use speak so much, good mother. Joe better now, this morning. Sometime Better sometime very hard time

New London County Historical Society, New London, Conn., Correspondence of Esquimaux 919.8/C818

The dramatic survival and rescue of the twenty, marooned on an ice floe, when the partly unloaded *Polaris* suddenly drifted away, excited sensational attention in the United States. Newspapers devoted whole pages to the story and published detailed interviews with the survivors. Ipirvik's testimony was always sought after.

Ipirvik's Testimony to the New York Herald, 1873

Very fond of Captain Hall. We was crushed in ice. Didn't like Buddington; always talking behind back; asking story all time. Ship's stern broken. Blow hard when drove from ship. Couldn't get aboard. Some men here (in St. Johns) and some in ship used to quarrel. I went with Captain Hall purpose to go sledge to North. After Hall died Buddington wouldn't go. I see with two eye and two ear. I tell Buddington I come to go North. He wouldn't let me go. Buddington and I quarrelled good deal about it. I went with Hall on last sled and Hans and Chester (the mate). We went fifty miles north of ship on ice and land. Found musk ox tracks on land. Sun nearly gone when came back to ship. Hall told me when sick. Somebody give him something bad.

He was sick two weeks. Buddington did not take care of him. I think it not right; made me feel bad. Sick man good man too. Throat swelled something; couldn't drink. Said he burn inside. I stopped up with him every night with another man; he sleep I wake, I wake he sleep. Hall was in cabin. I talked to Hall much. He no talk to others much as me. I didn't see Hall in first night after he came aboard from sled. Came aboard with him in afternoon. He looked well, happy, and spoke nice. The four of us –

HALL, CHESTER, HANS AND JOE –

had coffee when came aboard. I had mine in my own room, underneath cabin. Hall in cabin and two others in galley. At 10 o'clock that night my wife told me

HALL VERY SICK; VOMITING;

eat something. Next morning I go see him and say, 'What matter?' He all alone in cabin. He say, 'You pretty well, Joe?' I say 'Yes.' He say, 'You drink bad coffee last night?' I say 'No.' I ask him, 'Did he drink bad coffee?' He say, 'Something bad in coffee I drink last night, making me sick and stomach bad.' Same morning he get very sick, vomiting. After five days he feel better: wake up and say he want to see my little girl, and say to her he think he would leave her, but didn't like. After he got better he get four doctor books to try and see what make him sick. He study hard, and say to me, 'That name is makin' me sick.' [Joe explained that he (Captain Hall) here pointed to a name in one of the books, which he read out.] It was

SOMETHING ABOUT POISON, I THINK.

After Hall die everybody watching one another. Me no understand what they mean. All afraid somebody put down poison in water, bread or something. It looked like he was poisoned to me all same ...

New York Weekly Herald, 24 May 1873

After the horrible ordeal, the United States government launched an investigation into the *Polaris* affair. Taqulittuq's responses at the official inquiry were self-effacing and forthright.

Taqulittuq's Testimony, 1873

QUESTION: Do you remember when you lost the ship?
ANSWER: Yes, sir.
QUESTION: How was that?
ANSWER: The wind blew hard. We were driven on ice. Captain Buddington thought the ship was going to be lost. Ordered everything ready to go on ice. I took my clothes. We tried to get everything off. We all worked like horses. Everybody tumbled over everybody. Then I went on the ice, and then came aboard again. I had left my trunk on board. I asked the fireman who was pumping how the ship was. He said the ship was all right. Was not tipped over at this time. He was pumping close to my door. He said, 'You need not carry anything more out, you will come aboard all right to-night.' I staid down in cabin a few minutes. Captain Buddington told me to go on ice, and to take my things with me. I told him that fireman said, ship all right. He replied, 'Never you mind; take little girl and go on ice.' Mr. Myers came on ice little after I did. In a few minutes ship went. Very dark. Snowing thick, wet. The ship broke away from us. The hawser slipped from anchor, which had

been planted in the ice. It was gone in a few minutes, it was so dark.

QUESTION: Did you see the ship again?

ANSWER: Yes, next morning. We tried to go on shore, to the ship, but we were prevented by the drifting ice. Then we got back on the same floe. That night we were blown away and floated off. We never saw the ship again. I think the ship would have saved us if she had come out after us in the first place, but the heavy wind carried us off. We felt bad enough.

QUESTION: Don't you think they tried to come to you?

ANSWER: Don't believe they saw us; we saw them.

QUESTION: Do you think the ship is all right now?

ANSWER: O, yes; it is safe. It is in a very good place. There are no icebergs there. They are behind a little island. They will be able to get out in the summer time.

QUESTION: Do you think they have plenty of provisions?

ANSWER: O, yes, some Esquimaux there. They can hunt for fresh meat. Esquimaux can come to them as soon as the ice is made. We floated off on this cake of ice. We were on it nearly five months. Then we traveled from piece to piece.

QUESTION: Who was in command of the party on the ice?

ANSWER: Nobody.

QUESTION: Was not Captain Tyson in command?

ANSWER: Well, he did not have much. He could not control them. He tried to do everything he could. He was a good man. We have known him a good many years. He tried to do everything for the best; sometimes they would not mind him; I sorry, and Joe very sorry too. Some time little provisions left; just before we were taken off, about a week, we thought we were going to starve, but the bear saved us; the bear came across the pack-ice. He smelt the seals, and the people. Joe chased him; the men laid down out of sight ...

Annual Report of the Secretary of the Navy on the Operations of the Department for the year 1873 (Washington, 1873) 69

Taqulittuq's Letter to Mrs Budington, 1873

Taqulittuq's brief letter to Mrs Budington displays an uncommon strength, decency, and loyalty. She dismisses her ordeal on the ice in one short sentence. Although she is very busy, she takes time off to reassure Mrs Budington that her husband who had been left on his wrecked ship was safe.

Wiscasset, June 22, 1873.

Sarah Mother Buddington: I shall never forget you. I now try to write you. I am well; Joe well; Punna very sick for thirty-four days, little better now. I like to see you once more. So good to me. I never have time to do anything. Hans four children here too. I got eight children; no go with them home. Oct. 15, 1872, we come home down on ice. Old man [Capt. Budington] come by and by; he well.

Hannah Lito.

New London Country Historical Society, New London, Conn., undated clipping from *New York Herald*

When Ipirvik was interviewed by J.A. MacGahan, a journalist aboard the *Pandora*, his steadfast loyalty and generosity shine through. Although the stranded men whose lives he saved were lazy and ungrateful, Ipirvik prefered to recall only their small gestures of gratitude.

Ipirvik's Reactions, 1875

They all vely good men – like me good deal – meet him – say Joe – how you do – you save our life – come take a drink – give cigar sometimes too ...

Kill him seal. No! never go out house – try keep warm – afraid go out – pretty cold – vely weak . . . not know how kill him seal – nothing but starve.

Just when the stranded party on the ice floe were at the point of starvation, Ipirvik killed a big Ugjuk seal. His description of what happened to those who ate the poisonous liver despite his warnings is amusing.

After while, all sick – skin all come off face, look very bad – one man black – nigger-man – (there was a negro in Tyson's party) – after while little skin come off here – little there – then he spotted – by'n by skin all come off – then he white man – he! he! he! he!

MacGahan, *Under the Northern Lights* 147, 148

O   **Hans Hendrik** (c. 1834–89), hunter, guide, dog-driver, interpreter, was another of those exceptional Inuit, like Ipirvik and Taqulittuq, who assisted polar expeditions. He saved the party of Elisha Kane from starvation in 1853–5, and in the winter of 1873 he too was with the stranded *Polaris* group and helped them to survive tht six-month ordeal. In his dictated *Memoirs*, Hendrik gives his impressions of New York and the Washington area where he and his family were taken after their rescue.

Hans Hendrik's Memoirs (an extract)

The following day we left for a place farther to the north and a little cooler, as they were anxious for us on account of the heat. First we touched at Boston, stopping, I believe, for one day, then we landed in New York. Here we stayed several days wondering at the crowd of masts, the large buildings, and heaps of people. While on board, we went on deck in the evening to have a view of the many vessels that lay intermingled, illuminated by thousands of lamps, some of them furnished with red, some with blue, and some with yellow glasses; and their whistles were heard, some very shrill, some less so. To be sure it was an amazing view, the lights of the houses glittering like so many stars. At last I began to think on the creation of the world, and I said to my comrade: 'How wonderful that all these people subsist from the trifle that the soil produces; behold the numberless houses, the charming shores yonder, and this calm sea, how inviting!' ...

Then our train arrived, and we took seats in it. When we had started and looked at the ground, it appeared like a river, making us dizzy, and the trembling of the carriage might give you headache. In this way we proceeded and whenever we approached houses they gave warning by making big whistle sound, and on arriving at the houses they rung a bell, and we stopped for a little while.

By the way we entered a long cave through the earth, used as a road, and soon after we emerged from it again. At length we reached our goal and entered a large mansion, in which numbers of people crowded together. It was almost stifling, I said jokingly to them 'Get out of the way.' On the same occasion we lost our companions, but on coming outside we found each other again. Here a carriage drawn by horses arrived with an old man, who now was to take care of us, the father-in-law of him who first had attended us. He invited us to seat ourselves and drive to the country of the farmers [cultivators], to be lodged in an uninhabited house. We came to a very fine land, over which lay spread the cultivators' houses. Numbers of horses, oxen, and sheep were seen all around, as if they were without owners, and the habitations scattered here and there offered a beautiful view.

The Captain who brought us to his father-in-law, had said: 'I will come back to fetch you,' and, bidding us farewell, he had left us. His father-in-law likewise was named Christian. He used to come and look after us; every third day he brought us provisions. Whenever he came his first words were: 'My children, how do ye do?' He was a very pleasant man indeed. When he left us, he inquired what sort of food we should like. He also used to send us lumps of ice. To be sure, it was very hot; in calm weather we did not take a walk without being provided with fans.

During our stay here in the country of the farmers, lodged in the empty house, we used to get eggs and milk from another house, where there lived people, our foster-parent having allowed us to fetch them there. We also frequently had visitors, who came in large carriages. Sometimes, at noon, when we were going to have our dinner, and people crowded in, we felt embarrassed. However, they were all very kind, and they used to give our children small coins and sweets ...

> Hans Hendrik also took part in 1875–6 in the British Arctic expedition led by George Strong Nares aboard Captain Henry Stephenson's *Discovery*. In this extract Hendrik reveals his sensitive reactions to the bullying and taunting that was all too often shown him and other Inuit.

While the dark season still lasted I began to perceive that some of the crew were talking about me, and had wicked designs towards me. We also used to collect at nine o'clock in the morning, and stand upright in a row near the ship in military fashion. But I being a native was not accustomed to this. Two officers then proceeded to examine our faces, arms and feet

[?] A little after nine o'clock the clergyman appeared to read prayers. This was repeated every day. Also in the evening they assembled to be inspected, but then without divine service. One evening I heard them talking thus: 'When Hans is to be punished, who shall flog him?' The boatswain answered: 'I.' To be sure, as I am not very clever in English, and do not know whether I have thoroughly understood their meaning, I only have written this without any particular purpose.

I also remember that in the beginning, when we took our meals, I was placed at the table of the first-class sailors [petty officers?] but afterwards I abstained [?] from their table. In this way I grew dejected, and the sadness of my mind was increased by my having no business on account of the terrible darkness. So when I took a walk near the ship I used to fall a-weeping, remembering my wife and little children, especially that little son of mine who was so tenderly attached to me, that I could not be without him even when I was travelling with the transport boat. However, I had one friend, a young man named Tage [Page, Captain Stephenson's steward]; he sometimes took a walk with me, and when I made him know my sorrow, he consoled me. But at length my thoughts grew on me, and I took it into my head to go away to the wilds. If I should freeze to death it would be preferable to hearing this vile talk about me.

Once when heavy with grief I thus walked alone, I again heard them gossiping in their wicked manner. I then said to myself: 'These people are all united as countrymen. I am the only one without any comrade of my nation, the only abandoned one' – and I ran away in the black night a distance of about 5 miles, when I stopped and meditated: 'Our Captain likes me; perhaps he will send people in search of me. I will return, and if I am to be treated ill, the All Merciful will pity my soul.' I turned back but resolved to stop in the neighbourhood of the ship, as I knew our Captain who was my friend would search for me. I went ashore, dug a hole in the snow and lay down. I had just fallen asleep when I heard footsteps, and as they approached I went out. They asked me: 'Hast thou slept?' – 'Yes, I have slept.' 'Dost thou feel cold?' – 'Only a little.' The two officers said to me: 'Our Captain was afraid thou wert lost, we have followed thy footprints, go home now.'

We went down upon the ice and met several men carrying torches. On coming on board the boatswain accosted me: 'Tomorrow morning sleep sufficiently; when we rouse thou needst not rise, only sleep in peace,' The next morning I did not rise before I had slept well. At noon I got something to eat, and towards two o'clock I was summoned by the Master, who questioned me: 'Why didst thou run away last night?' I made answer: 'I heard them talk badly about me, and thought they reviled me.' He rejoined: 'Whenever thou hearst them speaking thus, tell me directly.' I afterwards heard them speaking several times in the same way, but nevertheless, did not mention it, because I supposed that, if I reported it, none of them would like me more.

Hans Hendrik, 75–8, 89–91

O **Chimoackjo**, popularly known as **John Bull** (d. 1888), skilled whaler, was brought from the Hudson Bay area to testify at a trial that took place in the United States circuit court in Boston in June 1882. In 1879 New England whaling captain John Orrin Spicer put John Bull in charge of a crew searching for whales. Bad weather delayed Spicer's return to collect his cargo. Meanwhile two other New England whaling captains told Bull that Spicer was lost and offered to buy the stockpile. When Bull refused they just took the oil, bone, and blubber. Spicer returned and learned of the theft. When he arrived back in New England, Spicer sued the owners. John Bull's testimony won the case for Spicer.

With Bull came his wife Kimelo and five-year-old daughter Cudalarjo. Despite all the new sights and experiences, Bull was unimpressed. He disliked fences and walls. The climate bothered him and he begged to return home 'where there were no enclosures and where a man could go where he liked when he liked.' Three days before they were to sail, Kimelo gave birth to a baby girl whom she named 'American Girl.' When Bull and his family returned home, the other natives were afraid of him because they claimed he had too much knowledge and was a dangerous man. He was accordingly sentenced to death. Spicer family history records what John Bull told the New England captains.

John Bull's Testimony

You will take away what belongs to Spicer's ship and you must pay Spicer for it. You have no right to take it so long as there is someone to watch over it. I will tell Spicer when he comes.

S.B. Meech, comp., *A Supplement to the Descendants of Peter Spicer* 156

An official notarized statement states 'exactly what he [Bull] said:

Me bone gone Bone Capt Spicer bone ... Other white men took a large quantity without permission.

G.W. Blunt White Library, Mystic Seaport, Conn. Bull Deposition, Ms. vfm 1476

O   A group of fifty-seven Labrador Inuit, including **Zecharias** and **Gabriel Pomiuk**, were exhibited at the World's Columbian Exposition in Chicago in 1893 and then left stranded. When they finally arrived back home, through the good graces of the American physician-explorer Dr Frederick A. Cook, Zecharias, from Hebron, Labrador, confessed his state of mind to Brother Kahle, the Moravian missionary stationed at Nain.

Zecharias' Confession to Brother Kahle

I have returned quite a different man. Trouble has taught me to pray, and the only course left to me was to seek the Saviour, of whom you have so constantly told us ... We are glad to be once more at liberty, and not continually looked at as if we were animals. We shall never go again. Nowhere are we better off than with our missionaries.

Periodical Accounts, ii, 442

O   Gabriel Pomiuk (d. 1897) was the star attraction of the Inuit exhibit at the Chicago World's Fair of 1893 because of his skill with the dog whip. Visitors would place a coin on the ground as a target and the first Inuk who could hit it at thirty feet with the whiplash won it. Pomiuk always hit it first. Two years later Dr Wilfred T. Grenfell found Pomiuk crippled and dying on the Nachak beach in Labrador and took him to his hospital. While in hospital Pomiuk wrote many letters to his benefactors and to the Reverend C.C. Carpenter, known as Mr Martin, editor of the "Children's Corner" in *The Congregationalist*, who befriended Pomiuk from first watching him perform on the midway.

Pomiuk's Letter to Mr Martin, 1897

Battle Harbor Hospital, Labrador, March 20, 1897.
    Aukshenai Mr. Martin: I am glad that you sent me a book. I am very sorry I got no letter at all. I am a lot better now, and I walk about on my crutches. Sister make me trousers and slippers. I very glad. Sister teach me letters and writing. Me got a fine Christmas time, sweets, cake and book in the morning. Lot of little girls and boys got a tea. We had a big Christmas tree. Sister gave Tommy and me Jack-in-the-box. I opened box. I very frightened, and they all laugh very much. Room very, very pretty, lots of candles in lanterns, next day lot of people came to tea. After tea lot of singing. I sing *Takpanele*, I would like to see you here Christmas day. Tommy and me learn 'There is a better world they say.' I very sorry Dr. Grenfell stop in England this year. I want a letter more, please. You got my photograph? Thank you very much for the book we got. Aukshenai, Mr. Martin. Gabriel Pomiuk.

Forbush, *Pomiuk* 105–6

O   **Uisakassak** or **Uisakavsok** (1875–1910) was one of a group of six taken by the American explorer Admiral Robert E. Peary from Greenland to New York for scientific study in 1897. Within months of their arrival four of the six had died. Uisakassak returned to Greenland with Peary the following summer on board the *Windward*, leaving behind the only other survivor, Minik or Mene Wallace. Uisakassak was the first adult polar Inuk to see the 'white man's' land and return to tell about it.
    While in the United States, Uisakassak spent most of his time indoors because he had difficulty finding his way 'among the man-made mountains.' He was unhappy. 'It was too warm and there was a great lack of walrus meat and blubber.' Once

he was back home, however, he could not stop talking about his experiences: trains that sped 'like a gust of wind across the sea'; streetcars 'big as houses with masses of glass windows as transparent as freshwater ice, racing on without dogs to haul them, without smoke and full of smiling people who had no fear of their fate. All this just because a man pulled on a cord.'

Uisakassak's Impressions of New York, 1898

The ships sailed in and out there, like eiders on the brooding cliffs when their young begin to swim. There weren't many free drops of water in the harbor itself; it was filled with ships. You'd risk your life if you tried to go out there in a kayak, you'd simply not be noticed, and you'd be run down unmercifully. People lived up in the air like auks on a bird cliff. The houses are as big as icebergs on a glacial bank, and they stretch inland as far as you can see, like a steep chain of mountains with innumerable canyons that serve as roads.

And the people. Yes, there are so many of them that when smoke rises from th chimneys and the women are about to make breakfast, clouds fill the sky and the sun is eclipsed.

Such things were beyond the understanding of his incredulous listeners. And he was accused of being a liar when he told them that he, Uisakassak, had stood and talked to Peary, who was visiting another village. Without shouting to one another, they had talked together through a funnel along a cord.' Sorqaq, the tribe's old and respected shaman, told him to 'go tell your big lies to the women.' To be called a liar in Inuit society was the utmost disgrace and the unfortunate Uisakassak had to live with his stigma until the day he died.

Rolf Gilberg, 'Uisâkavsak, 'The Big Liar,' *Folk*, 11–12 (1969/70) 85–6

O   **Minik** or **Mene Wallace** (c. 1890–1918) was born at Smith Sound in northwestern Greenland. In 1897 he was one of six Inuit taken to New York by the explorer Robert Peary. Four of the six, including Minik's father soon died. The other survivor, Uisakassak, returned to Greenland, but Minik was adopted by the building superintendent of the American Museum of Natural History, William Wallace. He was sent to school and learned to speak English 'with remarkable accuracy.' His ensuing tragic life became legend among his people. In an article for the *San Francisco Examiner,* when he was nineteen years old, Mene related the pathetic details of his life. Curiously he does not mention Uisakassak.

Minik Wallace's Dilemma

When Mr. Peary came to us, twelve years ago, we had never seen a white man. Our tribe welcomed him and helped him with guides, hunters, dogs and every hospitality.

At the start Peary, was kind enough to my people. He made them presents of ornaments, a few knives and guns for hunting, and wood to build sledges. But as soon as he was ready to start home his other work began.

Before our eyes he packed up the bones of our dead friends and ancestors. To the women's crying and the men's questioning he answered that he was taking our dead friends to a warm and pleasant land to bury them. Our sole supply of flint for lighting and iron for hunting and cooking implements was furnished by a huge meteorite. This Peary put aboard his steamer and took from my poor people, who needed it so much. After this he coaxed my father and that brave man Natooka, who were the stanchest hunters and the wisest heads for our tribe, to go with him to America.

Our people were afraid to let them go, but Peary promised them that they should have Natooka and my father back within a year, and that with them would come a great stock of guns and ammuinition, and wood and metal and presents for the women and children. So that my father believed that for so much good and comfort to his people they should let him and Natooka risk the trip. Natooka could not part from Artoona, his wife, and his little girl, Ahweah, so he took them with him. My mother was dead, and my father would not go without me, so the five of us said a last farewell to home and went on Peary's ship.

We were crowded into the hold of the vessel and treated like dogs. Peary seldom came near us. When we reached the end of the sea voyage we were given the most miserable and unhealthy quarters on the steamship Kite, and lay off Brooklyn for several days on exhibition.

After this we were sent to the Museum of Natural History in New York. There we were quartered in a damp cellar most unfavourable to people from the dry air of the North. One after another we became ill and began to die off; during the fourth month my poor father died; at last I alone remained.

After my father died they took me out into the garden of the museum to see him buried. They lowered a big box into the ground and told me to say goodby to him. That box was filled with stones, and father – my father – his body even then was in the museum being prepared for exhibition. My father on exhibition!

Unexpectedly one day I came face to face with it. I felt as though I must die then and there. I threw myself at the bottom of the glass case and prayed and wept. I went straight to the director and implored him to let me bury my father. He would not. I swore I never would rest until I had given my father burial.

I have lived on and on and have made appeal after appeal, but none has been granted. Mr. Wallace has been good to me, but he can do nothing. Mr. Beecroft has been a true friend, but he has not the power to give me what I want. I prayed to Peary to take me with him upon this last voyage and leave me in my home in Greenland, but he refused me. I had tried to study at Manhattan College so that I could be wise and go North in good time and help my unhappy people, but I am not fitted for your ways or your life.

I have felt that I must go North, back to Greenland some-how, some way. I am a burden on my friends and I see clearly that as long as I live they will have me a weight upon their hands helping me always. I would die for Mr. Wallace and Mr. Beecroft, but I won't be a burden on them. I can never forgive Peary and I hope to see him to show him the wreck he has caused.

I have lost hope. I lost it when Peary refused to take me with him this last trip. And I have given up believing your Christian creed that you taught me was meant for one and all – Christian and savage alike. I gave that up finally when Professor Bumpus at the museum told me for the last time I could not have my father's bones to bury them. Where is your Christianity? My own people are kinder and better, more human, and I am going back to them. My land is frozen and desolate, but we can bury our dead there. What has your civilization done to my people and me but harm us? We are tens now where we were thousands, and what is left is dying fast through your work.

I shall go back to die with my people as soon as I am well enough again to start. My father knows that if I cannot give his bones burial it is not because I have not tried with all that is in me. I even went to Albany because I believed the Assembly would help me, but now I know they won't.

Let me tell you more about my father and me. They brought me down from my home, where I would naturally have fallen into the way of making a living, and where, no doubt, I would have been at least happy and healthy, and they set me adrift where everything is strange and nearly everything hostile. I am in no way fitted to follow a business life such as you people have been trained in for generations. I cannot bear the confinement of a public school class room – it makes me deathly sick in a few days – and I have no funds nor will I burden my few friends for them to secure tutoring or private instruction; so I can only grow into a nonentity, useless to myself and more or less a freak to those about me. It was so at Manhattan College and I saw it could never be different. So much for me.

My father was taken from me, a martyr to the cold-blooded, scientific study of your people. His body was refused a burial, even after he gave his life to your science, and is now degraded to a mere exhibition relic for no greater purpose than to amuse the visitors of a museum. He was dearer to me than anything else in the world – especially when we were brought to New York, strangers in a strange land.

You can imagine how closely that brought us together: how our disease and suffering and lack of understanding of all the strange things around us, and the ominous death of the three other Eskimo of our party, who one by one bade us a sad farewell, made us sit tremblingly waiting our turn to go – more and more lonesome and alone, hopelessly far from home, we grew to depend on one another, and to love each other as no father and son under ordinary conditions could possibly love. Every morning he would come and sit beside me until I wakened, almost crazy to know how I felt, and yet too tender to arouse me from my rest. How he would smile if I was a little better, and how he would sob, with big tears in his eyes when I was suffering.

Aside from hopeless loneliness do you know what it is to be sad – to feel a terrible longing to go home, and to know that you are absolutely without hope? Ah, you cannot know! And then add to this the horror of knowing that death was waiting near for us, and that one must go first and leave the other all alone – awfully alone; no one who even understands your language – no one except grief. Aside from these tortures my poor father was suffering frightfully from disease. His neck was terribly swollen from tuberculosis, and his chest ached so badly that he could not rest. And yet, in spite of all this, his whole thought was constantly of me. He watched over me night and day, denying himself sleep and even food, and when anything was brought for me to eat he insisted on giving it to me himself – coaxing me and praising the food – and if I seemed to like it big tears would come in his eyes and he would laugh – half laugh and half cry – and pat me on the cheeks.

He wanted to do everything for me with his own hands and watched every one who came near me. His greatest suffering was when he grew so weak that he was obliged to remain still in bed and could not come to me. And I cried all the time, and could no longer eat for fear my father would die. Then I grew better; probably because I was so anxious to be with him, and soon I was allowed to go to him and lie near him. He did not notice any of the doctors' torture after that.

One day a doctor accidentally or carelessly burnt my arm with an iron. My father saw the sore, and when I told him that it was a burn, he got out of bed, enraged, as weak and sick as he was, and I am sure he would have killed the doctor. I was terribly frightened, and for the first time I lied to my father. I told him that I had burned my arm on a gaslight. Then he took me in his arms and kissed me and said in Eskimo, 'Mene must be careful for his father's sake.' The next morning my father was dead. The strain had been too great for him, and he nearly suffocated during the night, and cried out for his home, his family his friends and me. I put my head under a pillow crying hard. They tried to take me from the room, and my father saw them and realized what it was. He called to me and I ran into his arms. He knew that he must leave me, and his grief was terrible. 'Father's spirit will stay with Mene always,' he said in Eskimo, choking hard. Father was dying then I know, but I think his poor heart broke and that is what killed him.

I thought my heart was broken, too! That sad, long lonesome day! ... Oh, they have given me a thousand deaths! When I could be of no further use to them and my illness frightened them, they turned me adrift – and yet I am not dead. I wish I was, I wish I was!

How can I get justice from those who took me from my home, robbed me of all that was dear to me and have made me a prisoner here.

Think of the injustice of it all. Think of that burial of stones or a piece of wood instead of what I thought was my father's body. When I found out can any one imagine what I felt? You see, we Greenlanders have some curious beliefs about burial. We think a spirit cannot rest unless it is safely in the earth. My father, who held to the beliefs of the tribe had begged me again and again to see that he was buried according to the rites of the tribe. But how could a child see to this? Since I have found out about the way they did, I have tried everything. What I wanted to do was to get the remains of my father, take them with his spear and sled and carry them with me up to Greenland. That would be the way I could have justice. Surely this country owes me justice; the State owes it.

Mene Wallace, 'Why Arctic Explorer Peary's Neglected Eskimo Boy Wants to Shoot Him,' *San Francisco Examiner* (magazine supplement) 9 May 1909

O   Migration has been a traditional way of life for the Inuit. Small groups of people would move away from their traditional territories for a variety of reasons: to look for better hunting grounds, to meet new people, to escape vengeance for murder, or to take advantage of whalers and missionaries. Whatever the cause, mobility played a crucial role in Inuit survival.

About 1856 the famous shaman, Qitdlak (Qitdlarssuaq), led the last recorded migration of Baffin Island Inuit to the northwestern coast of Greenland, following the traditional route to the coast of Greenland where they found the polar Inuit. The Baffin Islanders reintroduced such technological skills as the kayak, the bow and arrow, and fish spear to the polar Inuit who had somehow lost the skills. The Canadians subsequently intermarried with their long lost cousins, the world's northernmost inhabitants.

Merqusaq (c. 1840–), who participated in this important migration, told Danish explorer Knud Rasmussen about it in 1903.

An Epic Arctic Journey

After Qitdlarssuaq had once heard [probably around 1853 from Francis Leopold McClintock and Edward Augustus Inglefield who were both involved in the search for Sir John Franklin] that there were Inuit over on the other side of the sea, he could never settle down to anything again. He held great conjurations of spirits in the presence of all the people of the village. He made his soul take long journeys through the air, with his helping spirits, to look for the country of the strange Inuit. At last one day he informed his fellow-villagers that he had found the new country! And he told them that he was going to journey to the strange people, and he exhorted them all to follow him.

'Do you know the desire for new countries? Do you know the desire to see new people?' he said to them.

And nine sledges joined him at once, and ten sledges together they set out northward to find the new country that Qitdlarssuaq said he had seen on his soul-flight. There were men, women, and children, thirty-eight in all, who started ...

We started on our journey in the winter, after the light came, and set up our permanent camp in the spring, when the ice broke. There were plenty of animals for food on the way, seals, white whales, walruses, and bears. Long stretches of the coast along which we had to drive were not covered with ice, and so we were often obliged to make our way over huge glaciers. On our way we also came to bird rocks, where auks built, and to some eider-duck islands.

As we carried all our belongings with us, clothes, tents, hunting and fishing implements, kayaks, we used very long narrow sledges. (He gave me the measure of the sledges, which were twenty feet long and four feet wide.) We had to have our sledges so long because the kayaks were carried on them. We had fastened whalebone, or walrus tusks, to our runners. Whalebone in particular made extraordinary light running, especially in the spring, when the sun began to warm the snow and ice. But the lightest of all to pull, under a sledge runner, is the thick skin of the walrus. But this does not hold on pack ice. We had as many as twenty dogs for our sledges, with traces of varying length. It is not wise to drive so many dogs in a row with traces all the same length; they prevent each other pulling properly, when the number exceeds twelve. The outer ones, too, will pull at too sharp an angle from the sledge, unless you have impossibly long reins; and reins too long would not be wise, because the weight is felt more, the farther the dogs are from the sledges. We did not have uprights on our sledges. When we had to descend a snow-covered glacier we lashed thongs round our tires, so that they should not run too easily, and fastened the thongs to the back part of the sledge, so that we could pull at them as we went down hill. On these sledges, besides our baggage, we could also drive our wives and children; and we could ride on them ourselves, too, when there was good going.

At the season when the ice breaks up, we used to choose a good fishing place and strike permanent camp, and there we hunted supplies for the winter with our kayaks. Towards the autumn we built stone houses, which we roofed with turf; in these houses we spent the dark season, until the light came again, and we were able to continue our journey.

We had travelled thus for two winters, and neither year had we lacked food. Then it so happened that one of the oldest amongst us, old Oqé, grew homesick. He had long been grave and without words, then all at once he began to talk about whale-beef. He was homesick for his own country, and he wanted to eat whale-beef again. In our old country at home we used to catch many whales.

After he had once started talking, he began to accuse old Qitdlarssuaq, who had been the leader all through the journey, of cheating. He said it was all lies that Qitdlarssuaq had told about the new country, and he invited them all to turn back.

Then a great dissension arose between the old men. The travellers divided themselves up into those who held with Qitdlarssuaq and those who believed Oqé, and meanwhile the two old men argued, each in support of his own assertion; Qitdlarssuaq said that Oqé was envious, because he was not the leader himself, and Oqé declared that Qitdlarssuaq was simply deceiving his fellow-countrymen in order to gain influence over them. The quarrel ended by five sledges turning back, while five went on. Twenty-four people turned back, and fourteen went on, and amongst these latter was Oqé's own son, Minik.

This happened after two winterings.

Qitdlarssuaq and the people who believed in his words then journeyed farther north. He assured them that it was not much farther to the new country, and encouraged them to hold out. He was always the first to break up camp, and he always drove the first sledge. He was stronger than the young men, and more enduring, although his hair was white. Those who drove after him declared that often, as they toiled along after dark, they saw a white flame burning above his head: so great was he in his might.

Late in the spring we came to a place where the sea narrowed to a small channel. (Before this we had crossed two very broad inlets or fjords.) Here Qitdlarssuaq pitched camp and conjured spirits. His soul took an air-flight over the sea, while his body lay lifeless behind. When the incantation was over, he announced that it was here that we were to cross the sea. On the other side we should meet with people. And all obeyed him, for they knew that he understood the hidden things.

So we crossed the sea, which was frozen over, and camped on the opposite coast. There we found houses, human habitations, but no people. They had left the place. But we understood then that we had very little farther to go before meeting with people, and a great joy filled us all; our veneration for the man who for years had led us towards the distant goal knew no bounds.

It was decided that we should not seek further for the time being, but should first try to get in supplies, as the catch had for a long time been poor. The animals had been made invisible to us. And Qitdlarssuaq held an incantation to find out the reason of the failure of the fishery. After the incantation he announced that his daughter-in-law, Ivaloq, had had a miscarriage, but had kept the matter secret, to escape penance. That was why the animals had been invisible. And so he ordered his son to shut up his wife in a snow-hut as a punishment, after having first taken her furs from her. In the snow-hut she would either freeze to death or die of hunger. Before this came to pass, the animals would not allow themselves to become the prey of men.

And they built a snow-hut at once and shut Ivaloq up in it. This Qitdlarssuaq did with his son's wife, whom he loved greatly; and he did it, that the innocent should not suffer for her fault.

Immediately after the punishment had been carried into effect, we came upon a large herd of reindeer, inland, and had meat in abundance. This was at Etâ.

While we were there, there was a cry one day of 'Sledges! sledges!' And we saw two sledges approaching, sledges from a strange people. And they saw us and drove up to us.

They were people of the tribe we had been looking for so long. The one man was called Arrutsak, the other Agîna, and their home was at a place called Pitoravik, not far from where we were encamped. We shouted aloud with joy; for now we had found new country, and new people. And our great magician had proved himself greater than all who had doubted him.

Arrutsak was a man with a wooden leg. Once upon a time he had fallen from a bird rock, as we learnt later, and had had his one leg broken. His mother had cut off the injured part of the leg and made him a wooden leg which could be bound fast to the stump. He could run and drive just as well as if he had never lost a limb. But when we saw him come running up the first time with his wooden leg, many of us supposed that it was usual, and that the new people always had one leg made of wood.

We sat down at once to eat with the new arrivals, and they told us many things about the people we were going to see. During the meal a thing happened that amused us all.

It was customary in our tribe that, when eating together in a friendly way, all should eat from the same bone. When a piece of meat was handed to one, he just took a bite from it, and passed on the remainder to those with whom he was taking his meal. We call that Amerqatut. But every time that we handed the new arrivals a piece of meat, of which they were only intended to eat a mouthful, they ate the whole piece; and so it was a long time before we others could get anything to eat, as they were very hungry.

That was a custom the new people were not acquainted with, but now they have all adopted it.

After the meal all the men drove to Pitoravik, to visit the new people, the women being fetched only later. But during the jubilation of the meeting, Itsukusuk released his wife Ivaloq from the snow-hut in which she had been shut up, and thus saved her life. No one said anything, for they were all thinking only of their great joy. It was a long time before Ivaloq recovered. She had no flesh at all left, and was terribly exhausted.

Thus it was that Qitdlarssuaq led us all to new countries and new people.

Rasmussen, *The People of the Polar North* 27–32

O **John Aggâkdjuk** (c. 1864–) was headman on the expedition led in 1910–11 by the German ornithologist and explorer, Bernard Hantzsch, to investigate the unknown region along the west coast of Baffin Island by way of the inland sea Lake Nettilling. (This area was not fully surveyed until 1940.) During the harsh and difficult journey, Hantzsch died of trichinosis caused by a diet of bear's flesh. Aggâkdjuk wrote a report of the expedition in syllabics. A free translation in English of the report reveals the Inuk's affection and sorrow.

John Aggâkdjuk's Report

I write thus an account of my love for our friend, because he is dead in the wilderness, for I love him greatly, and ye also, I love you.

He was not frozen, and he was not starved, he was also well clothed, such were not the cause of his death. His death was caused by severe illness, his body, his arms, and his legs being very much swollen, his lungs also being affected. In this manner he died.

89

In the beginning, in Blacklead Island, my brother spoke in this way to me: Do you wish to travel with me, because you shall receive things from me? 'Yes, I answered, I wish to do so.' And so then we travelled together to Lake Kennedy (or Lake Netselik). We were very happy, because we were travelling together to Lake Netselik. We always kept the Sundays, and God was with us while we were alone, and He also caused us to be happy while we travelled. Then we reached Lake Netselik, when I who am an Eskimo, was very ill. Then my brother helped me, and I thank him and the medicines he used, very much. Indeed with much trouble he saved me, with the medicines and by God's help: When indeed I had but little flesh left on my body, my brother, the white man, saved me.

Then when I was recovered we began to travel together beyond Lake Netselik, and at last we arrived at the Kokjuak (or Great River), when the summer was ended and the winter was commencing. We were unable to travel on the sea, because there was so much ice, so we commenced journeying through the land. Then we reached a place where there were no animals to be found, and we lost most of our dogs. Then we travelled a little farther on, we found a place where seals could be obtained and upon this discovery we no longer despaired of our lives during the Winter. While there I made a means of helping ourselves, by constructing a canoe, covering it with sail-canvas, and indeed we found that canoe a great help in obtaining our livelihood. Then the midwinter was beginning, seals could no longer be found around our wintering-place. So we wished to travel still a little farther on, and then we discovered a place which had both seals and reindeer.

While it was completely Winter, I provided him (i.e. Herr Hantzsch) with food, seal-meat, because he liked seal-meat very much.

Indeed truly I was very much distressed, because he died in the wilderness, he who was as my brother. Because he desired to have me as a friend I consented, I could not think that he would die, of which death, truly his illness was the only cause. It was because he desired to make a Chart of the land which was far away, he said, that he wished to go. He did not live with me.

When we had only four dogs left, he said that he wished to

make a journey, being absent about four Sundays (i.e. a month), taking as his travelling companion Ittushakjuk, (because he had no children), while he [we] waited for him where we were. So they started off thither on this journey, he wished to make a chart of that coast; but they were away for a very long time, because my brother was very ill, and Ittushakjuk's wife also was very ill. Ittushakjuk brought him back to the place where I was awaiting them, and there in my tent he died. While he was there ill, whatever he desired we did for him, we complied with all his wishes. And he spoke thus to us: 'Thank you' he said, 'very much, (because he was helped and cared for by us), I am unable to write because I have no strength, but when you return, go and speak to Elatakou (i.e. the Missionary) because he is able to write, I cannot do so, I have no strength.' He said that he thanked Elatakou also, because he provided him with food.

This I must relate, that I was not able to help him with medicines, because I know nothing about the medicines, all I could do was to try to pray to God. Indeed truly, he is with God, for he believes God, he said so while he was very ill.

He also said this, while he was very ill, 'Go, when you return, and take my goods, which are brought from the white man's Land, for yourselves, because I am well cared for by all of you.' So he gave them to us then. We wept continually, while he was ill, because of our love for him: and I gave him water whenever he wished to drink, and generally assisted him. My wife and I, from the time he arrived to us ill, did not sleep at all for four nights. Then on the fourth day, he died. I sorrow greatly, because he is dead.

We made a suitable grave of stone, and it is in a good position. His body cannot be disturbed by foxes or a wolf.

We also did thus. We wishing to pray to God, when we committed his body to the grave, we used the prayers to God for the Burial of the Dead, that he might be taken to be with him truly, I know certainly that he is with God, because his faith was sufficient.

I thank you very greatly because I have received gifts from you. A great Farewell to you, I have very great sympathy for you, because our friend through great sickness is dead.

Elatakou also, I give him great thanks, because both him whom we loved, the white man, and us also, he also loves.

National Archives of Canada, MG30, B23, vol. 4 (translated by E.W.T. Greenshield, Blacklead Island)

O   **Tannaumirk** (1894–), 'a cheerful and companionable sort of fellow' from the Mackenzie Region, was one of the guides for noted Arctic explorer Vilhjalmur Stefansson during his second expedition of 1908–12. Usually, Stefansson would question his guides, but this time at Cape Parry in 1910, Tannaumirk asked the questions and gives his reaction to the explorer's response.

Tannaumirk's Reactions to Stefansson, 1910

Is it true ... that Christ was the only white man who could raise people from the dead?
Stefansson: Yes ... He was the only one; and some of my countrymen doubt that even He could.
Tannaumirk: I can understand how that might easily be so with your countrymen. If Christ was the only white man who could do it, and if you never knew of any one else who could, I can see why you should doubt His being able to do it. You naturally would not understand how it was done. But we Eskimo do not doubt it, because we understand it. We ourselves can raise people from the dead. You know that some years before you first came to the Mackenzie district Taiakpanna died. He died in the morning, and Alualuk, the great shaman, arrived in the afternoon. The body of Taiakpanna was still lying there in the house, Alualuk immediately summoned his familiar spirits, performed the appropriate ceremonies, and woke Taiakpanna from the dead, and, as you know, he is still living. If Alualuk could do it, why should we doubt that Christ could do it, too?

Stefansson, *My Life with the Eskimo* 420

O   On 15 September 1921, a party consisting of four young explorers and an Eskimo woman were put ashore on the bleak shores of Wrangel Island. They had been selected by Vilhjalmur Stefansson to claim the island for Great Britain as a strategic stepping stone for the era of commercial aviation on the polar route that Stefansson knew was coming. Besides taking possession of the uninhabited island, the expedition, a British-financed venture, was to test Stefansson's theory than any armed man could live on any of the Arctic islands for a year at least.

Two years later, on 19 August 1923, when the head of the Wrangel Island Rescue Expedition, Harold Noice, arrived on the island bringing twelve Inuit to begin a permanent colony, he found only one survivor. Three of the men from the original party had set out for Siberia on 28 January 1923 because they had despaired of rescue and their provisions were running out; they were never seen again. And the fourth man, Lorne E. Knight, lay dead in his deerskin sleeping bag. The lone survivor was Ada Blackjack.

Ada Blackjack Johnson (1898–1983), Arctic heroine, was hired in Alaska to be the expedition's seamstress. She cared for Knight when he was stricken with scurvy. At Knight's request, Ada wrote her diary, a daily record of her thoughts and activities that reveals her courage.

Ada Blackjack Johnson's Diary

Made in March 14, 1923. The first fox I caught was in feb. 21st and then second March 3 and 4th, 5th, that makes 4 white foxess and then in March 13th I caught three white foxess that makes seven foxess altogather. 14th I got headach all day I'm taking aspirin its seems didn't work. Oh yes in 13th I got new army pants. On 12th of Mar. I set eight placeses of traps two in each place.

15th. I was over to the traps no sign of fox fresh tracks. And I put new sole on my felt slipers and washed the dishess and I feel much better than yesterday. Very clear al day.

March 16th. I have not feeling well for three day frist I was headach and then I had stumpick trouble and today I feel much better. I was over to the traps with no fox or fresh tracks. And last night knight told me I can keep the bible he siad he give them to me, very nice day so far ...

26th. I was over to the traps today and fox has been in cold oil can traps and trap was sprung but didn't hold fox and this morning about 11 o'clock I sew a Polar bear on the ice, and I sew three foxess one with trap on her foot. And I haul one load of sled and saw four cuts of log and chop wood, and we look at knights legs my! they are skiny and they has no more blue spots like they use to be. And I pretty near finish my black belt ...

29th. My eye swolen up and one side of my face ach, it stard yesterdday and today it very much ach. I caught one male fox it pretty good meat, and I saw six cut of wood and I chop only three ...

April 2nd. I take ship poket out today one of my eye one that is swolen is going down a little, and one side of my throad out side of it, is hards a little. And knight wants me to go out to the traps but my eye is very ach so I cannot go out when my eye is that way because in evening I could bearly stand the ach of my eye and one side of head. If anything happen to me and my death is known, there is black stirp for bennett (Ada's son) school book bag. for my only son. I wish if you please take everything to Bennett that is belong to me. I don't know how much I would be glad to get home to folks ...

Apr. 6th. I made saw bock today and chop wood and I feel better today. And I open case of biscuits. Blowing today.

Apr. 7th. Blowing al day I didn't go out today and yesterday on account of wind blowing.

Apr. 8th. I got up early this mornig and then chop wood and I went out to the traps and caught one frozen fox nothing but skin and bone and I open can of cold oil. And I finish one side yarn glove for Galle [one of the explorers] and stard another side ...

Apr. 14th. I was out to the traps today and got nothing but I saw fresh track behind the camp, and I open case of biscuits and cut out skin for my boot soles and I made thread out of sinnew and I gather biscuit crums togather and take them out. Very clear and sunshine ...

Apr. 16th. I was out to the traps but see nothing and when I come home I starded chew my boot sole and then sew them on and I finish them by in evening. Wind from east ...

Apr. 24th. I didn't go out today I just wash my hiar and read the Bibil all day and think of folks are in church this morning and this evening and now I'm writing 11 o'clock in evening after I had cup of tea ...

Apr. 26th. I was out today and sawed wood and when I was hauling wood home I was almost fianting I guess I was so weak I was almost fianting. And this morning when I wake up from my deep sleeping I look at my watch. And it was 4 o'clock and the inside of the house was dark so I said to myself did I sleep that long because I went to bed early last night, and I was thinking that we haven't enough wood for today. And I siad to myself I'll sleep some more untill late this evening then I'll make cup of tea and go to bed again so about 10 o'clock I wake up again it was in the morning I was glad when I know its morning ...

May 1st. Still blowing a little but not much, I can see sun shining throught the little hoil. And I read the noted that I write some time ago this winter about Mr. knight and its says if knight live until May I would be glad so it happen that he is still living he was just dieing in frist part of February and now he still living untill May 1st day and if the ship comes next summer I don't know how much I would be glad ...

May 7th. I was out getting wood. I didn't go out to the traps and wind blowing from west. Clear and sunshine. On thrid of May knight eat Polar bear cup paw. And I dreamed last night I was with lots of people and Bennett and I was looking at some pictures and we see a picture the people swiming and Bennett says swiming pool and I ask him who told you these are swiming pool pictures and he siad to me Albert told me ...

May 12. I was to the traps today nothing at all. And I chop wood and haul wood and I took out some stuff from storm shad. And I fry one biscuit for knight thats all he eat for 9 days he don't look like he is going to live very long if I happen to live untill ship comes oh thank a living true God ...

May 22. didn't see nothing I didn't do nothing today.

May 23. I was over to little Islands to west end and some few roots I got for knight didn't see nothing but snow bird track. And I made pack for myself.

May 24h. I saw four flock of brant and long neck Black ducks five of them first I saw four flying south from over camp and one flying to west. All the flock of brant flying to west. And I fall in the water mouth of harper just to my Encle. And I saw one fox tracks front of camp over by big ice cake.

May 25th. I carry loges of about ten feet long and sawed up

half of it and I saw dodlie bird flying to east and I snow bird and I shot five times with knights rifle, I did shot better then I thought I would do I only hede my target twice I thought thats good enought for me for first time shooting with rifle.

May 26th. I took four shott with the rifle with three first shots I didn't hided my target with the last shot I hide my target I shoot with three sitting and last one I lie on my belly. And I took a shoot with shot gun standing up and I hide my target and I made shot gun case and knife case for myself and I saw flock of doidle birds flying east and flock of ducks flying way over old camp and I took two picture of camp and didn't work the camra right that was too bad. I was over to traps. Nothing.

May 27th. I was over to little islands and I saw two sea gulls flying and I saw flock of geese and two doidle birds flying and I saw another flock of geese this morning and I saw fox tracks over little Island. And I made myself a sun bonnert and I got some roots tea tin half full. To day I was going over to old camp but it was too windy and has been drifting last night in to storm shade.

May 28th. I over to the old camp and see if there is any birds a round but there is nothing it looks more winter then over here. And when I was on my way down I saw one fox way out of the ice going south west And when I come home I chop wood and clean fox skins three of them and put them strechers ...

June 6th. I was over to the Island and got some sweet roots I shot one doedle bird I saw only two and I saw a Polar bear it was way out on the ice first I saw him and from south of camp he turn tourch camp and just got about on the beach he went out to south again and then to west and went to the beach and it went out south again last I saw it and it got snowing and I cann't see him again. knight said he was fianting last night he is just dieing he could hardly talk. I shot three times today and got only with one.

June 7th. I going over to the Island get some sweet roots and when I got close to the end of the Island ——(?) the see gall and I took a shot at him and I got him dead shot. Oh my! it good and I eat no meat for long time and I saw two shadhurk (?) and I made smale little picks and I made rifle resting board so its handy if I seal hund when I'm ready to so I don't have to look a place to rest my rifle.

June 8th. I was over the and got some roots and I saw three doedle birds I took a shot at one doedle bird didn't get him and when I come home there two Idare ducks flying and got shotgun in my hands got the hammer ready and there were too far and I forgot the hammer was ready and I pull the tricker boom it went didn't hurt me. And I made shotgun cartridge bag and I made shide pan for knight he try to put the pan under him. He just bearly make it, I had to cut it open space on his sleeping bag so he can put the pan. And I can see tracks on the beach with the field glasses I think they are Polar bear tracks one looks fresh and one looks old.

June 9th. I was over to west end of the harbard I was boombarting over there but didn't get see gall and I found one fresh see gall Egg and when I was coming home there was geese fly over me and I took a shot I got one geese and she had three eggs in her one almost got shell on it and I took a shot at shid hwak but didn't kill her and I saw little summer bird ...

June 20. I was out to the west to get some eggs but there is no way to go to eggs water all around they are on smale sand Island see gall eggs that I found I made little sack for Idar downs.

June 21. I was trying to get Idar duck but I cann't get close to them and I carry rifle so I can shot but I cann't get any chance I boam with the rifle I didn't meant to but it want set knight is getting very bad he looks like he is going to die ...

June 26. I was taking walk over to little Island and I found three see gall eggs in one nest. and I cook them for my lunch I take tea and saccharine I had a nice picknick all by myself.

June 27. I was after a seal right out in the front of the camp she went down on me they were two of them in one place and I came back and took myself a picture try anyway and I went to the east and I saw a seal and I went after it and got it with one shot they were two but the other went down and I got the other. That's a frist seal I ever got in my life.

June 28th. I stay at home today and clean seal skin and let this afternoon I hear some funny noise so I look out thought the door and saw Polar bear and one cub. I was very afriad so I took a shot over them see if they would go so they went away and they were looking back and I shot five times and they run away. I thank God that is true living God ...

July 1st. I stay home today and I fix the shovel handle that I brack this spring and I saw Polar bear out on the ice and this evening I went to the end of the sand spit shot a eidar duck I shot him right in the head thank God keep me a live till now ...

July 4th. I was after a seal that was on the mouth of the harbar they were two and one on front of camp so they went down on me those two seals so I went after the one that was right front of camp and I got the rifle already and wait for him to put his head up and rifle was already hammer was ready so I look some thing and move around boam it went and the seal went down I stand up and say fourth of July. I was surprised rifle boan so I had my fourth of July. it was not rian this morning and this afternoon its rain ...

July 6. I was after seal over the harbar mouth and one on front of camp and I shot it second time I after it and when I got I went back and get pulling line and when I was close to the seal I saw bear out on the ice running tourch east and I ran back and they were dragging seal I took a shot over them because they were too far and they went west and then they went on the beach and came east and pass the camp over other siad of harbar mouth and it got very fogy and this evening it got clear and I saw that they ate the seal I shot. and I saw them not very far on the ice and I took one shot and they went west. and I cut a pair of sole for my boats and this afternoon I open box of shotgun cartridges ...

July 14. I sew fancy skin today and only 11 more it will be all ready to put around the parky I should say 11 pieces very nice day ...

July 21st. I put fancy trimming on my new parky and trimming around the hood, it look like a parky alright. and my new parky is all finished today ...

July 26. I made sort boats of raindeer skin and slepers I sqrieped the legens last night. and I got one little gray bird and I took the moldy biscits to the other box and clean ones to the —— box oh yes I dreamed last night I was singing three cheer for the red white and blue ...

Aug. 4. I finished Bennetts slepers today oh they are qured

looking things it look like ice is out I cannt see very far its very fogy but both ways out from beach it look clear the ice cakes don't drifting in around much. and today I found bear track east side of the tent thank living God is love ...

Aug. 12. I just knit seal net today this morning when I got up I found lard can was empty that was full seal blubber the Polar bear has been eating last night. I thank the lord Jesus keep me from danger the wind is from west first time for about whole monthe and I dreamed night before that the boss ask me if would have things creited from the store I said it will be case or nothing fore being stay here for two years ...

Aug. 15. I was knitting today. and this evening I saw bunch of walrus out front camp of about one mile off sore big bunch of them. I thank the savour Jesus Christ ...

Aug. 19. the wind blowing hard frome west and the ice is going out slowly few days ago I though it was going out but didn't go very far. I saw eider duck and four young ones back of the tent. I thank God through Jesus our savour.

Aug. 20. I finished my knited gloves today and I open last biscuit box. the ice is over little below horizon. I thank the lord Jesus and his father.

Shoo-Fly, as she was known to the whalers, wearing an atigi
adorned with pearls

Aua

Abraham's household;
clockwise from left:
Ulricke, Tobias,
Abraham, Sarah, Maria

Peter Pitseolak taken by his wife Aggeok, c. 1947

Monique Atagutaluk

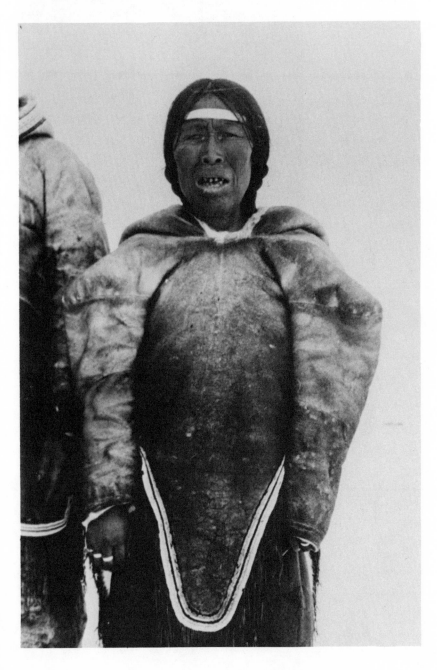

Peter Ernerk, 1983

Ohnainewk

Sister Pélagy

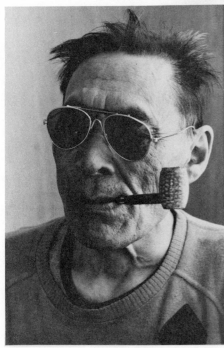

Eric Anoee,
Eskimo Point, 1985

Markoosie

Learning
to write

3 'When All Meat Was Juicy and Tender'

PERSONAL NARRATIVES, LETTERS, AND TRANSITIONAL LITERATURE

... when I chance to think of my childhood and recall all the old memories from those days, then youth seems a time when all meat was juicy and tender, and no game too swift for a hunter. When I was young, every day was as a beginning of some new thing, and every evening ended with the glow of the next day's dawn. Now, I have only the old stories ...

Rasmussen, *Intellectual Culture of the Iglulik Eskimos* 17

... we have our customs, which are not the same as those of the white men, the white men who live in another land and have need of other ways.

Rasmussen, *Intellectual Culture of the Iglulik Eskimos* 56

Once the first missionaries had introduced a written form for Inukti-tut, a new and important dimension of Inuit cultural expression evolved. The Inuit began to express their creative imagination in writing in such familiar forms as poetry and song and in such unfamiliar forms as the letter, the personal narrative, autobiography, memoir, reminiscence, novel, and diary. These non-traditional forms mark a break from the ancient oral traditions. Christian converts began writing their tales of conversion and testimonials about the advantages of life as Christians, using Christian images and motifs and the conventional Christian rhetoric. (These were often printed in mission reports and journals and undoubtedly used to raise money abroad as evidence of the success of the growing mission field in Canada.)

Many Inuit, like Opartok and Ohnainewk, started to keep diaries, making daily entries about the weather, animals taken, family activities, and other events. The earliest extant diary is that written by the Labrador Inuk, Abraham, in 1880. Others started telling their own stories and writing down their histories and experiences. The earliest published narratives were sponsored chiefly by religious and community agencies. Much later, beginning in the 1950s, they were sought after by various levels of government and commercial publishing companies. Although some were written in syllabics and later translated, like that of John Ayaruaq, the majority were recorded from 'as-told-to' life stories; for example, those by Aua and Atuat were related to Knud Rasmussen and the Reverend Guy Mary-Rousselière respectively. A number have been collaborative works, such as Peter Pitseolak and Dorothy Eber's *People from Our Side* (1975) and Davidialuk Alasuaq Amittu and Bernard Saladin d'Anglure's *La Parole changée en pierre* (1978).

If their parents and elders were writing their memoirs, young people were turning to poetry, short story, and essay to express their feelings of frustration and loss caused by the realities of social change. Thus Abe Okpik asks: 'What does it mean to be an Eskimo,' and Markoosie integrates a story of the old, nomadic hunting life into the new prose narrative form to create *Harpoon of the Hunter* (1967), the first novel by a Canadian Eskimo.

Letters became popular; young and old alike wrote to missionaries, family members, and government officials and later to editors of Inuit newspapers and periodical press. Letters often provided the only communication between homesick Inuit children in boarding schools and worried parents. Paper was always scarce and Mary-Rousselière tells of how he received letters, 'written on old soiled sheets, on ends of wrapping paper, even on pieces of cardboard preciously saved from an old package of tea or tobacco.' Sometimes letters would be folded 'the size of a postal stamp' and encircled 'with a tight net of wire or caribou nerve' or put 'in a clipping of seal hide' (Mary-Rousselière, 'Yvonne,' 6).

But autobiographical narrative and its allied forms dominated during this intermediate period. The themes that emerge from these personal restrospectives are the importance of the family and the establishment of kin relationships; preoccupation with the seasons and the weather; the complex, rich, and sometimes terrifying spiritual dimensions of this life; the significance of psychic travel and dream visions; the love of story, dance, and song; and a sound respect for the practical and pragmatic. The theme most noteworthy, however, is the Inuit's unique sense of the land. Land was not a backdrop, but a vital, dynamic presence, a partner in life. As a people who saw themselves participating in a cosmic relationship with all other living things, the animals, plants, rocks, and wind, their attitude towards land, towards nature, is one of stewardship. This special symbiotic relationship called for gentleness and co-operation rather than aggression and confrontation.

Such themes are reminiscent of the old nomadic way of life. Alongside these pre-contact themes appear those that have emerged from contact with the white newcomers: the influence of Christianity with the resulting loss of traditional religious ideas and practices; the decline of the importance and influence of the shaman; the terrible onslaught of white diseases and the acculturative influence of southern hospitalization. The importance of ships from the south in the post-contact lives of the Inuit is also evident.

Even though the Inuit writers were using new literary forms, they retained many of the oral features of their pre-literate culture. They told their stories in a loosely episodic and discursive structure and a plain, unadorned style. They juxtaposed traditional stories and songs to personal experiences. Although personal experiences are central, a story is never told sequentially. They moved backward and forward recounting private history along with communal stories, the collective advice of generations, little essays on how to acquire such specialized skills as how to make good mud runners or a proper igloo, and mythic folklore, creating a distinctive literary style. Thus, history, traditions, beliefs, skills training, and personal experiences were all woven into unified works.

The literary accomplishment of this transitional stage – the cultural odyssey of written reminiscence, letter, poetry, essay, and song – is amazing because it comes from a society that relied on a totally oral form of communication until a few decades ago in some regions.

O   The Moravian mission field in Laborador was so highly successful that it expanded from its first mission station founded in 1771 at Nain, to Okkak in 1776 and Hopedale in 1782. Other stations followed so that by 1862 most of the Inuit of Labrador belonged to the Moravian Church and could read and write. The introduction of Christianity radically transformed native beliefs and religious practices. Converts often gave testimony of their Christian piety and devotion. The following three pieces date from the early nineteenth to the early twentieth centuries.

Christian Testimony

O   **Jonathan** (c. 1754–) was regarded by the Moravian missionaries at Hopedale as one of the most skilful commanders on the whole coast of Labrador. He was captain of the missionaries' 1811 expedition to explore the Labrador coast 'and visit the Esquimaux in that unknown Region' of Ungava Bay. When Jonathan was told that the Ungava Eskimo would kill him, he answered:

Well, we will try, and shall know better when we get there ... When I hear people talking about the danger of being killed, I think: Jesus went to death out of love to us, what great matter would it be, if we were to be put to death in His service, should that be His good pleasure concerning us.

Kohlmeister and Kmoch, *Journal of a Voyage* 8

O   **Peter** (fl. 1824) was a member of the Moravian mission at Hopedale who, on a sealing expedition with another seal catcher, was carried out to sea on a field of ice and for nine days was driven about at the mercy of the waves. He reveals his trust in the Lord in his account of his perilous journey.

When, on the 4th of June, we were driven off the coast, upon the field of ice, I was not much alarmed, for I did not apprehend much danger. At night, when we lay down to rest, we commended ourselves in prayer to God our Saviour, and gave up our lives into His hands, which we always continued to do.

On the 5th as we were floating pretty near to the point of Tikkerarsoak, I hoped that our brother *Conrad*, who had been with us, would come to help us with kayaks. We repeatedly thought that we heard the report of fire-arms, and therefore fired off our pieces; but, towards evening, we perceived that we had been mistaken. Now I began to feel great fears about the preservation of my life, and thinking of my poor forsaken family, I wept much. With many tears, I cried fervently to Jesus to save me. I could speak with Him as if He stood by me, and said: 'I pray that I may not be carried to the other side of the water, nor to the south, nor too far to the north, among the unbelievers; but that my body may have decent burial in the earth. O shew mercy to me; and do Thou, the only Helper in need, take care of my poor family!' Then those words occurred to my mind, *'Hold that fast which thou hast, that no man take thy crown;'* which made me shed tears of gratitude and love to our Saviour, like a child, though at so great a distance from home. I entered our snow-house, weeping, and we both joined in calling upon Jesus for help and comfort. This we did, every morning and evening.

On the 6th in the morning, finding ourselves carried far away from the land, into the ocean, we again looked for comfort to Jesus, and prayed to Him with many tears to help us, and direct our course. We sang that verse together, *'O lift up thy countenance upon us, &c.'* and those words were impressed upon my mind, *'I am the good shepherd, and know my sheep, and am known of mine.'* I felt my unworthiness deeply, and nothing but the words of Jesus could give me joy. I prayed fervently to Him, that He would give His angels charge over me. I spent the whole day in prayer, and as I walked about alone, several parts of Scripture occurred to my recollection, especially the account of our Saviour's being taken captive.

The prayer He offered up for His disciples, (John, 17th Chap.) was peculiarly precious to me, and gave me great comfort. Frequently I felt joy in my heart on remembering our Saviour's words, and that He said to His disciples, *'Receive ye the Holy Ghost!'*

On the 7th, the fog was so dense, that we could not see whither we were driven. I cried to Jesus, O help me, and His words came sweetly into my mind: *'Come unto me all ye that labour and are heavy laden, and I will give you rest. Take my yoke upon you, and learn of me, for I am meek and lowly in heart.'* Then I felt comforted.

On the 8th, 9th, and 10th, we could see nothing on account of the fog. I wept, and longed only to enjoy the inexpressible love of Jesus. I remembered how the apostle Peter was frightened in the storm, and was comforted by our Saviour. Thus, also, He comforted us in our dreadful situation. I cried continually to Him to bring us again to the shore, for the thought of my poor bereaved family caused many tears to flow from my eyes; but I felt confident, that they were under the protection and care of our Saviour. I remembered St. Paul's shipwreck, and how for many days he saw neither sun nor stars, and was delivered. At another time, the poor thief's cry to Jesus on the cross, *'Lord! remember me, when Thou comest into Thy kingdom,'* and again, St. Peter's deliverance from prison, when an angel came and said to him, *'follow me;'* proved a comfort to me. Thus I also hoped we should be brought out of the great ocean, back to the land. Once I recollected the story of the prodigal son, who had spent all his living, and said, *My father's servants have bread enough to spare, and I perish with hunger. I will arise and go to my father, &c.* This I felt to be my case, and that I was as unworthy to be received.

On the 11th, when we saw land through the fog, we wept for joy, for it was clearly manifest to us, that we were guided by the hand of our Saviour; we were still surrounded by broken pieces of floating ice. On the 12th, in the morning, we again saw the land before us, but as we did not trust the fragments of drift ice, we remained upon our large field, and returning into our snow-house, felt comforted in prayer. Having examined more fully whether the drift ice lay close together, it appeared, towards evening, as if we were approaching the firm ice. But just as we were again entering our house, our ice field sustained a terrible shock, and a large portion of it broke off. We now left it, being quite convinced that the Lord would direct us. In passing over the drift ice, whenever we were in danger, I cried to Jesus, and He provided a way for us till we were in safety.

On the 13th, in the morning, we arrived with our own people, thankful to our Saviour for this wonderful preservation, nor shall I ever in my life forget it.

Periodical Accounts' IX, 231–3

O   There were others who sent letters thanking benefactors in Europe. **Simeon** of Nain, Labrador, writes:

My dear Brethren and Sisters ... who live on the other side of the great water, it is not possible for me to see you in this life, therefore I desire to meet you hereafter at the feet of Jesus; for I hope that I and all my children will one day be happy in His presence. I know that you do not understand our language; but I have a great desire to send you a few words in my own handwriting to thank you ... I am quite astonished at your love for us, and distressed that I am not able to make you any return. I have requested my teachers to translate my words into your words, that you may understand that I feel great gratitude towards you. I am Simeon.

Davey, *The Fall of Torngak* 283

O   **Abraham** (d. 1881) was one of a party of eight Inuit from Labrador who were taken to Europe in 1880 by Carl Hagenbeck, the well-known wild animal exhibitor from Hamburg, Germany. His travelling exhibition included kayaks, dog sleds, and native housing and attracted huge crowds in Germany, Austria, and France. But by the time the party reached Paris, the Inuit had contracted smallpox and all died.

Abraham was described as a highly intelligent person who had a fair knowledge of world geography and could play violin, guitar, and organ. The Moravian missionaries had taught him to read and write in his own language and to speak a little English as well. While in Berlin in mid-October, Abraham began keeping a diary written in Inuktitut of his thoughts and experiences.

Abraham's Diary

In Berlin it is not beautiful because with all those people and trees it is impossible ... The air is constantly buzzing because of the walking and driving.

... One day a big gentleman came to see us. He had many gentlemen with him. They came into our enclosure to see the kayak but immediately everything was filled with people and it was impossible to move anymore. Schoepf and Jacobsen [Hagenbeck's agents] shouted with big voices and some of the soldiers left but most of them had no ears.

Since our two masters failed to achieve anything they came to me and sent me to chase them out. I did what I could. Taking my whip and the Greenland seal harpoon I made myself terrible. One of the gentlemen was like a crier. Others quickly shook hands with me when I chased them out. Others went and jumped over the fence because there were so many.

Several thanked me that I did this and our masters thanked me very much.

Ulrike [Abraham's wife] had locked our house from the inside. The entrance was plugged up so that nobody would go in. Those looking in through the windows were pushed away with a piece of wood.

On one occasion 'some believing women' visited Abraham's home in the fair grounds to sing and pray. Abraham described the religious fervour of the visit.

Yes, the believers here in Germany are our brethren. They even called us brothers and sisters. They even cried in front of us so that we would not get lost through Satan. They even kneeled in front of us and greeted us to give us strength. They even brought us tasty food and thought in this manner to give strength to our souls.

... Something sad happened to us [Abraham reported in a November entry]. Our companion, the single man Tobias, was beaten with a dog whip by our master, Jacobsen. Mr. Jacobsen was very furious because Tobias did not do what he was told ... If Mr. Jacobsen does that once more I shall write to England as I have been told.

Afterwards, he (Jacobsen) was very friendly with me so that I would not write ... Even our two women were bought silken ribbons.

The weather in Berlin had grown so cold that Abraham reported:

... the Kablunat (Europeans) are freezing and even we are freezing very much ... This is a good place to get sick with a bad cold ... the daily work is getting difficult because of illness.

A whole year is too long because we would very much like to return to our land. We cannot stay here forever. Yes, it is impossible!

On 15 November the party moved to Prague, where although Abraham was afraid to leave home because, 'if we did, we would be caught by the Catholics,' he did report that 'we are truly appreciated here.' The highlight of the Prague visit was a seal hunt.

I have caught a seal in a pond near Prague. An enormous crowd was watching – an unbelievable number of people. When I harpooned the seal the people all clapped with their hands, loudly like the eider ducks. When I was finished with it the musicians started up with violins, drums, trumpets and flutes. It was truly impossible to speak to each other because of many voices.

The exhibition returned to Germany in December. In Frankfort two Inuit houses were built indoors within a fenced enclosure.

During our stay there we were guarded day and night by soldiers who relieved each other. There are many Jews there and the Catholics are very despised. There we paddled our kayak very often on a pond.

... In Darmstadt [their next stop], we had one beautiful house in one huge round house. This is a playground for skating with wheels. We have often gone sled riding around on the inside of this house. All of us were sitting on the sled.

Just as the group was preparing to leave for Paris, Abraham's four-year-old daughter Sarah contracted smallpox. And in the last entry of his diary Abraham leaves his sick daughter:

While she (Sarah) was alive she was taken to a hospital and I was taken there with her. She was still conscious when I was with her. She prayed very nicely the hymm 'Ich bin ein kleines Kindelein.' When I wanted to leave she sent greetings to her mother and small sister. When I left, she slept and never woke again. This was a great consolation for both of us. While she was still living we left for Paris and have travelled all day and all night.

Adapted from J. Garth Taylor, 'An Eskimo Abroad, 1880: His Diary and Death,' *Canadian Geographic*, October-November 1981, 38–43. The excerpts from Abraham's diary were translated into English by Dr Helga Taylor from a nineteenth-century German translation of the Inuktitut original.

On the day before he himself was committed to bed, Abraham wrote to Brother Elsner, a former Labrador missionary who was living in Bremen, Germany.

Abraham's Letter to Brother Elsner, 1881

Paris, January 8th, 1881

My Dear Teacher Elsner,
  I write to you very sadly, and am much troubled about my relatives, for my child which I was so fond of lives no more; she has died of the bad small-pox, after being for four days only ill. By our child's death my wife and I are strongly reminded that we too must die. It died in Crefeld, although many doctors saw it. These men can indeed do nothing, so we will above all look to Jesus, who died for us, as our Physician. My dear teacher Elsner, we kneel daily before Him, and ask Him to pardon us for coming over here; and do not doubt that He will hear our prayer. Every day we weep together for the pardon of our sins through our Lord Jesus Christ. Even Terri-

aniak, who is now alone [his wife and child had died], when I speak to him about conversion, tells me – I think with sincerity – he desires to become our Saviour's property. He joins us daily at prayers, as also our little Maria. But her life is in danger, for her face is much swollen. Tobias is very ill. I remember that Jesus alone can help us in the hour of death. Yes, indeed, He is with us everywhere. I wish I could tell my people beyond the sea how kind the Lord is. Our master buys much medicine for us, but all seems useless. I hope in the Lord, who sees my tears daily. I care not for worldly advantage; but I do long to see my friends once more, and, as long as I live, to speak to them in the name of the Lord. I did not formerly understand these things; now I do. My tears come often, but the words which He has spoken always bring me fresh comfort. My dear teacher Elsner, pray for us that this sickness be removed, if it be His will; but His will be done. I am a poor man like the dust.

It is very cold in Paris, but our master is now very kind to all of us. I salute you, so does my wife; and with you the members of the church at Bremen. Tell the great teachers [the Directing Board] that we salute them very much. The Lord be with you all. Amen.

I am, Abraham, husband of Ulrika.

Gosling, *Labrador* 310–11

O   **Lydia Campbell** (1818–1907) was a native of Hamilton Inlet, Labrador. Her 'Sketches of Labrador Life,' printed in the *Evening Herald* of St John's, Newfoundland, in 1893 and 1894, was the first diary written by an Inuk to be published. It provides the reader with glimpses of female life in the early history of coastal Labrador. Mrs Campbell had 'never been to school ... had no school book ... nothing but a family Bible and a common Prayer.' In their biblical undertones and phrasing her sketches reveal some almost poetic lines.

Lydia Campbell's Autobiography (an extract)

Maligan River, Dec. 25, 1893. Christmas Day, as this is a holy day for us, the Campbell's and Blake's – my family – I think that it is a nice time to write a few loins, a beginning of this winter. I have been very busy all this fall in particular, for I has a lot to do with 3 little motherless granddaughters to work for, beside their poor father and a big son, going off hunting and wood choping, and the weather so cold as to need all the warm clothing possible to warm them. The weather 30 below zero often, and myself off to my rabbit snars, about 4 miles going and coming, over ice and snow, with snow shoes and axe and game bag. Some days I has 3 rabbits in one day, caught in snears, for I has about 24 snears, made myself to set them up, and I gets pretty tired some days. Often the snow is deep and soft, just now about 3 feet deep in the woods, but it can't be expected otherwise with me to get tired, for I am now the last birthday 75 years old, last month, first November. I have seen many ups and downs, but the Good Lord has safely brought me through. I have been bereaved of my first husband and 4 of his children. One is left me, Thomas Blake. It is his little children that I has to look to now. The present husband that I has now is nearly as old as me. We has 3 children left by him out of 8 – 2 boys and a girl. They all has a family to look to. We have a meeting some times, and when our large rivers freezes over hard enough to go on, then comes the time for trouting, as we call it, then most of our grandaughters and grandsons gather together here to trout. One family, John Campbell's children comes along shore, about 4 miles he lives. My eldest son, Thos. Blake, my first husband's son, and his motherless children, is near us, next door – none near us but them and our dear children's graves. We can see their head-stones at a distance, over on the cranberry banks, so pretty it looks in the fall when we come home from our summer quarters, above 70 miles from here. When we are sailing up in our large boat, to see the ducks in our bay when we are nearing the river, and when we get ashore to the pretty river banks and walking up the path under our large trees, some 50, and some 60 or more feet high, we often meet with a flock of partridges flying up to the trees. Before we get to the house, so pretty, then is the scramble among the young ones who will see the first turnips and potatoes, and sure enough, all around the house is green with turnip tops, and between them and the wall of the house is hanging red with moss-berries, some falls, then we get home to our winter house for 10 months or more.

Lydia Campbell's Hunt in the Year 1894
I was out the other day walking in the woods with my snow shoes on all alone, looking up at the pretty trees, at the high spruce and birches looking so high and steatly. I saw in the sun shine such a pretty sight high above the highest trees, a flock of the beautiful white partridge, how pretty it lookt and the snow glistening and ice and trees and me – poor old mortel – drinking in all the beautyful scenery, which will soon be out of sight of it all, but not lait, ah no, only going the way all the people has gone before ...

Muligan River, Jan. 22, 1894
Now for all the superstition in the olden times. When i was a little girl my mother used to tell me and my sister how when she and her little sisters and brother was left alone, orphans, that the older Esquimaux took them and used them very hard. and while any of them – the master or mistress – got sick, that they would take hold of their hands and cut a place in it, to draw blood to cure the sick. They thought that was a cure for them, as the orphans was witches. If that was not enough of superstition, i don't know what to say – to see the poor little ones bleeding in that way – the friendless was used pretty hardly. I suppose it is the case in many a country besides this. Poor mother, when she grew up to be a woman she ran away from them before there was any ice to keep her, in October some time, and she went along shore, crossing rivers on drift sticks and wading in shalow water, crossing points, throu woods, meeting bears, no gun, no axe, no fire works, but lye down under juniper tree and spruce tree. Who does it represent in the Bible. She had to travel all the way – 70 miles – on foot. All she had to eat was 2 dry fish and berries, and the only wepen she had was a mooloo, a woman's knife. She went on until she came to a large river called Mulligan in French language. There she got stock, (as the people call it about hear), but while she was standing and wondering what to do and gathering some sticks to make a raft, she saw a French boat with 2 people in it – Frenchmen – and she took off her outer

114

garment and waved to them, and they thought it was a deer, and when they rowed towards it and saw it was a person, and, what a strange sight, miles and miles away from any habitation, and the mountaineers went into the country. When they came to her they could not understand each other, but they took her in their boat and went back to their trading post, and she stayed a winter with them, and was loved as a sister to one and a daughter to the other. How she did their things, and how did she pick and gather berries in the fall, for the winter how she drest and reflen and tap their boots.

In the spring they came up the bay sealing and took her away again. She was sorry to go. That was the custom of the Esquimaux, to go up the big bay to kill and hunt seals and pitch their tents on the ice near the seals with dogs, komatiks tents, men, women, and children. What a time they would have when it would come bad weather. The women firing to let the sealers know whereabouts they were, the women going ashore for wood to cook their meat, and the seals was inumerable at that time. The reason that they pitched their tents on the ice, was that they was afraid of the mountens [Indians] might come out of the woods and kill them. So we was told when we was young, and in that way they would go to a french post called Muligan, at the point of Muligan. There things for their seal, and going ashore they found my dear, good mother and carried her off, and as there was no other kind of women to marrie hear, the few English men each took a wife of the sort, and they never sorry that they took them for they was great workers, and so it came to pass that I was one of the youngsters of them.

O **Igjugârjuk** (c. 1875–) was a man of great authority among his people, the Caribou. A shaman of great skill, he described to Knud Rasmussen how he became a shaman. It is interesting to compare Igjugârjuk's shamanic experiences with those of the Iglulik shaman, Aua.

How Igjugârjuk Acquired His Shamanic Powers

When I was to be a shaman, I chose suffering through the two things that are most dangerous to us humans, suffering through hunger and suffering through cold. First I hungered five days and was then allowed to drink a mouthful of warm water; the old ones say that only if the water is warm will Pinga and Hila notice the novice and help him. Thereafter I went hungry another fifteen days, and again was given a mouthful of warm water. After that I hungered for ten days, and then could begin to eat, though it only had to be aklɛrnän̩icut, that is to say the sort of food on which there is never any taboo, preferably fleshy meat, and never intestines, head, heart or other entrails, nor meat that had been touched by wolf or wolverine while it lay in a cache. I was to keep to this diet for five moons, and then the next five moons might eat everything; but after that I was again forced to eat the meat diet that is prescribed for all those who must do penance in order to become clean. The old ones attached great importance to the food that the would-be shamans might eat; thus a novice who wished to possess the ability to kill had never to eat the salmon that we call hiuʳlχit. If they eat hiuʳlχit, they will, instead of killing others, kill themselves.

My instructor was my wife's father, Perqánâq. When I was to be exhibited to Pinga and Hila, he dragged me on a little sledge that was no bigger than I could just sit on it; he dragged me far over on the other side of Hikoligjuaq. It was a very long day's journey inland to a place we call Kingârjuit: the high hills, which are at Tikerarjuaq (by the southeast shore of Hikoligjuaq). It was in winter time and took place at night with the new moon; one could just see the very first streak of the moon; it had just appeared in the sky. I was not fetched again until the next moon was of the same size. Perqánâq built a small snow hut at the place where I was to be, this snow hut being no bigger than that I could just get under cover and sit down. I was given no sleeping skin to protect me against the cold, only a little piece of caribou skin to sit upon. There I was shut in ... The entrance was closed with a block, but no soft snow was thrown over the hut to make it warm. When I had sat there five days, Perqánâq came with water, tepid, wrapped in caribou skin, a watertight caribou-skin bag. Not until fifteen days afterwards did he come again and hand me the same, just giving himself time to hand it to me, and then he was gone again, for even the old shaman must not inter-

116

rupt my solitude. The snow hut in which I sat was built far from the trails of men, and when Perqánâq had found the spot where he thought it ought to be built, he stopped the little sledge at a distance, and there I had to remain seated until the snow hut was ready. Not even I, who was after all the one to have to stay there, might set my footprints in the vicinity of the hut, and old Perqánâq had to carry me from the sledge over to the hut so that I could crawl in. As soon as I had become alone, Perqánâq enjoined me to think of one single thing all the time I was to be there, to want only one single thing, and that was to draw Pinga's attention to the fact that there I sat and wished to be a shaman ... Pinga should own me. My novitiate took place in the middle of the coldest winter, and I, who never got anything to warm me, and must not move, was very cold, and it was so tiring having to sit without daring to lie down, that sometimes it was as if I died a little. Only towards the end of the thirty days did a helping spirit come to me, a lovely and beautiful helping spirit, whom I had never thought of; it was a white woman; she came to me whilst I had collapsed, exhausted, and was sleeping. But still I saw her lifelike, hovering over me, and from that day I could not close my eyes or dream without seeing her. There is this remarkable thing about my helping spirit, that I have never seen her while awake, but only in dreams. She came to me from Pinga and was a sign that Pinga had now noticed me and would give me powers that would make me a shaman.

When a new moon was lighted and had the same size as the one that had shone for us when we left the village, Perqánâq came again with his little sledge and stopped a long way from the snow hut. But by this time I was not very much alive any more and had not the strength to rise, in fact I could not stand on my feet. Perqánâq pulled me out of the hut and carried me down to the sledge and dragged me home in the same manner as he had dragged me to Kingârjuit. I was now so completely emaciated that the veins on my hands and body and feet had quite disappeared ... For a long time I might only eat only very little in order to again get my intestines extended, and later came the diet that was to help to cleanse my body.

For a whole year I was not to lie with my wife, who, however, had to make my food. For a whole year I had to have my own little cooking pot and my own meat dish; no one else was allowed to eat of what had been cooked for me.

Later, when I had quite become myself again, I understood that I had become the shaman of my village, and it did happen that my neighbours or people from a long distance away called me to heal a sick person, or to 'inspect a course' if they were going to travel. When this happened, the people of my village were called together and I told them what I had been asked to do. Then I left tent or snow house and went out into solitude ... away from the dwellings of man, but those who remained behind had to sing continuously ... just to keep themselves happy and lively. If anything difficult had to be found out, my solitude had to extend over three days and two nights, or three nights and two days. In all that time I had to wander about without rest, and only sit down once in a while on a stone or a snow drift. When I had been out long and had become tired, I could almost doze and dream what I had come out to find and about which I had been thinking all the time. Every morning, however, I could come home and report on what I had so far found, but as soon as I had spoken I had to return again, out into the open, out to places where I could be quite alone. In the time when one is out seeking, one may eat a little, but not much. If a shaman 'out of the secrets of solitude' finds out that the sick person will die, he can return home and stay there without first having allowed the usual time to pass. It is only in cases of possible cure that he must remain out the whole time. On the first night after returning from such a spirit wandering in solitude, the shaman must not lie with his wife, nor must he undress when going to sleep, nor lie down at full length, but must sleep in a sitting position.

These days of 'seeking for knowledge' are very tiring, for one must walk all the time, no matter what the weather is like and only rest in short snatches. I am usually quite done up, tired, not only in body but also in head, when I have found what I sought.

We shamans in the interior have no special spirit language, and believe that the real angatkut do not need it. On my travels I have sometimes been present at a seance among the saltwater-dwellers, for instance among the coast people at

Utkuhigjalik (Back River, or Great Fish River). These angatkut never seemed trustworthy to me. It always appeared to me that these salt-water angatkut attached more weight to tricks that would astonish the audience, when they jumped about the floor and lisped all sorts of absurdities and lies in their so-called spirit language; to me all this seemed only amusing and as something that would impress the ignorant. A real shaman does not jump about the floor and do tricks, nor does he seek by the aid of darkness, by putting out the lamps, to make the minds of his neighbours uneasy. For myself, I do not think I know much but I do not think that wisdom or knowledge about things that are hidden can be sought in that manner. True wisdom is only to be found far away from people, out in the great solitude, and it is not found in play but only through suffering. Solitude and suffering open the human mind, and therefore, a shaman must seek his wisdom there.

But during my visits to the salt-water shamans, both down about Iglugârjuk and Utkuhigjalik, I have never openly expressed my contempt for their manner of summoning their helping spirits. A stranger ought always to be cautious, for – one may never know – they may of course be skilful in magic and, like our shamans, be able to kill through words and thoughts. This that I am telling you now, I dare to confide to you, because you are a stranger from a far away country, but I would never speak about it to my own kinsmen, except those whom I should teach to become shamans. While I was at Utkuhigjalik, people there had heard from my wife that I was a shaman, and therefore they once asked me to cure a sick man, a man who was so wasted that he could no longer swallow food. I summoned all the people of the village together and asked them to hold a song-feast, as is our custom, because we believe that all evil will shun a place where people are happy. And when the song-feast began, I went out alone into the night. They laughed at me, and my wife was later on able to tell me how they mocked me, because I would not do tricks to entertain everybody. But I kept away in lonely places, far from the village, for five days, thinking uninterruptedly of the sick man and wishing him health. He got better, and since then nobody at that village has mocked me.

Rasmussen, *Intellectual Culture of the Caribou Eskimos* 52–5

○ **Aua** (c. 1870–) was an Iglulik shaman who impressed Rasmussen when they met in 1922. Rasmussen praised Aua who, he
claimed, was always 'clear in his line of thought, and with a
remarkable power of expressing what he meant.' The spiritual
leader of his group, Aua told Rasmussen how he acquired his
shamanic power.

How Aua Became a Shaman

I was yet but a tiny unborn infant in my mother's womb when
anxious folk-began to enquire sympathetically about me; all
the children my mother had had before had lain crosswise and
been stillborn. As soon as my mother now perceived that she
was with child, the child that one day was to be me, she spoke
thus to her house-fellows:

Now I have again that within me which will turn out no
real human being.

All were very sorry for her and a woman named Ârdjuaq,
who was a shaman herself, called up her spirits that same evening to help my mother. And the very next morning it could
be felt that I had grown, but it did me no good at the time, for
Ârdjuaq had forgotten that she must do no work the day after
a spirit-calling, and had mended a hole in a mitten. This breach
of taboo at once had its effect upon me; my mother felt the
birth-pangs coming on before the time, and I kicked and struggled as if trying to work my way out through her side. A new
spirit-calling then took place, and as all precepts were duly
observed this time, it helped both my mother and myself.

But then one day it happened that my father, who was going
out on a jouney to hunt, was angry and impatient, and in
order to calm him, my mother went to help him harness the
dogs to the sledge. She forgot that in her condition, all work
was taboo. And so, hardly had she picked up the traces and
lifted one dog's paw before I began again kicking and struggling
and trying to get out through her navel; and again we had to
have a shaman to help us.

Old people now assured my mother that my great sensitive-
ness to any breach of taboo was a sign that I should live to
become a great shaman; but at the same time, many dangers

and misfortunes would pursue me before I was born.

My father had got a walrus with its unborn young one, and when he began cutting it out, without reflecting that my mother was with child, I again fell to struggling within the womb, and this time in earnest. But the moment I was born, all life left me, and I lay there dead as a stone. The cord was twisted round my neck and had strangled me. Ârdjuaq, who lived in another village, was at once sent for, and a special hut was built for my mother. When Ârdjuaq came and saw me with me eyes sticking right out of my head, she wiped my mother's blood from my body with the skin of a raven, and made a little jacket for me of the same skin.

He is born to die, but he shall live, she said.

And so Ârdjuaq stayed with my mother, until I showed signs of life. Mother was put on very strict diet, and had to observe difficult rules of taboo. If she had eaten part of a walrus, for instance, then that walrus was taboo to all others; the same with seal and caribou. She had to have special pots, from which no one else was allowed to eat. No woman was allowed to visit her, but men might do so. My clothes were made after a particular fashion; the hair of the skins must never lie pointing upwards or down, but fall athwart the body. Thus I lived in the birth-hut, unconscious of all the care that was being taken with me.

For a whole year my mother and I had to live entirely alone, only visited now and again by my father. He was a great hunter, and always out after game, but in spite of this he was never allowed to sharpen his own knives; as soon as he did so, his hand began to swell and I fell ill. A year after my birth, we were allowed to have another person in the house with us; it was a woman, and she had to be very careful herself; whenever she went out she must throw her hood over her head, wear boots without stockings, and hold the tail of her fur coat lifted high in one hand.

I was already a big boy when my mother was first allowed to go visiting; all were anxious to be kind, and she was invited to all the other families. But she stayed out too long; the spirits do not like women with little children to stay too long away from their house, and they took vengeance in this wise;

the skin of her head peeled of, and I, who had no understanding of anything at that time, beat her about the body with my little fists as she went home, and made water down her back.

No one who is to become a skilful hunter or a good shaman must remain out too long when visiting strange houses; and the same holds good for a woman with a child in her amaut.

At last I was big enough to go out with the grown up men to the blowholes after seal. The day I harpooned my first seal, my father had to lie down on the ice with the upper part of his body naked, and the seal I had caught was dragged across his back while it was still alive. Only men were allowed to eat of my first catch, and nothing must be left. The skin and the head were set on the ice, in order that I might be able later on to catch the same seal again. For three days and nights, none of the men who had eaten of it might go out hunting or do any kind of work.

The next animal I killed was a caribou. I was strictly forbidden to use a gun, and had to kill it with bow and arrows; this animal also only men were allowed to eat; no woman might touch it.

Some time passed, and I grew up and was strong enough to go out hunting walrus. The day I harpooned my first walrus my father shouted at the top of his voice the names of all the villages he knew, and cried: Now there is food for all!

The walrus was towed in to land, while it was still alive, and not until we reached the shore was it finally killed. My mother, who was to cut it up, had the harpoon line made fast to her body before the harpoon head was withdrawn. After having killed this walrus, I was allowed to eat all those delicacies which had formerly been forbidden, yes, even entrails, and women were now allowed to eat of my catch, as long as they were not with child or recently delivered. Only my own mother had still to observe great caution, and whenever she had any sewing to do, a special hut had to be built for her. I had been named after a little spirit, Aua, and it was said that it was in order to avoid offending this spirit that my mother had to be so particular about everything she did. It was my guardian spirit, and took great care that I should not do anything that was forbidden. I was never allowed, for instance, to remain in a snow hut where young women were undressing for the night; nor might any woman comb her hair while I was present.

Even after I had been married a long time, my catch was still subject to strict taboo. If there but lived women with infants near us, my own wife was only allowed to eat meat of my killing, and no other woman was allowed to satisfy her hunger with the meat of any animal of which my wife had eaten. Any walrus I killed was further subject to the rule that no woman might eat of its entrails, which are reckoned a great delicacy, and this prohibition was maintained until I had four children of my own. And it is really only since I had grown old that the obligations laid on me by Ardjuaq in order that I might live have ceased to be needful.

Everything was thus made ready for me beforehand, even from the time when I was yet unborn; nevertheless, I endeavoured to become a shaman by the help of others; but in this I did not succeed. I visited many famous shamans, and gave them great gifts, which they at once gave away to others; for if they had kept the things for themselves, they or their children would have died. This they believed because my own life had been so threatened from birth. Then I sought solitude, and here I soon became very melancholy. I would sometimes fall to weeping, and feel unhappy without knowing why. Then, for no reason, all would suddenly be changed, and I felt a great, inexplicable joy, a joy so powerful that I could not restrain it, but had to break into song, a mighty song, with only room for the one word: joy, joy! And I had to use the full strength of my voice. And then in the midst of such a fit of mysterious and overwhelming delight I became a shaman, not knowing myself how it came about. But I was a shaman. I could see and hear in a totally different way. I had gained my qaumaneq, my enlightenment, the shaman-light of brain and body, and this in such a manner that it was not only I who could see through the darkness of life, but the same light also shone out from me, imperceptible to human beings, but visible to all the spirits of earth and sky and sea, and these now came to me and became my helping spirits.

My first helping spirit was my namesake, a little aua. When it came to me, it was as if the passage and roof of the house were lifted up, and I felt such a power of vision, that I could see right through the house, in through the earth and up into the sky; it was the little Aua that brought me all this inward light, hovering over me as long as I was singing. Then it placed itself in a corner of the passage, invisible to others, but always ready if I should call it.

An aua is a little spirit, a woman, that lives down by the sea shore. There are many of these shore spirits, who run about with a pointed skin hood on their heads; their breeches are queerly short, and made of bearskin; they wear long boots with a black pattern, and coats of sealskin. Their feet are twisted upward, and they seem to walk only on their heels. They hold their hands in such a fashion that the thumb is always bent in over the palm; their arms are held raised up on high with the hands together, and incessantly stroking the head. They are bright and cheerful when one calls them, and resemble most of all sweet little live dolls; they are no taller than the length of a man's arm.

My second helping spirit was a shark. One day when I was out in my kayak, it came swimming up to me, lay alongside quite silently and whispered my name. I was greatly astonished, for I had never seen a shark before; they are very rare in these waters. Afterwards it helped me with my hunting, and was always near me when I had need of it. These two, the shore spirit and the shark, were my principal helpers, and they could aid me in everything I wished. The song I generally sang when calling them was of few words, as follows:

Joy, joy,
Joy, joy!
I see a little shore spirit,
A little aua,
I myself am also aua,
The shore spirit's namesake,
Joy, joy!

These words I would keep on repeating, until I burst into tears, overwhelmed by a great dread; then I would tremble all over, crying only: 'Ah-a-a-a-a, joy, joy! Now I will go home, joy, joy!'

Once I lost a son, and felt that I could never again leave the spot where I had laid his body. I was like a mountain spirit, afraid of human kind. We stayed for a long time up inland, and my helping spirits forsook me, for they do not like live human beings to dwell upon any sorrow. But one day the song about joy came to me all of itself and quite unexpectedly. I felt once more a longing for my fellow men, my helping spirits returned to me, and I was myself once more.

Rasmussen, *Intellectual Culture of the Iglulik Eskimos* 116–20

Aua's philosophical ideas about the nature of death, the existence of reincarnation, and the origin of the cosmos, interested Rasmussen. Here he tells the famous Danish explorer about the nature of the human soul.

The Soul

We ignorant Eskimos living up here do not believe, as you have told us many white men do, in one great solitary spirit that from a place far up in the sky maintains humanity and all the life of nature. Among us, as I have already explained to you, all is bound up with the earth we live on and our life here; and it would be even more imcomprehensible, even more unreasonable, if, after a life short or long, of happy days or of suffering and misery, we were then to cease altogether from existence. What we have heard about the soul shows us that the life of men and beasts does not end with death. When at the end of life we draw our last breath, that is not the end. We awake to consciousness again, we come to life again, and all this is effected through the medium of the soul. Therefore it is that we regard the soul as the greatest and most incomprehensible of all.

In our ordinary everyday life we do not think much about all these things, and it is only now you ask that so many thoughts arise in my head of long-known things; old thoughts, but as it were becoming altogether new when one has to put them into words.

Rasmussen, *Intellectual Culture of the Iglulik* Eskimos 60–1

○ **Peter Tulugajuak** (c. 1870–c. 1935) was a prominent and influential leader among the Inuit of Cumberland Sound. He became an Anglican catechist in April 1904 and from 1912 to 1925, when there were no white Anglican missionaries in the region,

125

he was the leading Anglican catechist. He was employed as the whale-boat leader for the whaling station at Blacklead Island, until it closed. And from 1922 until his death he was principal hunting leader at Kingmiksok. He was reputed to be 'one of the finest whalers and dog drivers in the country while in the handling of boats or canoes in any sort of weather he was unsurpassed.'

His letter to the commissioner of the Northwest Territories complaining about the trading practices of the Hudson's Bay Company at Pangnirtung is typical of ones written by Inuit to government officials complaining about whites.

A Letter of Complaint, 1922

Truly I am now at a loss to understand my Captain, the White Man [the HBC manager at Pangnirtung] who dwells above there with us. He is going after women, it is not at all good.

I think it would be a good thing thus, if they are spoken to by you. We also who are Eskimo teachers ought to speak to the White Men who are accustomed to come here.

I cannot understand how that White man who is up there is acting in relation to all of us here. He is not good to those who are endeavouring to trade. Sometimes their payments are small. Sometimes they are more adequate. That is how he is.

Yet, it is true, his manner of dealing with them thus, so it is not at all good if we are overcome in this way, we being only Eskimos.

For I have known White Men who were accustomed to share out even small portions, when they had got seals, to those who traded with them. They never altered. they were always the same.

My payments are contemptible, for fox-skins, for seal-skins, and for wolf-skins, for reindeer-skins also, and for various things. So also I am frequently hearing from those who dwell above there, sometimes they receive not enough, sometimes enough. It has been so now all this winter, to all of us Eskimos here. So they have been dealt with.

And truly I know this same White Man, he who is seeking after Eskimo women, because we generally know these things. I know well. Let his name be told to those who come here.

We also frequently speak to the women that they ought not to do evil in seeking after men, and they generally assent to what we say.

That White Man above there, who is seeking after Eskimo women, and only wants to kill reindeer, wishes also to have seals. But I am at a loss to know where he wants the seals he gets to go, whether to White Men, or to Eskimos. That is known only to himself.

We shall only endeavour to get things, if we have sufficient materials for clothing, and also if we get sufficient food. That one who lives above there is one who only wishes to kill reindeer.

National Archives of Canada, RG 85, vol. 610, file 2712

O   **Thommy Bruce Opartok** (c. 1902–), adopted by Nivicennar (Shoo-Fly), was one of the best hunters of Southampton Island. Alone in one year, 1926–7, he caught 180 foxes, 63 caribou, 40 seals, 6 white bear, 6 walruses and 4 bearded seals. Opartok kept a diary between 1 September 1926 and 1 November 1927 in Inuktitut syllabics that were later translated into French by the Reverend Arthur Thibert. It is a dry piece of literature but it does give information regarding the cycle of occupations of a group of Eskimo at a time when little attention was given to socio-economic surveys in the north.

Opartok's Diary

Feb. 8, 1927: Little wind. Pameork and Joe go to the sea; I go to visit my traps; John stayed home and the others stayed home as well; it is beginning to snow and in the evening there is a heavy blizzard.

Feb. 9 It is snowing and we are forced to stay at home; there's no one who could travel in such weather; we do not do very much.

Feb. 10 We go to the sea in spite of the wind. Makik caught three seals and I two. Joe and Pameork both caught one. Krakoluk caught nothing. John and I caught a fox each. Those who remained in their homes worked some seal skins in order to bleach them outdoors.

Feb. 11 There is little wind, we go to the sea but we caught nothing. Makik nevertheless fired on an *udjuk*. Joe took the seal spear. John and I went by canoe. Nevertheless we hooked it and pulled again however the hook slipped off and it went straight down, we lost it. Krakoluk goes to see his traps at Ittiyuardjuk; he caught four foxes one of which belongs to his father Makik. The weather is nice and the wind is from the North West. In the evening the sky becomes cloudy.

Feb. 12 Pameork and John leave to visit their traps. We go to the sea, Krakoluk, Makik and I, but we catch nothing. The sea is not good; while staying at the seashore we hunt the seal through the breathing holes (aglous). In this way, I caught a seal. It is very cold.

Feb. 13 Joe and I leave for our home at the same time as Makik and Krakoluk. While visiting our traps we each take two foxes while Pameork only catches one.

Feb. 14 In two's we go visit our traps; during the morning my companions saw some caribou when I was not with them. I have also seen some twice and I fired my rifle. I fired at one but I missed it. Nevertheless I had seen twenty-one all together. I missed them twice. I go to the traps and I catch five foxes. Kayardjuark takes seven. I met him at the traps. Krakoluk and Makik also return passing by their traps.

Feb. 15 We return home and we pass near the caribou which Makik killed. Visibility is very poor and we have wind in front. Pameork and John have been back for quite a while. We arrive having left Krakoluk and Joe far behind us ...

May 20 We remain in camp. It is snowing lightly. In the evening, we set off again once the snow has stopped falling. We camp out in the morning. It is snowing heavily from the south east.

May 21 We sleep during the day. Snow is drifting and falling. We are not any father out.

May 22 The heavy blizzard keeps us on the spot. In the evening, the snow is no longer drifting. My dogs have left. Krakoluk and Akrearok leave. I stay with Joe, we wait for the dogs.

May 23 In the morning, the weather is mild. My dogs had come back. We leave in the evening. We left a seal there and towards midnight we arrive at the spot where we were this winter: Nanuraktalik.

May 24 Krakoluk and I stay on the spot; Akrearok is on the way home by way of Mount Minto. Joe goes to look for a bear which he has in cache (a hiding place) at Mount Minto. He has killed a seal on the other side of the mountain. The weather is nice.

May 25 We go to look for our boat, but, it is impossible because it is trapped in the snow. We leave it there. Our clothes are soaking. On the way back, Joe takes a seal and I take a bear which I had in cache. The others leave. Joe goes to my caribou cache and Krokoluk to my bear cache.

May 26 We spend the day on the spot where we are because it is snowing. We clear the snow from a bear cache. We have seen a swan. The wind is from the north west and the sky is overcast.

May 27 We set off again. Krakoluk is going to pass between the two ... (word is illegible). Krakoluk takes a caribou and I one also. Krokoluk takes two seals.

May 28 We try to sleep during the day.

May 29 We set off from there and in the evening we camp out at Tunnermiut after having travelled in the blizzard.

May 30 We set off once more. I kill a seal. Krakoluk, while walking, has passed across the ice. We camp out at Kredluark. Snow is still drifting.

May 31 We depart again and we arrive at the whites' (the summer post). We meet each other again all four brothers ...

June 18 We do not leave on a journey. I went bird hunting during the night. I killed 14 geese, 3 ducks, 3 mauves, 2 loons and a white magpie. I came back in the morning and I found 3 duck eggs. It is cloudy and the wind is very strong from the west.

June 19 Sunday. We stay at home. No one travels. We play ball (aitaiyartut) ...

July 23 (at the trading post) They make us carry rocks to the stock store with wheelbarrows. The wind is faint. Akrearok arrives with his family.

July 24 We spent the day doing nothing. In the evening some Okkomiut arrive with their families. They are coming from Nunareark. The wind is fierce and from the West. In the evening, however, it dies down and blows from the north west. Our children are baptized (Southampton's first Christenings by E. Duplain, o.m.i.)

July 25 We work cleaning the surroundings of the white people's homes. We put in order the empty barrels. I do some painting. The families of Keviartok, Kangualuk and Sapagnak arrive. The wind is from the west.

July 26 We work for the white people. Kreunerk wants to cross the bay but he is unsuccessful. The newcomers trade in the evening. The wind is blowing fiercely and always from the west. The rain is coming down in torrents, buckets, this evening.

Archives Deschâtelets, Oblats de Marie-Immaculée, Ottawa, typescript copy (translation from the French by Tonina Costanzo)

O **Harry Gibbons Ohnainewk** (c. 1900–54) was born near Wager Bay. Between 19 September 1945 and 11 June 1948, while living near Rocky Brook, Southampton Island, Northwest Territories, Gibbons kept a diary. The type of wind is so crucial to the hunter that Gibbons began nearly every entry with the wind. His diary contained valuable data on hunting, weather, animals and daily tasks. Gibbons was awarded the Queen Elizabeth II Coronation Medal.

Ohnainewk's Diary

09/08/47 Wind West in the morning North in the afternoon. We seen two flocks swans flying south & 1 flock geese or wavies all hands building house. We now have 32 people at camp 10 men 10 women 6 boys 6 girls.

09/09/47 Wind E.S.E. moderate. The tide has been so low that we have not been able to get out with the boat however the whale boat was out today got 6 jar seals the rest of us still laying the foundation of the house. We got 2 geese, radio not very good. Harry Jr not feeling well legs acking. Seals shot by Harry Jr, 2 Kaloojak 2, Natchik 1, J.E. Joe 1 & 2 geese.

09/10/47 Wind East strong. Raining in the afternoon all

hands working in the morning at the house. We had seal meat for supper & bannak Poridge in the morning.
09/11/47 Wind East very strong snowing & raining all at home making a karakade for a barkour in the afternoon. We had seal meat for noon meal & walrus at night.
09/12/47 Wind S.E. very light. We went out with the two boats all day we got 4 sqwear flippers & 4 jar seals our food consists of seal meat and bannock.
09/13/47 Wind East strong & snowing all day Savgak was out in the bay all night. We took her in at noon high tide & cachshing meat every body wet water very cold.
09/14/47 Wind N.E. very strong. We fixed the fly wheel again. I hope it stay this time. Out meat seal and walrus & bannock.
09/15/47 Wind North very strong and snowing all at home hammering nails strieght & (Restling) our meat seal & walrus & bannock.
09/16/47 Wind N.W. very strong partly cloudy tides very high all at work on the house. Freezing at night.
10/27/47 Wind North very cold & cleer in the morning. Natchik Joe, Akaat & myself working on the lining of the house the rest doing odd jobs such as dog harnesses.
10/27/47 Wind North very cold & cleer in the morning. Natchik Joe, Akaat & myself working on the lining of the house the rest doing odd jobs such as dog harnesses.
10/28/47 Wind N.E. not too cold. Kalojak & Jasper left for a fish hunt. The rest of us seal hunting got nothing. Was out with the boat. Had a hard time getting back to shore. Natchik off with his dogs got 17 partridge. Kukilasak had an attack of bronckitis very bad.

Canadian Museum of Civilization, Ottawa, 1030.1/B20#2/IV-C-6

O **Poovlaleraq**, baptized **Pélagy** (1931–), was the daughter of Joseph Okatsiak, a former sorcerer. The first Inuk girl to become a member of a religious community, she made her profession in the Institute of the Grey Nuns of Montreal at Chesterfield Inlet on 15 February 1951. She later left the order and in 1988 was living in Eskimo Point, N.W.T.

A letter which she wrote in Inuktitut to Father Arthur Thibert a few months after taking her vow reveals a touching simplicity.

Sister Pélagy's Letter to Father Thibert, o.m.i., 1951

Hospital of the Little Flower,
Chesterfield Inlet,
Today, July 13th, 1951.

From Naya Pelagy Inuk
to Father Thibert,

I am writing to you again so that you may well understand, and also to greet you. Your letter has reached me. The sea ice went away on the day marked July 9th. At the same time, the lakes are not covered with ice any more. How pleasant it is for us! Towards the last part of winter I received some news. Here it is.

Teresa Swannak, my elder sister, died, and so did her little baby boy. Her husband got lost last fall and perished. Teresa walked outside (to go and secure help) and died from hunger and cold. She froze to death while carrying her baby on her back. How pitiful it is! Here too, Maurice who was at the hospital, froze to death. His mother had sent for him, and he left for home. Why didn't he stay here where he was confortable? He would probably be alive today, who knows? The good Lord is the Master.

Also, near Padley, an Eskimo by the name of Oookadlerk (the Arctic hare) committed a murder by shooting somebody at point blank range. They say he has been arrested by the Police. However, all is well at Chesterfield, excepting this Maurice, the son of Shooweserk, who died from exposure.

As for me, I am always very happy here. At last I can be of help to the Eskimos. Also, I play the organ when the children sing. A few days ago, for the first time in my life, I played the organ in the chapel. It is Sister Piché who taught me music. I would love also to learn many more things, out of love for my countrymen and for the children whom I wish to help. By my prayers I can aid them a great deal, and this thought makes me feel good.

Now I have a request to make, if it is not asking for something too difficult. I often wish to read, but I cannot do it for lack of books. (Naya Pelagy speaks a little French, but cannot read it well as yet). Would it be possible for you to translate in Eskimo the life of St. Teresa of the Child Jesus [patron of missions, especially honoured in the Arctic], and explain her writings to me? You will tell me if you are too busy to do it. If I knew better the life of the Little Flower, I could make more efforts to perfect myself, therefore, I could be of more service to Jesus and the Eskimos. I wish to imitate the Little Flower, for I know her life was perfect. The Priests at Chesterfield Inlet are unable to answer my request, since they have many more things to do. They go and visit the Eskimos, sometimes by dogteam, sometimes by canoe. They could not very well translate the book. Many babies to be baptized have been born in distant camps. The Priests take turns going, when one returns from a trip, the other one goes in some other direction. However, both of them are now at the Mission.

Let us pray often, so we may have more Priests! The natives would receive better instruction. As for me, although I am staying here at the hospital, I am certain that through prayer I can greatly help the Eskimos and the Priests. Prayer in itself can accomplish a lot and inspires confidence. With Jesus helping us we can aid greatly our neighbors.

I know where my strength lies, in Jesus Whom I love, He loves me too, since He wants to use me to be of service to others. It is for that reason that He gave me my religious vocation here.

Although they are baptized, many Eskimos do not understand their religion very well as yet. They are those I must aid through my prayers and works, and especially the children, so they may understand what is good for them, follow the commandments and, in brief, lead a devout Christian life. Our Divine Saviour has inspired me to direct and guide them on the right path. Whever I think of it, I can only be grateful to Our Lord for this Mission.

Also, two of my Eskimo friends wish to become Sisters, and I want very much to help them in their religious training. This is why I would like to have, in syllabic writing, the Eskimo translation of St. Teresa's life. I will take her for my model, for I know that she had a great love and devotion to Our Lord.

This is the end.

Naya Pel., In., s.g.m.

'Naya Pelagy writes ... ,' *Eskimo*, 24 (March 1952) 13–15

O   Written in the 1950s, this letter by a young Eskimo girl from
     Chesterfield Inlet is a typical example of a request letter. Made-
     leine makes certain that the request is repeated and repeated
     in precise terms.

Madeleine's Letter of Request

Madeleine is writing to Father Philippe. I am writing to you
because I want a comb. How I would be happy if I had a comb;
that is why I am writing to you. My little brother would very
much like to have woolen stockings, and I have asked the
Sisters, but they replied that they did not have any. If I write
to you, it is because I want them. My father is very good to
me, my mother expects a baby. Do not forget, I want a comb.
   There are no caribou, no foxes either, there is nothing we
can do about it. At this moment, my little brother's ears are
aching. I write to you because I want a comb. But this is
enough. Good-bye. This is Madeleine writing to Father
Philippe.

'Ask and ... you shall receive ...' *Eskimo*, 20 (March 1951) 9

O   **Thomas Umaok** (1879–1965) was ordained an Anglican deacon
     at Herschel Island in 1928, the first Inuk to receive Anglican
     orders. He was the representative and leader of the Inuit in the
     western Arctic for many years, leading his people through
     times of great change.

Interview

One time when I was small boy, maybe May time, lots of
people say they want to go west, set snare for caribou. We all
go place where there little creek between two hills. Hill on
west side not so steep. They say going to build snow house
there, snow maybe six feet high, then skin tent on top. They
wait for caribou to come. About five miles away, they set up
sticks, maybe five feet high. They put nigger heads on top and
snares between. They put long line of sticks – hard to see
end. Then wait for caribou – maybe one week. Some of them
say – caribou coming. Some people then have real good eyes.
I look around, I couldn't see them. We go near on end of
sticks. One man, Chicksi's father, say follow me. We start

after him. He go fast, lots of loose snow kick up, pretty soon we couldn't see. One boy and me, we go home, we scared. Lots of caribou run around. Ladies take their oolus, go to caribou. Some of them quick run. They try to kill caribou, can't do it. My mother slow run, but plenty strong. When she get there, take caribou by horns and twist it over, kill it right away. When some of the caribou caught in snares, others try to turn back, men behind them, kill them with bow and arrow. The caribou turn back, run round and round. The ones the ladies kill, from the snares, they skin right there, then haul them back to the house and divide them up. The ones the men kill with bow and arrow, they bring them all back to the house and divide them before they skin them. They skin them, take sinew from leg, hang up meat to dry, pound bones and take out marrow and store it in caribou stomach. After meal all ready start to travel. Snow nearly all gone. Travel night time, when sun low. When sun get high, make camp. Go back to Herschel Island.

Long time ago, people of Herschel Island and Shingle Point try to live like this. Before white people come, I see them live like this. Bow and arrow they carry all the time, when they hunt around for caribou and for bear they use it, bow and arrow. Sinew they braid for the bow. Ivory hook they use, to twist the sinew. Then, when it gets tight, ivory pointed piece. They make it real tight. That's what they use before white people come. The bow would be pretty near one fathom, sometimes little shorter. For arrow they fix piece of stone, from the mountains, real sharp, on end of stick about three feet long.

Before white people come to the coast, I see gun, muzzle loader. When they see something come, maybe caribou, they put little bit powder on plate, then when it gets closer, light it, put it in gun. They wait until it gets hot, then it comes out. This kind they use on polar bear and brown bear. After they put in powder, plug it up with shavings, sticks or anything. Then they put in little round one, look like marble. Then put again shavings. When it get hot, hammer come down. Little one like stone at end of hammer hits and it goes off.

Seal skin they hang in the house to rot. When the hair come off, then they dry it. Then they cut it, and soak it in fresh water. They could tell when it was ready to stretch – then they dried it again. They used this to back the fish nets. It never get rotten quick in salt water.

If they take care of net, last all summer. They set net near mouth of little creek – good water. So families are all separated. In July time they set the net. They make stage to hang up the fish to dry first skin side out, then when a little dry, turn it flesh side out. They make smoke house – like Indian tent (teepee) but all of wood – chinked with moss. When fish little dry then put it in smoke house and make fire and smoke it ...

When start to snow look like snow never go away (may be October time) pull up the net. Start to make house. Big house, different rooms for each family. Walls sloping in, roof and walls of log, chinked with moss, then covered with sand, no mud, just sand. On top, window made from intestines of oogyuk (seal) dried, cut and sewed. Window maybe two feet square. Need new window each year. Easy for frost to come off. Liked to have new house each year. Suppose not much wood, then use old house and fix it up. Dig ground, maybe ten feet, like ditch, to door. Ditch go under wall of house. Fix it some way so log doesn't fall down in ditch. Inside house make round frame from two large logs for hole in floor.

Outside put two long logs, near house maybe one foot high, away out, maybe 3–4 feet high, make them strong over the ditch. Make the ditch real smooth. Cover long logs with roof and sides to make porch. At outer end make more porch, no ditch under. Every house got ventilator. About four inches diameter. Inside house, sleeping bench around three sides. Each family on one blanket. Rest of floor covered with logs. Door frame in floor, near wall, smooth thin ones. Use three lamps, seal oil, for heat and light. Cook in porch. Men and ladies both help make house. Men do logs. Ladies put moss and sand. Everyone work together. Maybe take not quite ten days. Get up soon as start to get daylight. Quit when get dark.

When house finished, ladies start to make clothes. First make men's clothes. Then make ladies' clothes. Make pretty ones, too. When ladies busy sewing get up early – long time before day light, men still sleep. Men hunt seal and caribou. Lots of different things to eat, never get tired, fresh caribou, caribou from lake, little bit rotten, fresh fish, rotten fish seal.

Sewing and hunting, fall time, like October and November until sun goes away. Sun go away, start to play, all different kind of play. Make something look like bear head, maybe real bear head, put stick like teeth, put long stick like pipe (with hole in it) cut through mouth. Blow through it, make funny sound, try to scare the children. Maybe play in the house. Man like bear run around on sleeping bench. When look like going to get warm, others stand near door, try not to let him get out. If he does get out, then everyone follow, go in another house. Sometime play all night, till early in morning. Then dance. Everyone happy ...

Thomas Umaok, 'The Reverend Thomas Umaok,' *The Arctic News*, 6–60 (June 1960) 4–5

O   **Victor Allen** (1928–) was born near Letty Harbour in the western Arctic. From 1970 to 1977 he worked in oil exploration and from 1977 to 1985 in the oil fields at Tuktoyaktuk. Since 1985 he has been employed with the Canadian Broadcasting Corporation and Environment Canada, Parks Yukon. In 1967 he was working at the Canadian Forces Base, Inuvik, when, as a delegate representing the western Arctic for the Indian-Eskimo Association, he spoke at the fourth National Northern Development Conference held in Edmonton in early November. His speech won a standing ovation; the opening anecdote follows.

The Snow Goose and the Mosquito – A Question of Development

Long ago on the Yukon Coast when the whalers first came to Herschel Island, an old Eskimo admired a whiteman's sports coat. So he bought it for a few skins. One of his fellow Eskimos bought himself a rifle.

As time went on the Eskimo with the sports coat was quite popular among his people for nobody else had such a coat. He used to hang it in his sod house in summer and his igloo in winter where everybody could see it.

Now, his neighbour was the Eskimo who bought the rifle. He wanted to trade his gun for the sports coat in the worst way. Against his wife's wishes he did trade his gun for the sports coat. After all, it was summer and he didn't need the rifle in the summer. His wife used to tell him that he'd need it

137

in the winter, but he didn't listen, saying 'So what, I got a coat, haven't I.'

Winter came and they were living in an igloo as Eskimos did. Late one night the man's dogs started making a great disturbance outside the igloo. He woke up and put his skin pants on and lit the seal oil lamp.

A polar bear was coming into the porch tunnel where there was some seal meat and blubber. The Eskimo was getting more and more frigtened, for he had no gun. So he asked his wife. 'What am I going to do'? And the bear was coming into the igloo, getting closer and closer. Now the Eskimo was really scared and he asked his wife again, 'What am I going to do?'

His wife told him, 'Put on your coat.'

Today, all my people are wearing the White man's coat.

Victor Allen, 'The Snow Goose and the Mosquito – A Question of Development' *North*, 15, 1 (January/February 1968) 28

○ **John Ayaruaq** (1907–69) was the son of Uvineq, a shaman and a fine hunter who had often worked for whalers wintering at Fullerton or Depot Island. An outstanding guide and hunter, Ayaruaq travelled extensively, accompanying the Roman Catholic missionaries at Chesterfield Inlet. In 1938 he was one of three Inuit selected to assist at the Eucharistic Congress at Quebec and at the Marian Congress at Cap-de-la-Madeleine. To journalists who asked him if he would readily change his homeland, he replied: 'Certainly not. At home we have freedom and time to think and live' (*Eskimo*, 84 (fall/winter 1970) 14). At the age of 42, Ayaruaq was stricken with tuberculosis and spent some time in a sanitorium in the south.

In 1968 his autobiography was the first book to be published in Inuktitut syllabics. In this excerpt he recalls a tragic incident on a boat trip in July 1912 when the ice in Hudson Bay was breaking up.

John Ayaruaq's Autobiography (an excerpt)

Because there was no route to Qattitalik we decided to return to Repulse Bay. Two boats were on their way back, ours and Mirquirsinilik's. Then while we were crossing Ukkusissalik we found out there was no route on account of the pack of ice. When we reached the shore we were not able to get on the land so we had to go through two pieces of ice to land because the ice was hard to move to make our way. Taqaugaq went to see if he could find a way to open water, while the women went by the side of the boat to relieve themselves. I remember that there were four of us in the boat at that moment, and that I was looking at rocks and seaweeds moving with the motion of water at the bottom of the sea.

Suddenly the ice, moved by the currents of the water, fell on the boats and destroyed them. And all we could see was the sail pole, and the rear of one of the boats. Shortly after, both of them disappeared. A father and a son, Ikkitinnuaq and Igunaassiaq, were killed. We could also see Haakuluk holding on to her adopted child in the midst of smacking ice. My father, Taquagaq, Kanguq and Sammurtuq tried to get hold of her but it was difficult because of the moving ice. Finally they reached Haakuluk. I came up right beside my little sister and when I saw her I recognized her. I had one foot on a piece of ice and this I will never forget, although I was maybe three years old when this happened. While I was floating on the piece of ice I could see others gathered around Haakuluk who was dying. They reached her adopted child who was still alive but all torn and broken bones. But my real mother, Iquaq, was gone! The others told me that my mother jumped back in the water on purpose when she couldn't see me and her body was never seen but her intestines floated with the motion of water and ice. And a voice could be heard under the ice and we could not move the ice to search for the person and it was pathetic! And we lost all our belongings.

After the ice had calmed down we saw Angutimmarik and his family coming back in his boat. When they saw us and realized what had happened they hurried (but not as fast as they would have with a motor), battling and paddling as fast as they could. First they just went by us to the island and left some passengers behind; then they came back and got us. I don't remember being frightened when they arrived. But we could still hear a voice underneath the ice. They broke the ice with an axe and there was Sissaaq, his hip all ruined and two others who were brought to land and both dying.

Because of the taboo, Haakuluk's body was left on the ice for I don't know how many days, and it was awful to see it lying on the ice. Five people died and five got badly hurt, my father, Kanguq, Taqaugaq, Sammurtuq and myself. My eyes went out of place and I was told they were red.

We stayed on the island maybe five days to mourn. After the five days we continued our journey and the ones that were not hurt badly walked by the shore and the others went by boat. Whenever they had to cross a river they came into the boat, because they knew which rivers were hard to cross by foot. Then I felt frightened because my father began to have a reaction from the shock while he was still in the boat; it was caused by grief and pain of his broken leg, but mostly from losing his two wives. They were fighting and crying in the boat trying to calm him down and to save him from killing himself. That was the episode that frightened me most. I often talk about this, but this is the first time I have written it down in detail.

Ayaruaq, 'The Story of John Ayaruaq,' *North*, 16, 2(1969) 3–4

O   **Abe Okpik** (1929–) was born near Aklavik in the Mackenzie Delta in the traditional way. Hunter, trapper, interpreter, radio announcer, and reporter, he has held a number of government positions and travelled extensively around the territories. In 1969 he headed 'Project Surname' which the government of the Northwest Territories introduced to persuade Eskimo adults to adopt a family name to eliminate the old government disc numbering identification system. He was appointed the first Inuk member of the Northwest Territories' council and served on it during the years 1965–7. A member of the Order of Canada, he was living in Iqaluit in 1988. This passage closes his much quoted essay, 'What does it mean to be an Eskimo?'

What Does It Mean to Be an Eskimo?

The survival of the Eskimo people depends on the survival of the language. When people meet Eskimos, they are disappointed if they cannot show their knowledge of Eskimo ways. The Eskimo language is big. It could be used to give many great thoughts to the world. If the Eskimos themselves don't use their language more, it will be forgotten, and very soon the Eskimo too will be a forgotten people.

140

It is up to the Eskimos of today to use their Eskimo strength of word and thought. It is up to the young people. If they don't learn and use the language and the stories and songs, they will have nothing special to give to their children.

It's no good looking like an Eskimo if you can't speak like one.

There are only very few Eskimos, but millions of whites, just like mosquitoes. It is something very special and wonderful to be an Eskimo – they are like the snow geese. If an Eskimo forgets his language and Eskimo ways, he will be nothing but just another mosquito.

North, 9, 2 (March–April 1962) 28

O   **Atuat** (1894–1976), adopted daughter of Tagornaq and Padloq, was with her parents and others when they discovered, in the middle of Baffin Island, Monique Atagutaluk, the lone survivor of a group of twelve, who lived on the bodies of her first husband, Qumangâpik, and her children, Atagudlik, Niviarsarainuk, and Sigluk in the winter of 1904–5. Some sixty years after the event, Atuat recounted the grim details to the Reverend Guy Mary-Rousselière.

Atuat's Grim Tale of Cannibalism

On returning from our trip, we settled under a tent, I remember. It was at the time when a tent begins to be used, in the month of May. At that time, we did not have a proper calendar however it was certainly in May. My father who had no more ammunition for the hunt decided to undertake crossing the land (towards Pont Inlet). We began to prepare for our departure. My father had several caribou caches on the way because we had spent the preceding summer on the land.

As it had rained in the middle of winter during that year, Amarualik, our oldest man, the husband of Akvapialuk, spoke those words which made a deep impression on me: 'Alas! such bad weather is a bad omen when a hunter disappears. There are somewhere people who are in great trouble.' In all truth, he meant those whom we were to meet on the way.

So, we got ready to leave. Amarualik and his wife came

with us at the beginning in order to take part of the caches because we had not many dogs.

We had four in all: Anisinuk, Suviitok and Kauktitaq. The fourth was Ayarpertoq, the only female. We camped at the place where we were to leave the sea in order to get on the land and, there, our only female dog died from an injury to her foot.

After we had been accompanied and the meat duly loaded, we left for the inner land. Together with the dogs, my parents were pulling the sled. As for me, I would sit from time to time on the sled, whenever I felt tired. Anisinuk, the small grey dog given to us, was not pulling much but the two other male dogs did their share well, so did my parents.

I have forgotten our camping sites but we had not yet camped ten times when we began to observe strange things – it was indeed in old times. When our sled was going on flat land and downhill, it would sometimes stop as if someone had grabbed it. That was how we journeyed that day. My parents observed all that.

We made camp. That was the day before we were due to meet the one who had eaten human flesh. That night, my father had a dream that he told us when he woke up: he had seen a big black sled dog, trailing his harness, coming towards him from the direction we were taking. It vanished right at the time when it would have reached the stone holding the rope of our tent: it vanished in the ground and the end of his harness switched the air before disappearing. It was thus that Qumangâpik, Ataguttaaluk's husband, fearing that no one would be aware of their fate, had wanted, prior to his death, to give knowledge of what had happened so that his wife might live.

While we were advancing as well as we could, we heard like a strident human shout. What I heard was like an echo coming in front from a small rocky tong of land, way over there. The side of the sea on which we were travelling was much more even.

Shuddering with fright, I cried: 'Mum! I hear a loud voice. Is it a fox, a wolverine or a wolf? I don't know.' I had never heard a wolverine but I knew the peculiar calls of the fox and the wolf. Thus, I shouted without taking time to think. My mother replied with a simple yes. My father who was not much of a talker said nothing. We kept on going ahead. Suddenly, as we were getting more visible and, as it was impossible not to see the sled and the dogs, we heard the voice again. It was like a noise in the air, like a shriek not resembling a man's voice. We stopped and listened. The shriek no longer was indistinct and we heard: 'I am not destined to liiiiive ... ' And it was as if her breath had died.

My parents looked at each other and my father said: 'Uma! It is someone who has eaten human flesh.'

– 'Is there any danger?' said Tagornaq. She was most anxious to talk but she asked only if there was any danger.

Suddenly, I thought: how stupid can I be? That woman is probably devouring a man's leg. That was what I was imagining.

Then my mother said: 'Is there anything to fear? Uma! Who can those people be who were crossing the land? Perhaps it is the family of my *qagge* companion; they probably ventured into the land in summer and a misfortune has befallen them ... Who can it be? ... Perhaps the family of Torngaq. They must have tried to go across the land ... Who can it be? ... People who have spent the summer in the land? ... Thus spoke my mother while we were advancing.

And, while we were going forward, we saw a man standing, over there, among the igloos ... but we were mistaken; it was nothing ... We could see igloos, between them, a dog seemed to appear and disappear, then he would reappear and disappear again ... But no! it was Ataguttaaluk's head and we mistook for men the hunting implements of her husband Qumangâpik, stocky guns with an iron bar beneath them. The telescopes were big but less long than the guns. The latter, firearms coming from the white people, were rather short.

A short time before dying, the man had told his wife: 'While you have still strength to walk about, you will go and plant my rifle and my telescope in the snow. They will survive as landmarks for people: they will be seen and you will be found.' Thus, it was the one who was to die and be eaten who had directed the proper placing of the arms.

We could see somebody outside. In the hole where she was, looking for something to eat, she had slowly pulled out small blocks of snow in order to dry on them bits of clothing from which she had cut the hair in order to eat them. As a matter of fact, she had practically nothing left but some of Iktuku-suk's intestines.

We stopped. My parents started walking and I was about to follow them when my mother told me: 'My nice little brother – she had given me the name of her brother, Atuat, who had been killed and whom she called thus – my nice little brother, do not follow us now. When we have learnt what has happened, you will come.'

Standing on the edge of the hole, perhaps because the snow had accumulated on what was left of the walls of the old igloo, I could see my parents. After talking for some time, my mother turned towards me and said: 'My nice little brother, your little cousin – it was the name I had given Atagudlik. Ataguttaa-luk's daughter who was my playmate. Being of about the same age and living at the same place up North, we were used to amuse ourselves together and to play with dolls; she was my great friend – your little cousin has been eaten by her mother. Come!'

I advanced. When I reached the edge of the hole, I grabbed my mother's clothing. Ataguttaaluk was there in it. However, what a horrid sight! She was like a bird in its egg. She seemed to have a beak and like some sorts of miserable small wings because she no longer had sleeves, having eaten part of her 'atigi.' Her hair was cut and her skin had no longer a human appearance. She was the very image of an embryo in the egg. Yes indeed, now I know that a human being, be it ever so thin, cannot die unless it has been afflicted with a sickness.

On the snow on the ground were two skulls.

We went back to the sled. As she had no shelter, my father said to her: 'Kikkak! – he had her for kikkak[1] – I will carry you. Uma and myself, we will build you a shelter and we will put you in it.' It was beginning to get dark.

He took down the skins closing our tent and, as the snow was frozen, he cut some blocks and built a small circular wall which he covered with the skins in the form of a tent.

---

1 Literally: a bone on which there is meat left to chew. The kikkaq were those who presented this choice morsel to their partner when they would visit each other.

She did not really walk but bending deep forward and leaning with her hands, she dragged herself following the tracks on the snow. She had so little of a human appearance that our dogs started barking when they saw her.

As we had left our bedding skins behind, my parents made her a couch with the old seal skin on which we placed the load on the sled. My mother put some of her pants on her and an attigi which my old grandmother, Ataguarjukutseq – my true father's mother – had sent Saumik and we took over what was left of her old clothes to the place where she had eaten.

What she told us, I have never forgotten. I was beside my mother when Ataguttaaluk, having eaten, began to tell us what had happened.

As they were not sick, Iktukusuk, Kunuk and she had taken Sigluk's body outside. He had not starved to death but his parotid glands had swollen up. He was the true son of Eqipereaq; Ikuma bears his name. So, his body had been taken out and carried to a point of land, a little towards back of the seaside.

Qumangâpik was walking, looking for caribou rumens, picking up those that he could find. When there were none left, he said: 'My little sister – it was the name he gave his wife – when I shall have died, you will also eat me, won't you? There are always some who escape. You who have so many relations, you will eat me and you will be found when people will cross the land.'

But, she did not want that and, as he mentioned going down towards the sea in order to catch a seal and to come back with some food, she asked him not to do so because she was afraid to be attacked by wolves. Thus, she was the cause of their desperate plight. Yes, that was what I heard.

Her husband who had come back after trying to walk a little around, laid down and died during the night.

They tried to place his body on the side of the platform but, lacking strength, they could not lift it up. After their vain endeavor, she said: 'Well, he is dead now, he who wanted so much that he would be eaten. Let us put him on the ground and we will eat him.' The three of them then proceeded to place the body on the ground.

Kunuk, who was carving the body of his father, began to

wail and to cry. Having opened the body, as he was trying to cut his head off he began to howl and to sob, struck by the horror of having to carve his own father's body ... He was a good boy, that one ...

After the body had been eaten, they also ate Atagutlik's who had also starved to death. The last one they ate, while they were still the three of them, was Niviarsarainuk, the little boy. Then, they fetched Sigluk's body and ate it frozen. They had just finished it when Kunuk died. Both women ate him.

Spring was coming and the sun was beginning to melt the top layer of the snow. Left alone, Ataguttaaluk and Iktukusuk had no longer an igloo. They had finished eating Kunuk's body. Iktukusuk had often said: 'Since people died, let us go to it and eat the dead.' She had even lost the taste for ordinary game. As she was often speaking in that vein, Ataguttaaluk was on her guard and was hiding the big pocket knife of her husband.

One day as the sun was getting warmer, she was looking for lice in the hair of Iktukusuk when she perceived that she was no longer breathing. She uncovered her face: Iktukusuk was dead! A trickle of blood was running from her nose. Ataguttaaluk was lying; she had merely feigned to look for lice in Itukusuak's hair and had killed her with the knife.[2] However, it was much later that she acknowledged having killed her companion.[3] As for my mother, she knew very well that she had killed her but did not want to mention it because she was afraid of Kuatsuk, her victim's brother. Yes, indeed, I am telling everything that happened. I sang Ataguttaaluk's songs while she lived with us after we had rescued her.

So she ate Iktukusuk and remained five days without eating until we arrived, or so she said. She was still lying. My mother who had gone to fetch her stone lamp from her old igloo discovered human entrails which she had hidden when she had

---

2 According to Atagutsiaq, Ataguttaaluk's niece, the latter had killed Iktukusuk as her aunt had told her, by sticking in her ear the one-pronged Eskimo fork. That was perhaps the awl, often part of the whalers' pocket knives.

3 During one of those witching sittings when the angatkoq tried to find the guilty parties for a sickness or bad luck in hunting and succeeded in wretching a confession from one of the participants.

seen us coming. And those are not merely an old woman's tales.

My father, Padluq, who had no longer any ammunition, wanted to continue towards the North because, by now, we were nearer Tununeq and he could not hunt any more but 'the one we had found' did not want to go. Of course, she did not want to see Kuatsuk, whose sister she had killed. Iktukusuk was the youngest of her family and, as her parents were dead, her brothers and sisters loved her well. Ataguttaaluk had two brothers at Iglulik and, although she had one at Tununeq, she was obstinate in her refusal to go there.

On the way back, as she was still ravenous, she almost became dangerous. When my father killed a seal, she began to have stomach cramps on account of her hunger. My mother said: 'Yes, in all truth, her stomach aches when she is hungry because she ate her own people; sure, it is because she ate so many of her relatives.'

I who knew that she had eaten Atagudlik, my little playmate, I was very much afraid. During the rest of the trip, I lost my appetite.

My parents continued to pull the sled since we had only three dogs. Every time we met people, Ataguttaaluk would begin to howl. It was frightening; when she cried, her voice became like the voice of a wild animal.

'History of a Case of Cannibalism in Baffin Land,' *Eskimo,* 78 (summer 1968) 9–18

O **Luke Issaluk** (1944–) was born at Chesterfield Inlet, Northwest Territories. He was manager of the Co-operative at Whale Cove from 1964 to 1967. In 1988 he was secretary-manager of Rankin Inlet. He has worked also as a translator. Romantic love is a new subject for Inuit writers, and 'I See Your Face' was one of the earliest love songs.

I See Your Face

I see your face,
It is always near me, though I
Am days away from you.
In dear memory, I always see your face.

I see your face.
Alone, in the dark night
I turn down the light and
In the darkness, I see your face.

I see your face.
You did not want to cry, but I
Remember now, tears as we said goodbye.
That is how, I see your face.

I will see your face.
Only wait, when spring birds fly
Home to nest and mate, so shall I,
And I will see your face.

Luke Issaluk, 'I See Your Face,' *North*, 16 (September/October 1969) 35

○ **Markoosie** (1941–) was born near Inukjuak. In 1953 his family moved to Resolute Bay, Northwest Territories, where, at the age of 15, Markoosie began his studies at a government school. In 1967, his novel, *Harpoon of the Hunter*, first appeared in serial form in Eskimo syllabics in *Inuttituut*. In 1970 McGill-Queen's University Press published the English version, a milestone in Canadian publishing because it was the first original work of fiction by a Canadian Eskimo.

Markoosie's second novel, 'Wings of Mercy,' draws upon his experience as a bush pilot. In the first instalment a plane carrying Seeko, a young boy who accidentally shot himself in the stomach while on a hunting trip, his father Mannik, a nurse, Doreen Moore, and the pilot, Norris Mann, is forced down over Lancaster Sound. This is the second instalment.

Wings of Mercy

In Baffin Island Fiord, Constable Swart scribbed Charlie Delta's position across a yellow message pad. Once again he tried to contact pilot Norris Mann in his stricken aircraft. There was no reply.

Norris opened the side window and tried to see ahead and below. He saw a large icepan, before the extreme cold forced his eyes shut. He pulled his head back inside and as calmly as possible fought to keep control of the aircraft.

Constable Swart continued to try and make contact with the plane without success. Then he switched his frequency and said; 'Devon Island Base. This is Baffin Island Fiord. Do you copy?' After several repeats he received an answer.

'Go ahead Baffin Island Fiord.'

'Charlie Delta has been forced down.'

'Oh my God! Did you get his position?'

'Yes, when I got his May Day, he was at latitude 74 degrees, longitude 80.'

The pilot's face lost all feeling as he strained his freezing eyeballs for a glimpse of the icepan. It was rough surfaced as he had feared. As soon as the tires touched the ice, he pulled the power all the way back and turned off the power switch at the same time. The plane bounced once, came down hard and bounced off the ice again. It came down hard the third time and everything seemed to break apart. Norris heard a muffled cry from Nurse Moore, before he blacked out.

'Baffin Island Fiord this is Devon Island Base. Do you copy?'

'Go ahead, Devon Island Base. I hear you.'

'Did Norris say he was ditching in the water or on the ice?'

'He said he was going to try for an icepan.'

'OK. Baffin Island Fiord, we will contact National Defence for rescue service.'

'Is there anything we can do to help from this side?'

'Afraid not, we will do everything possible from here.'

Constable Jim Coleman was called to the radio shack. The radio operator outlined the situation.

'We have a downed aircraft in about here,' he explained, tracing the location on the map tacked to the wall.' There is a very slim chance that they are still alive. Norris Mann is a skilled pilot but I don't think he has had much winter experience. Nurse Moore was tending the wounded boy and I understand his father Mannik is aboard. We called National Defence for rescue service and an aircraft is on the way from Frobisher with a doctor and supplies.'

'I hope he made it to an icepan. But even so, how can a doctor get there this time of the year?' the constable asked.

'The doctor will be a member of the Royal Canadian Air Force parachute team. We are hoping he can make the jump. Those Air Force boys know their business.'

'They are our only hope,' the constable replied quietly.

'Not quite, Jim,' said the radioman. 'You could organize the Eskimo rescue party.'

'I can try that,' said the constable, still scanning the map. 'That is about two hundred miles away and four days by dog team. Keep me posted on events. I am going to the settlement and talk to the people.'

Norris slowly opened his eyes. Slowly his memory returned and the terrible realization of their predicament. His head was pounding with pain as he turned it around without moving his body. He lay beside his seat. Slowly he got into sitting position. A sharp pain shot through his left leg. His boot was torn and a trace of blood showed through, 'Broken,' he thought to himself. He found a flashlight and flicked it on.

He looked to where his passengers had been and saw the nurse prostrate over the body of Seeko while Mannik seemed to be pinned against the wall. Norris tried to stand, but his legs refused to co-operate. 'Could both be broken,' he thought, surprised at his own calmness. He dragged himself toward the nurse with his hands. She was still and did not respond when he pushed her from Seeko. The boy was still breathing. He called for Mannik and was answered by a low moan. Mannik, bleeding from a cut on his forehead, began to crawl toward him and knelt beside Seeko. 'He is still alive' he said gratefully. Nurse Moore began to moan and then opened her eyes. 'Is everyone alright? How long have we been down?' The questions all came at once as she sought to understand the situation.

'I think my legs are broken, but there is no pain,' said Norris.

'Let me get those boots off. Have you got a knife?'

Norris pointed to the survival kit box. The nurse crawled toward the box, stopping to look at Seeko on the way. She listened to his breathing and was satisfied that his condition remained stable.

Doreen began to cut the laces on the pilot's torn boot. He clenched his teeth to keep from crying out as she removed it and the sock. A bone protruded. Quickly and skillfully, in spite of the cramped conditions, she applied a splint and bandage. She wrapped the leg in a blanket to protect it from the cold that she realized for the first time was creeping into the aircraft. She unlaced the boot from the other leg. A quick examination showed that no bones were broken but it was badly sprained and swelling. She wrapped it as best she could from the limited resources in the first aid box. Turning to Mannik she next wiped his wound clean and bandaged it.

'Anywhere else hurt?' she asked. She was relieved when Mannik shook his head and grinned.

They began to survey the damage and the full realization of their situation came to them. The aircraft door was broken off. One wing was broken and the nose buried in the snow and ice. The tiny finger of light from the flashlight disappeared in the blowing snow. How far they were from land or the size of the icepan was unknown to them. Above the wind they could hear the growing thunder of crushing ice.

'How long do you think it will be before we are rescued?' the nurse asked Norris.

He did not want to tell her that the chances were slim. He tried to be cheerful. 'It might take several days, depending on the weather. The only way to get off here will be by helicopter, and the nearest is about a thousand miles away. There is almost no daylight this time of the year. I hope they got the bearings I sent as we came down. We have to get out of here before we freeze.'

'I must build a shelter for us,' said Mannik. 'I will build an igloo.' He opened his pack and took out a snow-knife and a rifle, the hunter's tools.

When Mannik left the plane Doreen put an extra blanket around Seeko. 'I did not want to say it in front of his father, but I don't think he can live much longer without a doctor.' Norris nodded. He was thinking about it and about the food supply. He always carried emergency food – enough for one man for a week. He had a small pressure cooker and fuel for one man for two days. But there were four people. They sat in silence, listening to the beating of the wind and the distant grinding of the ice. Weak daylight crept into the plane with the cold.

Mannik returned to announce that the igloo was finished

and he needed blankets to cover the floor. They could move in. He took the blankets and the heater and soon had the little shelter warm. With the help of the nurse, he moved Seeko into it first. Together they returned and helped Norris down from the plane and dragged him through the small opening.

'We will make tea first,' Mannik said, 'and then I will go and see how big this icepan is. There is a chance I might get a seal. A seal will keep us fed and provide enough fat to keep Seeko and Norris warm.' There was something in his calm and determined manner that gave strength to all of them.

Far away from the little igloo and the wrecked aircraft Constable Coleman was explaining the situation to a group of Inuit hunters.

'We have no way of knowing if they are alive. They could be on the ice and it would be impossible for a plane to land near them. That is why I am asking for volunteers to make up a rescue party. Are there any questions?' Coleman asked.

'You think they are about two hundred miles away?' asked one of the men who was called Nuki.

'Yes, but we are not sure if that is the correct position.' The constable returned to the map, and pointed to the probable spot. 'It's somewhere here, between Kikitalook and Toononik.'

'That is a lot of land and water from here,' answered Nuki. Turning to the other men for approval, he said simply: 'We will go.'

Nuki turned again to the hunters in the room and began to give instructions in their own language. 'We will start in two hours. We will need twenty men and if possible, make up fifteen dog teams. We should take the six kayaks because there is still a lot of open water. Pack enough food for a week for ourselves and the dogs. We may have to hunt later but our first job is to get to the site.' The men stood up when he stopped talking and went to their homes to prepare themselves.

Four hours after the call for help went out, an RCAF Boxcar landed on the Devon Island Base strip. The first person down the ladder was a tall man in a flight suit, carrying a bag. 'Hi!' he greeted the constable. 'I'm Doctor Carl Poole. I would like to speak to the radioman who has been talking to Baffin Island Fiord.'

Inside the radio hut over a cup of hot coffee Doctor Poole gathered all the details of the accident.

152

'Can you tell me what really happened. How long ago and what has been done?'

The radioman outlined the situation. 'The boy is young. He shot himself in the stomach area. The bullet is .22 calibre. The nurse said he lost a lot of blood. It has been about ten hours since the accident and we have no way of knowing what his condition is now. Just that he is somewhere out there if he is alive,' he said, pointing to the map on the wall.

Thirty minutes later the Boxcar was refuelled and again airborne. At two thousand feet they lost visual contact with the ground. The doctor studied a map with the navigator.

'Let's go up to nine thousand feet and then descend under the cloud when we get over Lancaster Sound,' the navigator said. 'That will be in forty-five minutes.'

Over the Sound, the plane dropped to 800 feet. Fog rolled up to meet them, blocking out the thousands of floating icepans, except in a few spots. For two hours they flew a pattern over the area, all eyes straining for signs of wreckage. 'There is no hope of finding them under these conditions,' the pilot said. 'We will return to base and try again later.' The big plane gained altitude and headed back to Devon Island Base.

On the icepan the three people heard the plane passing over them but they could not see it. When the sound faded away for the last time, Doreen Moore began to cry.

'At least they are looking for us,' Norris said, trying to comfort her. 'They made a good try but the clouds are too low. They will be back.'

'Don't worry, nurse,' Mannik said. 'They will come again and again until they find us. We have a saying that no matter how sadly a day ends, another new day will come to the land tomorrow.'

Inside the igloo, which was warm but cramped, Norris was making plans. 'Mannik, look in the baggage compartment of the plane. Collect all the rags or anything else that will burn. There is gasoline in the belly tank. Push up the drain valve and fill up a bottle or oilcan with it. Soak the rags and leave them outside in the open and the next time you hear a plane run out and light fire to it.'

'I will give you a hand,' said Doreen. Together she and Mannik crawled out of the igloo.

Back at Devon Island Base the pilot and navigator listened

to the latest weather reports. They were not good. The meteorologist charted the path of an approaching storm. 'It is now over Melville Island and was over Prince Patrick Island yesterday. That means it is moving pretty fast. You won't have much time before you are grounded.'

The ice was rugged and made travelling slow. The barking of the dogs and the creaking of the sleds were the only sounds in the darkness. Nuki was ahead of the party, because he remembered the way from his early hunting years. They had been travelling for several hours and the dogs were growing tired when Nuki called a halt.

'We will stop a while and eat,' he said to Shinak, his closest companion.

'Are we going to keep on all night?' Shinak asked.

'We will have to go as far as the dogs can last. It is going to be rough but lives depend on us,' Nuki answered.

Inside the small igloo, the shadows of three silent people were cast upon the ice walls. They all looked anxiously at Seeko who was fighting for breath. Doreen decided she had to say the words that she hoped she would never have to say.

'Mannik,' she began, 'I have to tell you the truth. There is nothing more I can do. I don't think he will live till morning.'

Mannik looked into the eyes of the nurse and said: 'I have been expecting those words for sometime. I am old enough to know when death is near.' Then he turned away and wept quietly. For many hours that was the only sound in the silent cell, while the wind mourned outside.

'Listen,' Norris said suddenly. 'Hear it? It's an aircraft up there! Quick, Mannik, light the fire!'

Norris dragged himself out after Mannik. The fire was already blazing. Norris lay on his back on the ice and looked at the sky. The clouds were patchy now and the sound of motors was getting closer.

The pilot was the first to see the pinpoint of light on the floating ice island. 'Look over there!' he shouted to his co-pilot. 'We have found them! Tell the doctor to prepare to jump. Get the engineer to prepare to drop supplies.'

The big aircraft circles wide and turned back toward the welcoming light on the ice below. They were at 700 feet with the clouds above them. It was too low for the doctor to jump and he would have to go 'blind.' Directly over the fire he turned and went up to two thousand feet and into the darkness of the clouds. The turn continued for three minutes, then he signaled for the supplies to be dropped.

'OK, Doc. If you're ready we will do that again. I will go in over the fire and then climb and circle. We can let you go at two thousand feet in three minutes.'

The doctor signaled that he was ready. He wanted to look at his watch for some reason. He went to the back of the aircraft and stood in his bulky clothes under the blue light to wait for the signal. 'I hope that is one big icepan,' he thought to himself.

Markoosie, 'Wings of Mercy,' *Inuttituut* (autumn 1972) 19–22

O **Joe Panipakuttuk** (1916–70) of Pond Inlet was a well-known hunter and guide, and special Royal Canadian Mounted Police constable. In 1944 he and his family joined the RCMP vessel, *St. Roch* under the command of Henry A. Larsen at Pond Inlet for what was to be an historic trip through the Northwest Passage. After centuries of attempts and failures, the dream of navigating the Northwest Passage in one vessel during a single season was finally realized. In this article Joe recalls the memorable voyage.

The Historic Voyage of the St. Roch

I remember I left Pond Inlet on the RCMP boat in the summer of 1944, on the 17th day of August. On our way we stopped at Nalluaq where I got two dogs. Captain Larsen obtained two narwhal tusks at this place. I shot one bear when we were leaving. On crossing Lancaster Sound from Nalluaq a very heavy gale set in rocking the boat on either way. We sheltered near an iceberg on the leeward side. The iceberg was very big and long. The boat was headed against the wind and the engine running all the while, but the wind was so strong the water was as white as in a snow storm.

With the wind not so strong, we left the following day, but the swells were big and the bow of the boat would disappear from time to time in the water. I was very frightened. We arrived at the island (*Devon*) where the police used to have

155

a detachment. It was very windy and where we anchored it seemed we were on land. The police looked over the vacant buildings. Next day we left and followed along the coast close to the high cliffs of the island. Another gale arose and we were forced to anchor in another cove (*Stratton Inlet*). Ashore we walked around and found some old, old Eskimo houses made of whalebone and sod (*Thule culture*). Mr. Larsen and the crew built a landmark (*inukshuk*) and put some papers in it. That night we had a snow storm. We moved farther along the coast with heavy squalls so that sometimes we could not see the land. We did see some icebergs.

On August 20th we arrived at a small island off the west end of the big one we had been sailing alongside (*Beechey Island*). It is said that in the old days some white men got lost and the head of the expedition was never found although many ships had called here searching for him. The name of the man was Franklin. On the island I saw some stone markers and graves of white men (*Franklin cenotaph placed here by McClintock, 1858*).

Two days later we left for Resolute Bay and on the way I killed three walrus and a fourth at a place where the boat was touching the bottom because of the shallow water. I killed another walrus when we were anchored on the west coast from Resolute Bay. The white men climbed up the cliff and built an inukshuk and left a note in it. We left from there because there was a lot of ice. We travelled only a short distance at a time because there was so much ice. Sometimes we would stop and I would hunt. I shot three seals, but one bearded seal sank. We stayed overnight and left the following day travelling around the north side of the small island (*Byam Martin Island*) and anchored where the white men put up another inukshuk with a note. This inukshuk was taller than a man.

When we left again we travelled through a lot of rough ice. The floating ice was old ice. We came to a large island (*Melville Island*) and a small island (*Dealey Island*) on which there was once a building. It is said that here there was once a shipwreck. The building was made of rock with a wooden roof. They had a lot of firewood inside and quite a lot of food. The crew of this wreck had been found, it is said; they did not starve. There we found old clothing and canned food which

156

they had left. (Captain H. Kelle's Expedition, *H.M.S. Resolute,
1852–53. Remains of a large cache left by him.*) We stayed
here for part of the day.

Mr. Larsen, whom we called Pallursi, made notes and another inukshuk. We left to cross to the big island and during
our travel Mr. Larsen told me that there were musk oxen on
the land. I went to where he directed me. I searched the land
with a telescope and saw no sign of live animals. All I could
see were huge rocks. Mr. Larsen said that these were musk
oxen, these very things I thought to be rocks. So I looked again
through the telescope and the rocks began to move. We got
near the musk oxen and I found out that they were carrying
something on their backs. I thought to myself they must be
carrying their little ones, but I soon learned that this was part
of the animal. When you see musk oxen for the first time
they have such a huge back on them!

We travelled on through a lot of ice and came across an old
building. The building belonged to Kapitaikallak (*Captain Ber-
nier*), where his ship used to winter (*C.G.S. Arctic 1908–09 –
revisited 1910*). There was a pole standing with a model of
a fox attached to it which signified that the land was very rich
in foxes. The man left the boat, rifles and such, because he
caught a lot of foxes. We slept there for approximately three
days. On August 30 we left and met heavy ice as we were
crossing to Bank's Island but we got lost in a fog. We turned
back to a little cove (*Richard Collinson Inlet – Victoria Island*).
In the morning we were again on the right route and we were
in a long inlet (*Prince of Wales Strait*). We travelled all day
and night and when we woke up Mr. Larsen told me that we
would get to Holman Island that day and see people. About
mid-afternoon on September 4th we could see a building on
a point. For the first time since leaving Pond Inlet we would
now get to see a strange people and we began to feel shy.

The Eskimo people on the boat were myself and my wife
and Aariak, my son; Pallug, my daughter; Kalluk, my son;
Soopi Viguq, my daughter; Panipak my mother, and my grand-
daughter Mary Panigusiq [Mary Panegoosho Cousins].

On the day of our arrival at Holman Island a person had
died. We could see all the people climbing a hill where they
were burying the body. We anchored after the people had fin-

ished the burial. All the white people and ourselves waited in the bow of the boat and I felt nervous to be among strange people. But at last I went to a group of people when they asked me to come and I was told not to fear them. I shook hands.

They wanted us to come to their settlement which we did and we went to the house of Kanguaq. The settlement had only two white people, the missionary and the Hudson's Bay Company man. We stayed overnight here and left the following day for Tuktoyaktuk.

One of the narwhal tusks which belonged to Mr. Larsen was stolen by someone. I was frightened when Mr. Larsen found out that one of his tusks was missing. I was afraid to tell a lie so I told Mr. Larsen about the white person who stole the tusk and I also told him at what time. Mr. Larsen got very angry and when he went for lunch he started asking us again who had stolen the tusk. Though he knew who had taken it the rest of the crew tried to blame me. They told Mr. Larsen that it was me but he got more angry with them and he said 'Some of you people are not honest. This man already knows who has taken the tusk and he is the one who told me who did it. So you had better tell the truth right now.' They never said anything about the tusk again.

For the next two days we sailed through a lot of ice on our way to Tuktoyaktuk. We anchored near Tuktoyaktuk when we hit shallow water. A boat came out to welcome us and I saw that there were many white people in the boat and I thought there was only one Eskimo with them but when they came up to our boat it was the other way around. These people were all Eskimos and there was only one white man with them. That was the first time I had ever heard Eskimos talk English. The white man in the boat was the Hudson's Bay Company manager.

The next day it was very stormy and the wind was coming down hard against our boat. Another Eskimo came aboard with us and he and Larsen steered the boat together as the wind was blowing that hard. We faced the wind and the boat rocked as though it was going to turn over so we had to anchor it with two anchors.

The people slept on the boat and the next day they went

ashore. The people in Tuktoyaktuk were building houses. There had been a flood there. There were some dogs on an island and they had all died, all thirty-five of them. Across the Bay there was a house and there were two rooms in it. When the water started to come into the house they went outside and brought in a canoe. They sat in the canoe inside the house for two nights because the house was full of water. The ten-gallon oil tanks were all blown away and the Hudson's Bay office was also blown away. There were some people out in a boat during the storm and they never found them. They only found a young child on the shore wrapped up in a blanket. The boat had been trying to get to Bank's Island. The people went out looking for it but it was never found again. There was a white man on board also. While we were there I fished most of the time and we stayed for a week.

We left for Qikirtarjuaq (*Herschel Island*) where again we got caught in a storm. We kept going southward and the wind was very strong.

We got to Qikirtarjuaq (*September 17*) during the night. There was a house ready for us to live in. Mr. Larsen said that he was going to leave us because he wanted to go on through to Vancouver in the south. He left and we were alone there. When I looked through my binoculars and saw there was a house, some dogs and people, I became nervous. The people looked so different.

All summer long I went out sealing and caught quite a few. In the fall a man came to our camp who said he was from Alaska. My mother called him 'son' so after that I called him my brother. He said that there were many caribou where he came from. He was going out hunting and said that I would always be welcome to go along with him. He talked to me a lot and he told me not to be scared to talk to the people that I saw. I understood very well the way he talked except for a few things; sometimes he would have to try to explain to me, even in English.

The next day we went on a hunting trip. When we were getting quite close to the houses I again got nervous. The people there were very nice. They asked us to come into their house which was very interesting as the house inside looked like a white person's home. After spending a little time with them we left in our sled again. Not too long after that we spotted another house where there were only two ladies. They told us that their husbands were out hunting. We left expecting to meet them, but didn't. We stayed overnight in another camp. The next morning we went to hunt again and I got four caribou to take back home.

All winter long my son and I would go out hunting and there were caribou all of the time. I went to Aklavik with another man. It was quite a way and we slept nine times before we got there. There were many white people, Indians and Eskimos in the town of Aklavik and a school and hospital. We stayed there for three days before returning back to Qikirtarjuaq. I had sixteen dogs when I started on the trip but they began to die off and I returned home with only eight.

During the summer I caught a lot of seal, caribou and fish. In a day I would get sixteen to eighteen seals. There were also white and brown bear and many different kinds of birds. The Western Eskimos have ways very much like the white people and they would buy meat from me. I got $200 from the Eskimos there just by selling them meat. When they wanted seal they would give me $10 for it; caribou meat, $5, or if it was back meat of the caribou only they would pay me $10. I told them that we were all Eskimos and that they should not pay me for the meat, but they said that they had to pay for everything they take from someone. They even tried to buy dogs and that was the first time I found out that Eskimos buy things from other Eskimos for money.

During the winter I caught twelve foxes and in spring many seals including two square flippers and one whale.

On August 11, 1945, the St. Roch with Captain Larsen was back from the South and we were all happy to see him back. Larsen did not like it when he found out that we were not living in the house that he had got ready for us. We were living in a tent now. He asked me why we were not staying in the house and I told him that we liked a tent in the summer. We got all of our belongings together and loaded them on the St. Roch and when we left that night for Tuktoyaktuk we all slept aboard. We stayed at Tuktoyaktuk for two weeks.

Before we left the police found a white man who was almost starving. He did not have any food, tea or flour. He had an Eskimo wife who did not have any needles. My wife gave her some needles, clothes and soap. They had five dogs in a camp between Tuktoyaktuk and Coppermine. They had a big wooden house but I did not find out what he was doing up there. We arrived at Coppermine and stayed there for three weeks. When we did leave it was for Cambridge Bay and it took many days. We stayed in Cambridge Bay all that winter. There was a Hudson's Bay Company Store and an RCMP detachment there.

When spring came Mr. Larsen asked me to go to Pond Inlet by way of Gjoa Haven and Fort Ross. I had eight dogs with me and five pups when I left Cambridge. Kanayuk from Cambridge Bay went with me as a guide to Gjoa Haven. A man by the name of Tiitaa, a Nittillimmuit came with me as a guide from Gjoa Haven to Ikirasak. The following people were with me on the expedition: my wife and son, Aariak, who was now seventeen; my daughters, Palluq and Soopi, and my baby boy who was two years old, my mother and granddaughter, Mary Panigusiq. The total of us was eight and we had the same number of dogs as we had people on that journey. Our sled was twenty feet long and we had five pups besides the eight grown dogs.

The journey began on April 22, 1946 from Cambridge Bay to Gjoa Haven. When we finally arrived at Gjoa Haven we stayed for one week waiting for dog food.

We left with the young man Tiitaa and his wife for Ikirasak. During our journey I took very ill and with the windy weather it was difficult. We went for two days and two nights without food. Then the weather calmed down and I stocked up on seal as did Aariak and Tiitaa but I was so ill that I couldn't eat the meat. Though I was ill I wanted to keep on going so they all got ready while I was sitting on the ground. We left at night and the next day we made a camp. Aariak and Tiitaa had just left to go seal hunting when a large polar bear came to the camp. It was early morning and everyone else was still sleeping. So I took the gun and tried shooting it but missed and it started to run away. I unchained all the dogs and let them run after the bear but when I tried running I was so weak that I kept falling down. The dogs finally stopped the animal and I shot it. I walked back feeling very sick and my lungs were sore and burning. I walked for a while then saw Tiitaa and Aariak returning from their hunt. They put the bear on their sled and we rode home. It was only 600 yards from our tent that I shot the bear but it seemed so much farther. I had to stay in bed for two days feeling very weak. I found out that a shaman was trying to kill me, but he killed himself instead and I got better when he died.

When we were moving again we found the tracks of nine caribou. We went after them for quite a while and I shot four. We returned to our camp where everyone was waiting for us. My wife was the only one awake when we got there so we woke everybody up and had some caribou meat which tasted very good.

We left again, Tiitaa had only four dogs, and I told him to put the caribou meat on his sled. In June we started off for Fort Ross and were travelling on land but soon the snow was almost gone so we moved out onto the sea ice on June 29. On our way we met Taqulik a former Cape Dorset Eskimo. When we got to Fort Ross where there were also white people and we were told to stay there until the ship came in. All through that time I caught seals and earned money from the skins. In early summer Taqulik, Tiitaa and myself would go out in a boat and hunt. Finally the Nascopie came and soon we were all on our way to Pond Inlet. There were some RCMP officers, Mattaw and his family, Qillaq and his family, also on board and they were going to a place not far from Pond Inlet. We had left Pond Inlet in 1944 and here we were coming back in 1946. It was hard for me to talk with my own people when we first got back because I kept talking in Western dialect, I had been away that long.

Joe Panipakuttuk, 'Reminiscences,' *North*, 16, 1 (1969) 10–17.

O **Bernard Irqugaqtuq** (1918–), born at Pelly Bay, was a great leader and hunter. According to the Reverend Guy Mary-Rousselière he was a hunter and trapper 'who had intelligence, powers of observation and perfect knowledge of his group's customs' (*Eskimo*, fall/winter 1977, 22). In 1956 at Pelly Bay Irqugaqtuq composed a song about the airplane, adapting a traditional way of expression to a new subject. In the song, the propeller plane takes on bird and animal shapes.

The Song of the Aircraft

Aijaa ijajijaijajija
'Tis useless to ask what it is, ijaja.
Useless to ask what it is.
When it is heard, there is no doubt.
Ijaja ijajaijaijajaija jaijaajiaija
ijajaijajaija
This passes in front of my eyes
The flying machine and the winter.
Ijaja ... ...
At the time to cast off
It begins to crackle loudly ijajija
And to go off as a gun ijaja
It begins to jerk
And beat its wings
And to wing its tail
Ijaja ... ...
I cannot follow it
However it goes to a land where there are men ijajija.
I do not stop to think of it
While it goes away.
Ijaja ... ...
I begin to skip with joy ijaja
I begin to skip with joy
As on top of the hill
Ijaja ... ...
Has just appeared
Game, something to eat ijajaja
I begin to skip with joy and anxiety
As night falls.
Ijaja ... ...

Certainly, I will not fear a thing
When it is a matter of meat and food ijajija
However I am so often worried that I became anguished.
Ijaja ... ...
I have given them a whipping
To my poor dogs ·
And now at Fall
They howled with pain and fear
ijaja ijaja ijajaijaja ijajaijajai
ijaja ijaaji

Bernard Irqugaqtuq, 'The Song of the Aircraft,' trans. by Franz Van Der Velde *Eskimo*,
N.S. 6 (Fall/Winter 1974) 12

O   **Jimmy Patsauq Naumealuk** (1951–84) was born in arctic Quebec
     and raised in Resolute Bay, Northwest Territories.
     He attended Churchill Vocational Centre and worked for the
     Northern Quebec Inuit Association in Inukjuak. He froze to
     death on a hunting trip.
     In this poem, Naumealuk was concerned about the future
     of the Inuit people.

Wondering in Silence

A seagull is flying high in the summer breeze
A seal is swimming the calm cool sea
A caribou feeds on the mossy tundra
And I'm sitting here wondering about yesterday.

A jet plane flies high in the winter breeze
A ship travels the stormy sea
A snowmobile crosses the frozen tundra
And I'm sitting here wondering about today

I see not the seagull or the jet plane
I see not the seal or the ship
I see not the caribou or the snowmobile
And I'm sitting here wondering about tomorrow.

Jimmy Patsauq Naumealuk, 'Wondering in Silence,' *Inukshuk*, 16 (22 May 1974) 11

○ The poet, known only as **Dorothy** from Rankin Inlet, reflects on old age and death in the manner of her forefathers.

Old Woman's Song

I am old, now I must die
Me in my chair,
My body is tired I worked so hard
Old age is coming to kill me.
I cannot work for now I am old.
Me in my chair.
Death is waiting for me outside.
Old I am, old I am.
Death is here.
Old I am, old I am.
Me in my chair.

Dorothy, 'Old Woman's Song,' *Keewatin Echo*, 67 (1974) 6

○ **Alexis Pamiuq Utatnaq** (1951–), interpreter and musician, was born in Baker Lake, Northwest Territories. He attended school in Churchill and Ottawa and for a time had his own translation business in Baker Lake. In 1988 he was working for the Department of Education in Yellowknife. He is widely known in the Arctic as a singer/composer and has appeared at numerous concerts in the north. In his poem 'Blood Thirsty Enemies,' Utatnaq continues the ancient satiric practice.

Blood Thirsty Enemies

I am appreciative because of the fact that in Canada there is what you call 'Freedom of Speech,' and I am most happy to know that many people take that advantage. I, for one, will take this opportunity and write about my idea.

I am not asking that there be action taken about this but to reinforce to the public about how I feel about what I am about to say.

This may strike you as an inexpectation but it is about

enemies. Yes, I or we, have an enemy which have been irritating us, aggitating us, even terrorizing us for many years. Though we have weapons to fight them, it seems they are unconquerable. Their armies are many but weapons are few, like the Japanese suicide squad they are courageous, they are ... this poem should explain everything.

Our Enemy
Our enemy
They're so many
Our blood they spill
They make us ill
Help us, oh God
From their piercing rods
Our sworn foes
Those mosquitoes.

Alexis Pamiuq Utatnaq, 'Blood Thirsty Enemies,' *Keewatin Echo*, 7 (1974) 8

O   **Peter Pitseolak** (1902–73), photographer, artist, and writer, was born at Nottingham Island, Northwest Territories. He recognized early that traditional Inuit life was disappearing and tried to record its passing through his syllabic writings, drawings, and photographs. The story of his early life was published in 1975 as *People from Our Side*, which combines a taped interview with Pitseolak by Dorothy Eber and a manuscript written by Pitseolak. The excerpt below about the *Nascopie* was written by Pitseolak.

Built in 1911 and named for the Naskopi Indians of Northern Quebec and Labrador, the Hudson's Bay Company ship *Nascopie*, visited the HBC posts and RCMP detachments once a year, guided by Inuit pilots into her ports of call. It left the south in July and usually returned in October. 'Shiptime' was an exciting time for the Inuit and for thirty-three years the *Nascopie* brought joy until she was wrecked just outside Cape Dorset.

The Sinking of the Nascopie

I am going to tell the story of the 'Nascopie.' The 'Nascopie' was the ship that belonged to the Bay, and I'm going to tell how it hit the bottom on July 21, 1947. It was sad; that ship helped the Eskimo people. What it carried helped the people before we had the government. When it sank, we were really sorry.

When the 'Nascopie' came there was always a lot to eat. The old cook used to feed the Eskimo people.

When the ship arrived we went on and worked for two or three days. Today everyone seems to hate the ships, but then we loved them. The 'Nascopie' used to bring all the supplies for the store; if we hadn't had the 'Nascopie' there would have been no supplies. As soon as the ship arrived we ate. We ate outside; there was no other place. Those who couldn't work would cook on the shore. They were also paid. The cook fed us. His name was Storekeeper; they used to call out, 'Storekeeper!' Ahalona! He gave everything ... corn beef, stew ... everything. That cook loved to feed the Eskimo people.

In 1946 the old cook was replaced by another. The new cook did not feed the Eskimos. The Eskimo people felt unwanted. With the new cook, the 'Nascopie' was changed. There seemed to be nothing to eat on board! I was the only one who could get food. The new cook invited me – but not the others.

The next year there was a new captain also and with the new captain the ship was lost. The Bay manager had radioed the ship's captain that I should go down and meet the ship to pilot it into Cape Dorset. The captain said no. He thought he knew everything. If I had steered the ship, it would never have gone aground. I had been steering the ship for three or four years. The new captain did not want me to meet the ship.

Since it was such a nice day I went hunting for seal. I wanted meat! The captain did not want my help so I went hunting; I got two seals!

On our way home to Cape Dorset we saw the ship looking very high. It turned out that it had struck the rocks and was on top of them. The tide had left it behind. When we reached shore, Kululak said, 'Our big helper has hit the bottom.' So I joked and said, 'Then we will take all its possessions.' I only said this as a joke. I didn't know that she had a hole in her bottom. It turned out that she had a big hole through her. No wonder, as the ship was very heavy.

That night, when the tides had risen and the ship had let

loose its grip on the rocks, someone sent for me to come and help. Earlier that day my help had been refused; now, when it was too late, I was wanted.

On our way out to the ship we met a big barge full of kadluna heading for shore. It was full only of white men and they told us the ship had a big hole. I was the only person who heard this said – my companions missed it because of the noise of the motor. I told the kadluna in my boat that there was a hole in the 'Nascopie.' Our boss, the Bay manager, did not want to go to the ship after I told him about the big hole. So I told him, 'We must go; there are still people there – they are flashing lights because they want our help.' Then we went ahead.

When we got to the ship, our boss said to the captain, 'Peter has come to the "Nascopie" to help.' Then I was told to come aboard and told again that there was a big hole. The crew was trying to get the water out of the ship. The coal was being thrown away.

When we got aboard the ship, it was raining. The captain said to come with him. He took us to his cabin. He had the strong water – whisky – all ready for us. I did not want to become drunk so whenever the captain turned away from us, I would empty the glass into the pail. (Also our boss poured out his drink as he didn't want to become drunk either.)

Then the captain told me, 'Pitseolak, you are going to run the ship.' I replied, 'If I am to run the "Nascopie" let us start right now for Cape Dorset.' So the anchor was pulled and we started to move. We were moving towards the route when the Captain said, 'Let us not go into the deep water too much.' It turned out that the ship was slowly sinking. They did not want to let me know we were sinking.

Since I was steering the ship, I turned the ship around. We were then on the right route. The shallows were now behind us and I told the captain that I wanted a full speed. But after I gave the word, we started going backwards! The 'Nascopie' was going backwards. Then I said over and over, 'What are we doing?' Finally the boss answered, 'Ajunamat – it can't be helped!'

We were moving backwards so they could ground the ship.

The captain thought we might sink before we reached our land.

It turned out that we were to hit bottom. We were moving backwards towards a little island. We were sinking.

All the ship's boats were put into the water in a great hurry! I was told to get into one of the boats. The 'Nascopie' engines were already covered.

I was the only Inuk on the 'Nascopie.' My cousin Salamonie had come along for his own interest – he had not been asked to come by the kadluna. My cousin and I were the only Eskimos.

The captain was the last to come off the ship. He was told to come. He looked as if he was not getting off the ship into the boat. But our boss told him to come and then he came right away. All the 'Nascopie' boats were now on their way to shore. All of them were full of kadluna. More kadluna who had gone off earlier were already on shore.

It was not a happy time. I had been sick in the south. I was not feeling well and I was the only watchman. I had to watch that no one went to the 'Nascopie.' When the 'Nascopie' people were gone, then we were to pick up anything we wanted from the wreck. The kadluna said I was to be the first to take anything I wanted.

At last the ship 'Avatuk' arrived – the white people called this ship the 'M/V MacLean' – and we took the many kadluna out to the 'Avatuk.' My brother Pootoogook's boat also took some kadluna to the ship. Then the kadluna waited until my brother Pootoogook and companions were back on shore and told me, 'Go, take as much as your boat will hold.'

Soon my boat was full; it was not a small boat.

Then we had company – Simeonie and companions. They were also taking things. It was a happy time – until we reached shore. When we reached shore it turned out that we were to be scolded. My brother Pootoogook was upset because he, too, wanted things from the ship. It was unpleasant. He scolded us for taking things which he wanted himself. But I was the one who was to take what I wanted.

Our boss came to meet us on the shore. When he saw things he especially liked, he told lies. He said, 'That's my order.'

I was being pretty soft and giving things away. That's why there were many people at the shore meeting us. Then, all of a sudden, I got angry. I told the boss, 'These are all yours! Take them all – all the things in the boat!' I told him all this and then he left us alone.

There was also a silly policeman from Lake Harbour. He was also taking what he liked – taking things away from us. It was greedy. I told him he was taking the possessions of the Eskimos and then he slowed down his grabbing. He had been taking away whatever he liked from the Eskimo people.

Then those who wanted to drink got drunk. The police and Bay people had said not to touch the liquor. Eskimo people who were stubborn, they became drunk.

Of all the ships, the 'Nascopie' was the most appreciated by the Eskimo people. The 'Nascopie's' old cook used to feed the Eskimos, and the 'Nascopie' helped the Eskimo people by taking them along where they wanted to go. We were sorry when she sank. She carried many things to buy that were useful and helped us very much. Since the 'Nascopie' sank, the ships that come are not so much appreciated. When the 'Nascopie' could be seen in the distance, many people were happy.

The 'Nascopie' did not wait for the okiak – the 'time when everything is frozen.' By then she was no longer visible in the water.

For a time the people were rich with all the possessions they had from the ship. Today no one has those possessions; worldly goods do not last forever.

But even the people from the other side, from Eenookjuak – Port Harrison – came. They, too, came to collect from the ship. There were three boats – Sajueelee's boat, Johnny's boat and Kasaluak's. Also people came from Lake Harbour – Nuvolia's boat and also a short boat that belonged to Kepanik. Their boats were stuffed with things. Maybe the people from Port Harrison did not collect too much but the people from Cape Dorset gave them some of their collections. They couldn't collect themselves from the ship because when they came the 'Nascopie' was half sunk.

Pitseolak, *People from Our Side* 133–41

O **Kowmageak Arnakalak** (1951–c. 1979) was born in Iqaluit
(Frobisher Bay), Northwest Territories. He went to school in
Iqaluit and attended the Churchill Vocational Centre. Later he
worked for the Baffin Region Inuit Association. In 'Northern
Lights' Arnakalak draws upon several legends about the Aurora
Borealis.

Northern Lights

Dance, dance across the night skies
Dance, dance a tune unheard, to a tune uncomposed
Seemingly mystical, drawing fear to a child's mind
Drawing curiosity to a man of science
It is believed you will behead me
If I whistle and intrude in your dancing games
Mothers and fathers have told us so
We show respect to your dancing games
But still, we do not understand why you dance so
Fathers have said you light their paths
During their travels through the night
Mothers have said you have beheaded
And played games of ballet with the head of
    the foolish one
Oh may I hear the tune you dance to
Oh may I know why you exist so
Dance, dance across the night skies
Dance, dance to a tune unheard, to a tune uncomposed.

Kowmageak Arnakalak, 'Northern Lights,' *Inuit Today*, 4, 7 (July/August 1975) 47

O **Isa Smiler** (1921–) was born in Inukjuak in arctic Quebec. A
man of many talents, hunter, trapper, fisherman, sculptor, and
painter, he vividly brought to mind life along the east coast
of Hudson Bay in the years between the 1920s and the early
1950s in his reminiscences which he called 'Inukjuak.'

Inukjuak: Making Ready For Winter

We would go hungry if we stayed in an area for too long a
period of time, because soon the animals became scarce. Yet

we were unable to move until the lakes and sea were covered with ice. This was the time to get ready for winter; harnesses and ropes were made, kamiks were made for the dogs and the kamotiks were made ready. Once it got really cold, the men would go out to get mud to use on the runners of the sleds. They would always make sure to get the mud while they were close to a supply and while the ground was not completely frozen. Once they found a supply of mud, they chopped the frozen earth from it with an axe, then collected the soft mud with home made knives and put it onto a piece of seal skin that was once a part of a kayak. Before they started the job, they built a wind shield so the mud would not blow away. The men would always work together in groups. Each group had a job to do that was different from the others. Once the mud was collected, they would put it onto the runners of the sleds. Before they applied the mud they covered the entire sled with snow, leaving only the runners showing. Then, during the evening when the mud had frozen, they would smooth out the rough areas with a handmade axe. When this was done they would pour warm water on top of the mud. This was continued until there was a thick layer of ice. The runners were always watered again in the morning or when necessary. Once the mud was on their sleds, they were quite careful with them, so as not to break any chunks off, by hitting rocks, dog manure or landing too roughly. It was difficult to control the sleds when the dogs were going full speed and to try to prevent them from bumping too hard on the ice. It was great fun going full speed, but to protect the mud, we had to slow down. If a chunk broke off one of the runners, the men would always go back for it and make sure that the runner was mended when we camped. Whenever a long journey was planned, they would make sure that everything was in good condition: the mud on the sleds, the sleds, and the dog harnesses.

Many times when we went hunting we would sleep overnight in order to reach the hunting grounds, depending on if we were hunting for fox inland, seal hunting along the shore quite a distance from home, or hunting for caribou inland. We would leave home early in the morning and travel without stopping, unless it was for tea or a meal along the way. It was really enjoyable nevertheless. After a day's journey we would stop and look for the right kind of snow to build an igloo, then we would settle down for the night. If the snow was too hard or too soft and was not suitable to build an igloo, we would look around until we found the right type. There are different forms of snow and we have names for all of them. For example, stiluqaq, aqilluqaq, pokak, pokaqlak, and pokanaqyuk. The best type for making an igloo is pokanaqyuk, and the best kind to melt for water is aqilluqaq. When there is not enough good snow around to make water, any type is alright. As soon as someone saw a suitable spot to build the igloo, the dogs were guided there. First, the snow was tested to see if it was any good, then if it was alright, the dogs were unharnessed. The harnesses were folded in an orderly fashion and the kamotiks were unloaded, everything being put in order. When that job was done we would help the person who was building the igloo by filling the gaps between the blocks with soft snow. Sometimes it got dark while the igloo was still being worked on, so a lamp was lit to make it easier for the ones who were filling up the gaps. It was important to make sure all the holes were filled, otherwise we would be cold. When someone was taken on the hunt for the first time, he was taught how to build an igloo and how to fill the gaps properly. When the person building the igloo completed his work, the supplies were passed in to him, so that he would not have to go out to get them. The bedding was the first item passed, then the rest of the supplies followed. The dog food was the last. Besides building the igloo and receiving the supplies, the man inside was also responsible for starting the primus stove and boiling water for tea; with this done the dog food had a chance to thaw out. Once the igloo was completed, the gaps filled in and the supplies handed in, the rest of us would go inside and brush the snow off our clothes. Then the door was closed up.

If our food (seal or fish) was really frozen, the snow was brushed off it and it was cut into pieces and put on the stove. Before our tea was made, we would eat, having the tea last. Our igloo would get warmer after a while. Lastly, the dog food was thawed out, even if it took some time, so the dogs would have a proper meal. Then it was the dog's turn to eat. The younger children would go out and watch the rest of the dogs while the older men took one dog in at a time to feed it. The dogs were so anxious to be fed that sometimes they would try to get into the igloo and quite often they got hit, especially the greedy ones. Every one of the dogs had a name and when their name was called they got their chance for a meal. But quite often the ones who were not called would still go in, anyway.

After the dogs were fed, there was still more work to do before retiring, such as checking to see if there was mending to do on the dogs' harnesses and ropes. When this was done it was finally bed time. The next morning we would get up so early that it was still dark out. Our job was to make tea for the older men when they woke us younger ones up. After breakfast, the first one out of the igloo would start working on the kamotiks, smoothing out the mud runners with someone else warming water for him. The water had to be the right temperature and good water, too. Just before daylight the kamotiks were done; we would then pack up our belongings again and load them onto the sleds. The harnesses and ropes were then put on the dogs. The dogs were rested and anxious to get going. When we first started travelling, they would race along and those that fell behind would try to catch up to the others. The dogs were so happy that when they neared another sled they barked at one another and sometimes they almost got tangled up with the other sled. It was the only way to travel at the time, so if the dogs were healthy and well rested it was an exciting way ...

A Matter of Life and Death
One time, Samwillie, Noah and I were on a hunting trip, using one dog team, during the spring. It was one of those occasions where it was a matter of life or death. Noah was the eldest. We went down to Hudson Bay to look for open water. We had to go quite a distance before we could find any sign, and when we found it, Samwillie and I went to one opening while Noah found another. Samwillie and I spotted a square flipper seal and my companion shot at it and wounded it. It was right at the floe edge, which made it difficult to reach. We thought we could get to it by using a kamotik or a kayak, so I went to

Noah to ask him for help. He had caught a seal as well, but he could not get to it either. He had tired of waiting for us so he had gone on ahead to try and reach the seal. When I reached him, he told me to go on to a small ice floe. I was a bit scared because I was not able to stand, so I tied a rope around my self and tried to reach the seal. Just as I was about to reach it, a walrus appeared out of the open water. We tried to ignore it, and I was able to get a hold of the seal and haul it up onto the main ice. We then started to head back to where Samwillie had wounded the square flipper seal, which by this time had died. We had to think of a way to get at it and we could not use the kayak. We could have just forgotten about it but it was Samwillie's first catch and the first animal caught by a young boy is always important. So he and I got on the kamotik and Noah pushed us out towards the seal. (When kamotiks were frozen and they had some ice on the sides they were able to float. But this time the ice on it was soft.) We hoped to have our kamotik cross the open water but it did not quite make it. It went down into the water instead of crossing to the other side. We tried to push it with our feet but that did not help any. The ice was not safe enough to walk on so we were stuck; we threw ourselves onto the ice and landed on our stomachs.

Although we had got a hold on the ice, half of our bodies were in the water. I tried to get up onto the floe but failed, so I remained in the water. Noah, who was on solid ice, told us to stay put while he got a piece of rope that was long enough to pull us out. First he asked who was in the most danger. It appeared I was, so he started with me. When he threw over the rope I tried to help him by using my arms for leverage and holding the rope between my teeth. He pulled me ashore. Once this was done it was Samwillie's turn. He did exactly the same thing and by taking the rope between his teeth he made it, too. The next thing to do was to figure out just how we were going to get back our kamotik. Earlier we had spotted a walrus in the open water, apparently it had followed us from the spot where we had caught the seal, although we were not aware that it was beneath us while we were in the water. When Samwillie was in the water he could feel the kamotik moving beneath his feet, but did not worry about it too much.

Afterwards he realized that it was the walrus that had been moving the kamotik. It was a scary experience, because the walrus could have attacked us. In the meantime, it appeared again and was getting angry so we shot at it to scare it away.

We still had the kamotik and the square flipper to worry about. One of my companions got the kayak, pushed it into the water and used the paddles as foot rests. He gradually pushed himself to the square flipper. He had several ropes around his waist and we were able to pull him, the seal and the kamotik back to where we were.

With our wet clothes we were really cold. It was getting dark as well, so we started towards the land. Samwillie was really suffering, he just could not get warm, as for me, I was cold too, but not as cold as he was. It was night and we could not hope to reach the land because it was quite a distance, so we built an igloo on the ice. The following morning we started for home. We were close to death, but we survived. Today my two companions are no longer living.

Isa Smiler, 'Inukjuak,' *Inuktitut* (summer/fall 1977) 52, 56, 62

O **Eric Anoee** (1924–) was born north of Baker Lake, Northwest Territories. He has worked as director of traditional and cultural programs for the Inuit Cultural Institute, as a carver and painter, and has written several school texts in Inuktitut. A member of the Order of Canada, he was living in Eskimo Point, NWT, in 1988.

My Writings

My First Caribou Kill

The first summer we spent at Sarvartuq (Kazan River) was June, 1938, and we had two tents on the top of a hill. Our companions were the family of Qaarlugaasi with his wife, Kautaq. That woman also had two sons who were now men: the older named Issitaarjuk, and the younger, Aasivaarjuk, who was just a youth. The younger one was also called Kingaq and I would have him for a playmate – I think that he was more like a close member of my family to me. They also had one small sister called Mangilinaak, and the very smallest was being carried in the hood of her mother and her name was Narjaangiq. Kingaq and I, staying up late, would sometimes catch a seal and we would spy caribou on the land. We would indeed be jealous of the ones who went hunting and, although it was regrettable, we were stopped from doing this by our bosses. Perhaps, because of our inexperience, or ignorance, we were told not to try to shoot caribou. The day that we had longed for finally came around – that night the two brothers and my stepfather prepared for the hunt – and we were at last asked to go along. My night-hunting companion and I now started off walking down towards this side of the trails the caribou would take and, as we came to the bottom of a big lake, many caribou met us coming very close to us. My step-father handed me a gun, and holding it by the butt he told me to go ahead and aim at the nearby caribou. I had just taken one shot when, at this moment, my step-father stood up and was wanting to walk out there towards this side of the fleeing caribou. And I was thinking: 'I wonder what he's doing?' We walked out and came across a newly dead caribou and I was perplexed as to who had killed it. It was just a small one, a calf who had left his mother, and my step-father put it on his back without even first skinning it, he just wanted to take it home. So we went home with the caribou on his back, and I still didn't know whether I had shot it or someone else. When he got it home, he spoke to my mother and I gathered finally that I had apparently shot a caribou. Just at this moment, my mother, feeling happy, went out and came back in with our neighbour's wife, Kautaq, asking her to come in because, although I didn't know it, she wanted her to accompany them in customs of our forefathers. As she was cutting up the caribou with her ulu, she began saying: 'This caribou kill of my son's is not something that will harm or something forbidden in any way.' Some caribou kills would apparently be forbidden, and these customs while the meat is being cut up are called tuttungautit here amongst the akullirmiut.

The Sound of the Wolves Howling

A long time ago, our ancestors, the older Eskimos, would tell us that there were wolves in large packs, called kajjat. And they also said that, because of their very large numbers, their sides would even be rubbed bare of fur from touching one another and rubbing it off. On nights when we would be sleeping on the trail, if the weather was good and there was little wind, sometimes, as it would get dark, we would hear howling, and, in the deep night when one was sleeping, it would give one an uncanny feeling as if they were always on the verge of reaching one. Our dogs, however, tied up to the sledge-line outside, would be our guardians and, not being shy of or afraid of frightening things, they would make a noise or yap whenever they were threatened. Wolves, however, if they are not desperately hungry or if they have not been made crazy by sickness, are not usually dangerous, but are genuinely afraid as soon as they see men or are very quick to run away even if they smell them. There was one man by the name of Pingursak who had something to say at one time about this. In the early spring, he was walking to his fox traps and the weather was clouded and snow was falling heavily. He was apparently bitten from behind of his parka flap, even the back flap of his outer tunic was ripped. He had a crazy wolf to fight. He was carrying a gun on his back but the wolf was holding on so tightly with its jaws and was so strong that his gun apparently fell out of its case. He was also carrying a snow-knife on his back, and he grabbed at it first before start- ing to stab at the wolf. The blow just glanced off, however, hit but did not kill, and the knife apparently just bent, either the wolf being too hard or perhaps the knife that he had tried to use as a spear, was not sharp. Later he was thinking of wanting to force the wolf's head into what he was carrying on his back, and, throwing it to the ground, he put a hat on the wolf, forcing it into it by the head. While the wolf was thus in its bag, he quickly grabbed for his rifle. Just as he was putting cartridges in it, the wolf started to work violently to free itself and simultaneously got out of the hood. He started towards the man again but was shot by the same man who had just wrestled with him.

Since then, wolves have generally been killed by being led by their scent to meat which has been poisoned. The wolf that eats the meat that it has found in the beginning, having come this way just once, will perhaps die. In the past, Eskimo dog teams were slow and they would be followed by wolves, but now they use Skidoos and the wolves run quickly away and are even hunted through waiting until they tire out. Now, when we are sleeping on the trail, we no longer hear the howl of wolves. Perhaps, during the evening, they are now running away from the sound of engines or snowmobiles since there are no more wolves coming close to campers.

The Drum Dance

... a long time ago we had left Baker Lake for my mother's ancestors' land down there with the Paallirmiut. Here, while we were in between, in the place of the people we call Sarvarturmiut, for the first time I was seeing Eskimos who danced to the skin drum. Although they were Eskimos, I was usually afraid of them when they were drum-dancing, thinking that the dancers wanted the drum to break. I remember vividly a small man with a very black beard who would dance vigourously and would shout when he danced. His name was Akkiutaq. (I'm not sure what his name means – either 'that which slopes' or else we call a base or something to stand on made out of fresh-water seal an akkiutaq). I would be afraid of that little man, perhaps also because I knew that he was a shaman. Sometimes the shamans would be very frightening for a small child, but I discovered later that the dancing and the shamans were not frightening to the adults. Dancing was really something and a cause of joy to all those people who gathered together, even though the too young and the too inexperienced were not likely to be too happy about it. It was embarrassing when one was asked to dance on the floor all alone amongst those who would stand up. The worst and most frightening thing, being merely a visitor, was when one was asked to dance amongst those who were not his countrymen or neighbours – it made one shake from embarrassment because many Eskimos would be standing in front of the dancers. However, that would be only talk – those who were to dance did, and even the question of being easily frightened was a cause for joy. I have faith in these things, it is true. I never did make a song of my very own – I was not a song writer, and would always be too

179

incapable of that. Sometimes, even, I just borrowed someone else's song when I wanted to join in the play of the drum-dance.

Why is each one of all the assembled men apparently called on to dance? You can see the dancers, some of them seeming lively and not just staying in one spot on the floor – these are the ones that are more desirable to see; they are not lethargic and some of them accompany themselves with shouts and cries. Some of them also, the ones who can make songs, are delightful to hear, and they speak in their songs about the customs of their lives and about unusual events that have happened to them. Some of us, even though we were unable to make songs, would generally join in the dance, just trying to follow ... Anyone, or all, amongst the dancers, is generally asked to take the drum and dance. It was indeed regrettable to me that I didn't know how to make songs, and in spirit I wasn't able to join along in the merriment – I was never able to be happy as a child in my life about things like helpless-ness and hunger. I was able, however, to make enough noise crying when there was nothing else to do. I don't even know how to tell some of the real tales and stories. I had daily doubts about living, I think, just from being so helpless and wretched.

Eric Anoee, 'My Writings,' *Inuttituut* (winter 1977) 22–3, 46–7, 18–19

O   **Paulosie Kasudluak** (1938–) was once a prolific carver; exam-ples of his work are in the National Gallery in Ottawa. In 1988 he was living in Inukjuak, arctic Quebec, where as president of the Federation of Co-operatives in northern Quebec, he was deeply involved in community and regional activities. In this essay he discusses the art of Inuit carving.

Nothing Marvellous

It is not only to make money that we carve. Nor do we carve make-believe things. What we show in our carvings is the life we have lived in the past right up to today. We show the truth.

We carve the animals because they are important to us as

food. We carve Inuit figures because in that way we can show ourselves to the world as we were in the past and as we now are. That is why we carve men hunting and building igloos and women making something that they will use, maybe kamiks or clothing or using an ulu. No matter what activity the carved figure is engaged in, something about it will be true. That is because we carve to show what we have done as people. There is nothing marvellous about it. It is there for everyone to see. It is just the truth.

It is the same with the work which the women do with their hands. We do not reveal ourselves only in stone. The work of the women shows the type of clothing which we as people had. That, too, contributes to the truth.

We Inuit have had many experiences. We have used just about everything for clothing – skins and furs and modern day cotton and wool. We have eaten all kinds of animals and, for our hunting gear, have used their bones, fur and skin. Our clothing also came from the animals we killed. So, these carvings we make of the animals and the Inuk in traditional clothing, engaged in his work, all of them reveal what we were or what we are now. Nothing marvellous about it.

Carving means many things to us. One has to find stone in order to make carvings. Summer or winter, each brings its own difficulty in obtaining the stone. This is something which I believe the people in the South do not understand. You have to think of where the stone comes from and the problems one goes through getting it out. The problem of locating it in the first place and the distance one has to carry it. I could write many words about all this.

Before one finds the stone, it is useless. It just exists. Maybe it is exposed on the surface of the earth. Maybe it is beneath the water. One thing I know is that the best kind of stone is usually the hardest for us to get.

It is hard in summer because you have to carry the stone to your canoe all the way from the quarry where you extracted it by hand. It is tedious work but the thought that this will enable you to feed your family and develop your Cooperative provides you with the initiative and stamina to survive this trouble. As does the thought that in this way, we will be able to communicate to the rest of the world about ourselves. Even so, it is back-breaking work. Even when you do not have to carry the stone so far to your canoe at the shore, there is always a certain amount of danger in transporting the heavy rock by canoe. And you cannot even eat it!

Getting the stone out of the ground – even in summer when the ground is not frozen – is hard work because we do not have any fancy equipment. It is only because we help each other and work together to extract the stone that we are able to succeed.

In winter, it is particularly difficult to get at the stone. The snow can drift five to ten feet over the site so that you are unsure of the exact spot. You have to take a chance and when you shovel all that snow away you are still left to dig in the hard frozen earth.

The stone is never the same. Some is black and some is green. I really know the green stone because it is at a place where I grew up. The stone we are using now in Inoucdjouac is mined from a site about forty miles out of town. It costs a lot of money even to get to that place. You need proper equipment – ski-doo or canoe – to go there and proper mainte-nance so you will not break down.

If you go by canoe, you go through huge swells and waves along the way because part of your journey is through the open Hudson's Bay where there are no little islands to shelter you. It is not much better in the winter because your snowmobile needs gas which costs $2.25 a gallon now and your route lies over the unevenly frozen sea ice. But some sites, I hear, are even farther away than that from the settlements.

It is unfortunate but the stone which is close to our villages always seems to be of a poor quality and useless in our carv-ings. What I have said may be enough to convince you that making a carving is not play. It is man's work.

There is much that happens from the time the stone is found and the time the people in the south see it as a bird or anything. And everything is done with your hands. A man is dependent upon his hands when he wants to show what his life is.

Translated by Ali Tulugak, *Port Harrison/Inoucdjouac Exhibition Catalogue* (Winnipeg Art Gallery 1977) 21–2

○   **Felix Nuyaviak** (1892–1981), was a hunter and whaler, distinguished as a popular story-teller and a good entertainer who sang and played the Eskimo drum in Tuktoyaktuk. In 1971, he told Father Robert Le Meur this particularly gripping story of the heroism of his father-in-law, Mangilaluk. It was later broadcast on the local radio station CFCT.

Mangilaluk Adrift on the Ice

This is a true story which happened at Baillie Island and surroundings, Utkraluk, in the years preceding the 1900's. Utkrakuk, Baillie Island is located west of Tuk, some one hundred and forty-five miles, as the crow flies.

In 1905, Mangilaluk, tired of drifting here and there, and tired of living at Herschel Island, Baillie Island, Kittigariuit and many other places, decided finally to settle down and to take up roots at a place which seemed to his liking, Tuktoyaktik.

Tuk, then, was not even a village, nor a settlement, only a good place for fishing. A few sod houses still remained intact and of some use to the few Inuit who came for fishing in August and September. However, Mangilaluk prizing the location, the harbour and fishing grounds, set his heart upon a permanent home at this very place. So he began building himself a house, a real house, built with wood and logs, abundant along the shores of the Arctic coast. Soon however, he was followed by new comers, the Yitoariuk's, the Mangilana's, the Saputaitok's, the Sisksigaluk's, the Angisinaok's, and later the Nuyaviak's.

It must be said that Mangilaluk was well known and of good reputation, as well as a prominent hunter, a good provider, and also a good entertainer, a really good story teller. Last but not the least, he was considered as the best athlete in that part of the Arctic coast. In various competitions such as foot races, high jump, weight lifting, etc. he had no equal. He surpassed every challenger, even the whalers. It could be added that this stature, his demeanour prompted and aroused respect, admiration, love and even maybe a bit of fear. Indeed, he was a man among men, a true Inuvialuk. Of course due to all these qualities and gifts, he became a natural leader and chief in

Tuktoyaktuk, his place. He remained the uncontested and unchallenged leader til his death in 1940. For the old residents of Tuk, Mangilaluk is the real founder of the village. Even now, he is well spoken of as former chief and as an outstanding man.

Here now is a story about Mangilaluk and his adventures on the drifting ice field. This is the way Mangilaluk told the story of his unfortunate and forced journey, adrift on the ice. I heard him several times myself ...

One morning on a beautiful wintery day, very cold, but windless and clear weather, Mangilaluk went out to check on the weather and to scan the horizon and the frozen sea. Far out he saw plenty of black and darkened clouds, low over the sea ice, condensation caused by open water. That sight lifted his spirits, because over there was a chance to get some seals and maybe some polar bears. All foods were always welcome around Baillie Island. He then decided to go hunting on the ice. In a happy mood with good feelings, he left camp walking, and from land he stepped onto the strong ice. He was alone at the beginning of the trip, but not for long, as he heard some steps behind him and the voice of his friend and companion of many hunts, Kaobviak. This friend of his was a teaser, and of course even before reaching Mangilaluk, he began teasing him about his shooting.

They kept going, Kaobviak and Mangilaluk, talking and telling each other their last dreams and their hopes for that day. How would be the hunting? How many seals they needed?, etc. As they were pushing along at ease, behind them two other hunters, Sitorana (Alarpana's son) and Chiksak, followed them, stepping out at a smart pace til they also joined Mangilaluk. All four knew very well the treachery of the ice and constantly looked around them, ahead and behind, watching the ice. Nevertheless, unaware and without any notice or hint, what the Inuk hunter dreads the most happened suddenly and mystified them. The ice floe was on the move and they realized that they were being cut off from land and drifting, God knew where!

This happens quite often around Baillie Island. Winds become gales and the ice pack though thick and strong, does not last very long, as it battles against the pressure of the swift current. The violence of the wind, the breaking of the waves, the grinding, hitting and knocking of ice flow against ice flow, all these elements combined weaken the strongest ice field. Now, the four hunters, tense and afraid, dreading the worst, slowly plowed their way, searching for a safe passage in the blizzard and the blinding snow storm. Sitorana, though accustomed to hardships, couldn't even shed tears from his eyes which were blindfolded with ice and snow. They had only one recourse left to them, to keep going along and wander, at the mercy of the wind. They had to be alert in their movements, as the ice floe on which they had taken refuge, was getting smaller and smaller. So all watched carefully, especially Mangilaluk. He detected a bigger piece of ice passing by and jumped on it. His three companions did so also. They knew Mangilaluk very well, and in such circumstances as they were now Mangilaluk was for them the unchallenged leader. In fact he took charge of the party and was determined to go through this ordeal as he had several other times. After all, this was not the first time he had been adrift on the ice.

Time went by, how long? No one really knew and didn't care, while the wind increased in velocity and in roaring power, their main preoccupation being to stay on the ice. In order to do so, now and then leaving the ice pan for another, a larger one, to see it diminishing under the battery of waves and other ice floes.

Chisak, Kaobviak and Sitorana huddled themselves up to Mangilaluk, who placidly and without showing any emotion tried constantly to pierce the surroundings and the limited horizon. Suddenly, Mangilaluk jostled his near companion. No words were uttered at this time, words are useless and out of line, and with the other hand, pointed only to something, which looked like land. All looked ahead and lo, there it was, a high bluff? An iceberg? They were all tense and aghast, staring at that mass ahead of them and travelling its way toward them. Was it the end of their ice floe and a cold jump in the sea? They tried to guess and figure out what would be the next move from Mangilaluk. But as usual, he didn't show his emotions. Rather, he intently kept watching the movements of that iceberg, moving to and fro, now very near, then going away a little farther and then coming closer again.

At once, when the huge ice flow drew near the mark and almost accosted their floating ice boat, Mangilaluk jumped onto the moving white mass of ice and clinging and laying hold of the abrupt wall of ice with his hands and his fingers, climbed right to the top. Once up there he quickly threw his mannar (retrieving line for seals) and hooked it to the ice field he had just left. Then pulling and tying the line, he finally, after strenuous efforts, moved the two pieces of ice closer, at least close enough for his three companions to step onto the iceberg. Once aboard this new boat, or ark, they felt more secure, sheltered and safe from wrecking. Sure they were now in a better position, but not yet at the end of their trials.

During this time, at Baillie Island, their home, everything was at a standstill, they were aware of the storms at sea and more concerned with their relatives on the ice, than for themselves. Their anxieties and apprehensions increased, as no one came home. As time went by, sadness and sorrow as well as misgivings, crept into their minds, as well as fear for the hunters fate. How would they survive the storm? They had left on foot and didn't carry with them much food, just a little in their arrenat, their bags. Moreover, and worse yet, in Ularpana's mind, Mangilaluk left for his trip without any talisman or amulet, therefore without the help of his spirit protectors. Ularpana didn't waste any time, and taking his into his hands and stretching his arm, he breathed upon it, telling it to go forth and speed up to Mangilaluk and his companions and help.

As for Kaopkruna, Mangilaluk's mother, she thought a lot about her son and prayed for him in her own ways, humming and chanting some errenat, tunes. According to the old custom, inside their little dwelling, she hung her son's caribou boots on the ceiling, after filling them with shaving chips of wood. Although very upset, she was confident that her son would come through safe and sound. At night, her thoughts went to her son and sometimes she could hear the boots fastened to the ceiling just above her, dangling and swinging, moving to and fro, as a man walking. Then she felt relieved, 'my son is alive and safe on the treacherous ice, walking and on his way home.' A quick inspection of the interior of the boots confirmed her feelings. From inside the boots, the shavings had moved upwards. Cheerful and lighthearted, she told the Baillie Island people not to worry anymore.

On the ice berg, the hunters confined and walled in their rather small shelter, travelled and journeyed without effort on their part, fair wind, but God only knew in what direction. Their sole concern, and vital one, was to shield themselves from the wind and drifting snow, and not to fall asleep. Walking on that iceberg was out of the question, and even sleep evaded them, as the noises of the howling winds and the deafening roar of the grinding ice around them filled the air. Chiksak and Kaobviak were huddled together, cemented by iced snow, moaning and whining, afraid, frightened and freezing. On and on they went at the mercy of the waves and wind, til they met with an ice floe that looked like an ice field, or ice pack. Mangilaluk, constantly on watch and on standby, at first glance, sized it up. This was good ice, and the main ice. As far as he could see, this ice pack stretched far ahead. Safety, homeward at last, or at least landward maybe. Alas, the gap between their iceberg and what looked as a more suitable and walkable ice, although narrow enough, offered a too wide body of water, even for such a good jumper as Mangilaluk. Were they to be marooned on a now grounded island of ice, so near to a passway to escape? Mangilaluk's hopes had invigorated him, and renewed his resourcefulness, as well as his astuteness. He was ready for action almost immediately. This was for him another challenge and expertly he decided to tackle it. If a mank, a line, was useless on an ice-berg aground, and a boundless ice field was ahead, there was left a possibility to lessen the gap. Why not build a bridge with broken ice and his wooden staff?

Mangilaluk began slowly and painstakingly to assemble and lump together small chunks of floating ice and drifting snow, wetting them with water, cementing them together and hardening them with his hands. He pushed himself slowly and carefully forward, crawling on his belly, until with extended arms he could reach and touch the opposite side with his staff. Then he put the wooden staff in the water and around it, collecting more pieces of ice, sleet and slush he resumed the construction of his bridge. A bridge sufficiently strong enough to support his weight. Proudly he reached and landed upon the ice pack. If his companions watched intently the operation, once Mangilaluk rolled over and stood on the ice, one by one they followed, crossing the bridge. Once Mangilaluk had recovered his staff, they all went on with their travelling with more determination. However, due to sleeplessness, hunger and maybe weariness, they began to tire and fatigue.

Now the strongest and the fittest, Mangilaluk and Sitorana, were in the lead and following were the two laggers, Chiksak and Kaobviak. After awhile they met with another obstacle, another lead of water, this one far too wide to cross, even by a built up bridge. To make matters worse, this body of water seemed to extend as far as the horizon, be it on their right or their left. Taking into consideration this new unfortunate situation, the stranded Inuit didn't have much choice, no other alternative than to continue and to proceed one way or the other and hope to find a way to go across the crack. The decision was taken out of their hands, as suddenly before their bewildered eyes, a huge cake of ice sprung from the sea bottom ice covered with mud and rocks, a providential bridge, presenting itself at the right place and time. They didn't waste any time and speedily stepped on and hurried to the opposite shore, to resume again their journey.

There a disagreement arose as to which direction should be taken, and the party split and separated. Mangilaluk and Sitorana going one way and Chiksak and Kaobviak going the other way. Westward went Mangilaluk and his partner, marching and pushing along. Walking on sea ice, on rough ice that in their condition was rather exacting and demanding, even for them, hardened men. Therefore both decided to take a rest and halt for awhile. The location was appropriate, rough ice was easily found and set upright, providing a shabby shelter against the wind. They simply crouched there, so tired they were, too tired to sleep and too deeply involved, buried in their own inner thoughts and dreams.

Thus they remained in silence, each one respecting the other's privacy, til a voice startled them. It came so suddenly that they asked themselves if it was a dream, or a true voice? The voice seemed to address Sitorana, saying 'You are deceiving yourself and hurting yourself. Do not stay there, less you want to lose your foot. Walk man, walk a little bit and travel east.' Amazed and also in awe, both stood up and looked around, but nobody was to be seen around them, to be near them, on the ice, or in the air. Astonished certainly, and also maybe frightened and without any commentaries, Mangilaluk and Sitorana, immediately resumed their march, taking heed of their dream, or advice or warnings. Westward they went, beginning what would be the final leg of their trek. Tiredness and hunger were forgotten, as painfully and stalwartly they plodded their way, til land was sighted. This sight of land and of the point of Baillie Island, reinvigorated them. Both were now relaxed and strengthened, as the end of their ordeal came nearer and nearer ...

O   **Bessie Andreason** (1922–85), a cook, seamstress, and teacher from the western Arctic, recalled this tragic and poignant true experience when she was fourteen years old. In September 1937, Bessie's father decided to travel from the Coppermine to Kent Peninsula, a distance of 250 miles, to spend the winter there because foxes were said to be plentiful. On their way they stopped to visit at Wilmot Island only to discover that an epidemic of measles was ravaging the camp. Betty's father decided to camp there anyway, and almost immediately his wife and he were infected. Anxious to proceed with their plans, however, they left for their destination. But they never arrived. Both died en route. And the daughter, Bessie, was left all alone.

No Way Out

... I was now an orphan and also in the middle of nowhere with two dead people near me. I remember that I was then affected by an uncontrollable and involuntary trembling and quivering. It was now early morning, I think I could see some stars and daybreak, maybe. I felt an urge to withdraw from the tent for awhile and take a walk. This I did immediately and felt better, looking and scanning the horizon, the few stars still visible, the hills and all the surroundings. Everything around me seemed so quiet and silent, so unaware of the tragedies I had witnessed. Freely in the nature I let my tears

189

trickle from my eyes and I began gradually to get hold of myself and to overcome my agitations and achieve calm again. I felt stronger and capable. That walk helped me to dissipate all my despair and gave me a desire to live.

Another thought or inspiration suddenly infiltrated my mind – what about my prayer book? what about the hymns and songs I had used to sooth father's sufferings? Returning to the tent I began to hum some of the tunes. Once in, I took the book into my hands and first felt it with my hands, turning it one way and then the other, holding it, almost hugging it against my chest. Now I felt relieved at the thought that I was no longer alone. I still had a good friend near me, with me. This book was for me like a friend, present there and full of understanding. So enticed was I then, that I didn't notice the coffee pot boiling on the seal oil lamp. Having no desire to drink, I took the coffee pot and put it on the floor and came back to my prayer book, turning the pages now, here and there, trying desperately to piece together the ways to decipher letters and signs. At that time, I didn't know how to read yet, and being alone I thought that I should give it a try. An attempt that proved to be a trying experience, but not without some success – one word here, one word there and I found the key to reading and spelling. Then, as strange as it might look, alone in the tent I began to spell some words. Then more, even loudly, til it struck me that all made sense, words and sentences. I not only read, but also sang some hymns whose tunes I knew. Here I must confess that though in sorrow, I experienced joy and happiness and peace, such that I never before or since have experienced in my life time.

Fears, sorrow, sadness, grief, all dissipated and dissolved almost immediately, giving room to serenity and resignation. I observed also to my amazement and surprise that each time I sang I heard a noise, like wings fluttering over the tent. This rather, strange, unusual noise ceased as soon as I terminated my songs. It did not bring fear, just the opposite, joy. So I sang and sang, using the same hymns over and over again. Time elapsed that way without any other incident. The only worry I did have was to keep the seal oil lamp burning and now and then melting some ice for tea. At times, maybe only once or twice did I feel some pang of sadness and sorrow at my parents, whose corpses were so near me. Even at night I was calm and slept well, but always with my book near me.

However once during the night I got really frightened. It began with the dogs barking, growling, howling to the moon or maybe answering a call of another wild animal. Then I heard plainly a sound like some small dogs groaning, wailing around the tent and at the same time it seemed to me that some one was hitting the tent with a stick of wood. Alone in the tent nobody to talk with and in the silence, that noise scared me so much that I couldn't move, thinking to myself and searching the nature of such a noise. 'What is this now? What can I do now? The only thing I did was to lay down in my blanket and cover even my head and try not to listen. I began to sing loudly, yet the noise persisted and even came nearer, to the door or exit of the tent. As suddenly as it had started it also ended. Everything returned to quietness again to silence. That silence occuring after such a strange noise scared me. So even though it was still night, I got up and went outside to take a look at things and at the dogs. Everything was in order and nobody in evidence, the dogs at their dog line sleeping quietly.

Another night I had a beautiful dream, filled with joy and rich in future promises and expectations. I saw my parents, Ambrose and Lena, they were there as if they were alive, conversing with me. They spoke about all their concerns for me, about my anxieties and fears, apprehensions, etc. They said to me, 'Bessie, do not be afraid of us, of our dead bodies laying there near you, they are only bodies now, senseless and lifeless. Our spirit, our souls have left them and we are near you all the time, seeing you and following you. We want you to be a happy girl and live well. So give it an honest try. Remember if you are happy, we also will be happy, on the other hand if you are sad and disheartened, what do you think our feelings are going to be? It is up to you now Bessie,' and on they went with advice and words of wisdom. I do not remember how long that dream lasted, but suddenly I was awakened. I didn't even realize at first the cause, it seems that I was in a kind of dream yet ... where was I?, what was going on? It took me some time to find out that some noise outside must have disturbed me. Still half asleep and half awake, and yet under

191

the spell of my dream, I instinctively grabbed about in my blanket for my prayer book and little by little consciousness returned to my senses.

The noise was still there, not far away from the tent. Attentive now, I thought that I could detect a rattling of chains and snarling, as well as barking of dogs. I decided to investigate as fear had left me altogether. Perhaps it was the result of my dream which inspired me with confidence and security. Nevertheless I stepped outside the tent and looked around my surroundings. What I discovered made me shake my head, what a sight! All the dogs, seven adults and two young ones were bundled up, practically muzzle to muzzle, nose to nose, which explained the snarling and shrieking. One of the anchor lines gave way and of course the dogs took advantage of that lucky break to wander around and visit with each other. However, the result of their half freedom was a disastrous mess and an entanglement of dog chains and the dog line, so twisted as to resemble a big ball. I remember myself looking in bewilderment at that picture and almost in despair holding my hands around my head and thinking of the most effective and quick manner to rectify the situation. I searched for a pair of canvas gloves, but was unsuccessful in finding some. So with my bare hands I began the unpleasant task, first untying all the dogs and then undoing knots and twists til I had the dog line in order. Dad's dogs were very friendly and used to each other. They roamed around in a friendly manner. Now and then I had to take a break to warm up my hands which sometimes felt numb from handling metal and steel. We were now in October and the weather had turned cold. I was cold myself, but managed to share some of my warmth on my hands by blowing on them and then clapping them. As for my feet, stomping them on the frozen ground helped a little. I wanted to get that job over with as soon as possible, but had to take some breaks from time to time to remove the numbness from my fingers, especially the tips. During these 'thawing out' operations I faced the lake, so familiar to me by then.

Each day, sometimes even more than once, I walked to the lake to get some ice for water and for drinking purposes. I knew the trail by heart, knew where stood the nigerheads and rocks. As for the lake itself, it had no secret for me, its outline, the shore, the rocks and reefs in the water or in the ice then. But that day for some reason, something seemed to be amiss, something didn't fit with the picture printed in my mind and vision. I looked more attentively and intensely, as I began to be upset and it fretted me to almost irritation and impatience. All surroundings, as well as the ground was white, though only a bit of snow had fallen, but the boulders should have been dark and the largest one was white. I could see it now, and I must add it was also daring to my eyesight. Even more, it hypnotized me then. The more I stared at it the more I was convinced that it moved slightly perhaps, just a little, swaying with the wind maybe. It looked so strange, so startling, yet so seductive. Panic stricken I hastily finished untangling the dog line, stretched it on the ground and anchored it in a similar manner as I had seen my Father doing it. Piling some rocks on top of each other and covering it with snow. This done, I ran into the tent and sat on the blankets, my heart beating a tempo, thinking of my experience and trying to decide what to do about it. My imagination was maybe running loose, my mind and will out of control, maybe it was a trick of my own imagination. How I longed then for a living companion to discuss that problem with. Then I remembered my Father's binoculars. I took them and went to the door steps; mustering my courage I held the binoculars and settled them right up to my eyes turning them towards the lake. Yes, there it was behind the boulder, as standing up, it looked like a human form. A human shape, face sideways, arms extended and making signs as to call to approach. I couldn't make out the features and details but what I did see then, was more than enough for me, and all I could stand in my frame of mind. I retreated into the tent, a girl really frightened, quivering, ready to collapse into a nervous break down.

There I sat near the seal oil lamp and tried to steal some warmth from the flickering flames. Thinking, that was practically the only thing I could do then, nobody to talk to. What is it? Who is he? What is the meaning? Is it something or somebody who wants to help me, or to deceive me? All these questions raced in my mind at the same time and without any answers. Curiosity got the best of me, though I was very scared, I wanted to take another look at the object. Not from the outside but from the inside of the tent. I found a small hole in the canvas and with my fingers I enlarged it and peeped through the hole. There was nothing at all to be seen on the lake and I felt relieved and at the same time a bit disappointed! Anyway it didn't matter now and I resolved that given another opportunity, no matter the results I would investigate. With that resolution taken, I went out to tend the dogs and finish the job I had started. The dogs came to me but for a few exceptions. Those I wanted to call, however no sound came from my mouth – maybe I had been too scared. So turning to my prayer book, I stood for a little while til I was again calm and then tried again. That second time I had no problem and at my call the dogs came to me. Before entering the tent I double checked the line and anchors and satisfied with my work and after a last look at the lake, I went in calling it a day.

It was with mixed feelings that I thought of my experience, on one hand I would like to have it renewed, on the other hand there was in it something mysterious and mystifying, close to awe even. At any rate, no opportunity was granted me, this phenomena didn't occur again. Still up to today, some thirty-five years later, it remains a mystery, upon which I did meditate often without any reasonable answer. However, at the time of the above mentioned event, alone in the tent I kept pondering and searching for an explanation of course without success. It became like an obsession during a certain time. I couldn't find any answer, couldn't arrange the fact. It was like pieces of a puzzle too laborious to assemble. I managed one way or another to erase it from my mind as the days went by.

How many days did I spend in the tent? I do not have the faintest idea, no recollection at all. All I remember was that I kept busy each day, tending the seal oil lamp, melting ice, cooking my meagre meals, feeding the dogs, my routine trip to the lake for more ice, praying, singing ... and waiting, yes waiting – for what? I didn't know. I was not frightened anymore, no turmoil in my mind, no impatience, it was like living in an unreal world of my own. However, I was fully conscious of my ordeals and my sore plight – isolated in an unknown country. Cut off from other human beings, but in a way at peace and hopeful for the future, expecting a happy ending to my dreadful experiences.

Day by day the temperature dropped to freezing and now I could feel the cold at night in the tent. With winter and cold settling in, the sea water turned first into slush and rapidly, almost overnight into young ice. One morning I awoke and found all the bay frozen, evenly, without any rough ice. The weather had been so good, clear skies and the winds practically calm. I had been waiting for the change in the weather and I was grateful to see some ice. The life under the tent had become a bit monotonous and the close association with the dead bodies near me, weighted heavily on my nerves. Many times the sight of the schooner, the Nanuk, haunted me and attracted me at the same time. Now that the bay was entirely frozen, all obstacles in reaching it were gone and it was only a question of a day or two before I could venture stepping on the ice away from the shore. Already I walked along the shore and tested the solidity of the ice. After two or three days, although the ice was still black, I resolved to take a chance and go to the schooner. The urge to move into the boat became more and more pressing, almost imperative. I felt that I would feel more secure there, better sheltered from the wind and the possible storms, without mentioning all other dangers. There also I would find more comfort than in the tent, the galley being well equipped with stove, food, bunks – so I would also be safe from want.

Before leaving I tidied up the tent and fastened the door firmly. The only thing I took with me for the trip was an ax, as I knew I needed it to test the solidity of the ice as I went. Such a trip on thin and young ice was not new to me. I had done it several times with my father and the technique had no secret for me. Stepping carefully on the ice, I proceeded slowly, ax in hand, probing the black ice ahead of me, more careful yet when I approached the schooner. Everything went well and without incident I boarded the 'Nanuk' and helped my favorite puppy to come aboard. Those were the only things I brought from shore, my ax and that puppy, to be my companion in my new home. My home it would be for a long time I reckoned, til rescue came. When? I had no idea at all, only hopes. I made my quarters, my refuge in the galley. There was plenty of room for me and I lighted the primus. I thought that it would be sufficient to provide me with heat, without lighting the coal stove. However, I must confess that it produced me with just the minimum of heat. Even now I still wonder why I didn't use the stove, it was in good condition. The present was not too bright for me, so young and lonely in the middle of nowhere, in a boat stuck fast in the ice. Luckily I found some solace in my puppy.

Each day I took a walk around the schooner and also to the main land, the dogs had to be fed and ice was needed for drinking and washing. So even then, when I lived on the boat, I visited the small lake where a few days earlier I had experienced so much trouble. These occupations did me a lot of good, helped dismiss sad thoughts from my mind, and God knows how many there were! It was also good exercise and provided me with fresh air. Such was my daily routine, but if at the beginning I was looking forward to my promenade, little by little it turned out to be one long bore, devoid of interest. Often I gazed into the land beyond the lake and the shore line and yearned to survey a farther horizon ... The more I thought about it the more convinced I became that it would be to my advantage to take the chance. As it happened, before I made any decision, I was torn by conflicting alternatives, the security in the schooner and the unknown facing me and the remote possibility of locating my friends in the surroundings. Anyway it was a chance, a risk worth taking, a gamble in fact to come across someone in that desert of snow and ice.

On waking, before day rise, I was on my way towards land. For sole defence and support, my faithful puppy strolled along at my heels or ran around but never very far away from me, yelping with happiness. I carried also in my hand a stick, not so much as a weapon but as a cane. On the way I surveyed the ice and the land ahead of me, the distance had me fooled, I thought it was closer. From time to time I looked back at the schooner as it became smaller and lower in the horizon. Nevertheless, although tired I had no intention of turning back and giving up my search. I was determined to go through with it now. Once on land I walked and then scrambled to the top of a knoll and then almost collapsed, panting and tired. I threw myself on the frozen ground and rested awhile. Then I over-looked all the surroundings far below me for miles, but without spotting anything, no sign of human beings. I felt then not alarm but maybe a vague apprehension stealing over me, as I descended from the knoll to resume my journey inland and back to the schooner. I thought of myself as being a fool, like a person wishing for the moon. It was by then late afternoon, evening was gradually advancing. I realized that soon it would be dark, long before I could reach home, the schooner. So taking a last look I began my return trip, very tired, hungry and thirsty, I hadn't had any food since morning. The road seemed even longer now and my empty stomach ached and rebelled. I had to vomit on the way back, as I got nearer, my spirits were very low. A fruitless trip, resulting only in fatigue and deceptions.

In such a mood I boarded the schooner, lighted the primus, to get some warmth and immediately went to bed. I was so tired the food didn't even matter, only a cup of tea was greatly appreciated.

On the following days I resumed my routine trips to the mainland and around the schooner. I had decided not to go any farther in my search for my family's friends, deciding instead to wait there on the schooner for further developments. I do not remember how many days I spent in such a manner, alone with mingled feelings, with my ups and downs, my hopes. My walks on the ice helped ease the tensions and strain. The silence sometimes was oppressing and I felt gloomy and jumpy, apprehensive, but deliverance was near at hand and in one way I sort of expected it. It happened early one morning when I heard the dogs barking and howling. I knew that all that noise and fuss did not originate from fear of a wild animal, but rather translated it as frenzy and happiness on their part, a dog team probably. They could feel something new in the air. For me a mixture of various feelings filled me, rather difficult to analyse now. Joy and happiness of course, also a certain fright towards the unknown, to seeing human beings again after so many long days, lonely days. At that precise moment I just couldn't move. It seemed that I was glued to the stool on which I sat. I was even afraid to take a look through the portholes.

As usual in such circumstances, I held my prayer book and did pray on my own for a happy ending. It came suddenly. First from the outside, someone walking around the boat; then some steps on the deck. Still I remained silent, waiting for future events. Suspense grew progressively stronger. Delay became maddening. I feared I would shriek.

After touring the deck, someone approached the galley and opened the hatch. A head appeared, and I heard a voice. 'Anybody home?' Silence. I could feel my knees trembling and could hear my heart beating. A clear, high-pitched voice rang out from in front of me – a human voice at last! I was afraid to answer. Who were those people? Strangers maybe. Evil and harm could happen to me.

All initiatives were taken from my hands as someone descended the steps from the deck and slowly turned to face me. Staring at him, I shivered with joy and fear ...

Bessie was rescued by a group of people on their way to Wilmot Island, who had spotted the schooner in the ice.

Rose Pamack

Pitseolak Ashoona showing her grandchildren her book, 1971

Armand Tagoona

Mark Kalluak,
Eskimo Point, 1985

Sam Metcalfe

Tagak Curley, Ottawa, April 1985

Alootook Ipellie

Mary Simon, December 1984, Ottawa

Leah Idlout d'Argencourt

Martha Flaherty

John Amagoalik, 1982

Zebedee Nungak

4 A People Who Refuse to Disappear

MODERN WRITING

Too often, even today the whites regard us as only a people of hunters who have the strange habit of liking raw meat. But our culture cannot be reduced to such a single traditional element. Our culture provides a foundation and cohesiveness in our daily actions – yesterday we used to go hunting in dog sleds; today we build our co-operatives and tomorrow we will direct our government and other institutions.

My translation from *Les Inuit dissidents* (Povungnituk: Inuit Tungavingat Nunamini n.d.)

Nunavut speaks to the soul of the Inuit. It's like a promised land for the Eskimos.

Mary Carpenter Lyons

The years since the mid-1970s have witnessed an outburst of writing in English. Acculturated Inuit young people are articulating the feelings of a generation caught in a crisis of identity trying to determine a way of life that will protect their traditions and at the same time cope with the massive outside influences in their lives.

The various levels of political bodies, national and regional cultural institutes, and political organizations, as well as the native media – press, radio, and television – have all played important roles in the shaping of an Inuit literature in English. They have provided a forum for energy and ideas, thereby giving the first generation of Inuit writers, many of whom show great fluency in English, a literary identity.

Journalism dominates the imagination and absorbs the intellectual energies of many of these talented writers. And with a new political consciousness, unknown to their ancestors, they are writing a literature of opinion and information, largely derivative and imitative of western models, reflecting the new realities of political and social change. Political themes appear again and again: the vision of an eastern Arctic homeland named Nunavut, the need for constitutional and political reform, the settlement of land and water claims, the preservation of language, and resistance to total assimilation into the dominant society. Social themes also abound, created by changing contact situations, southern living, relocation, and modern settlement life; these themes are loneliness, alienation, the meaninglessness of the court system, and a nostalgia for the past and home. A directness characterizes their writing, whether it is John Amagoalik's closing remarks at the Federal Provincial Conference of First Ministers on Constitutional Matters or Peter Ernerk's letter to the editor defending the Inuit's traditional hunting and trapping rights.

As Inuit writers plead for their rights and opportunities, they are also protesting, as Mary Simon does, for the Indian and Métis people of Canada, for the peoples of the circumpolar world and indigenous peoples everywhere. This is a remarkable achievement for a people who, just three decades ago, were still the most isolated and widely dispersed in the world.

Although Inuit writers of the 1980s are using new themes and a variety of forms of self-expression, they have not forgotten their ancestral inheritance. They are restoring, reviving, and retelling the old stories and thus keeping alive the knowledge of a past way of life. They are still preserving 'as-told-to' narratives by elders like Aksaajuug Etuangat and Davidialuk Alasuaq Amittu about Inuit life. The traditional practice of using satire for humour and ridicule continues. Used for contemporary social and political themes, it is a powerful weapon in the hands of such writers as Zebedee Nungak, Alootook Ipellie, and Alexis Utatnaq. The traditional oral forms, too, are being adapted to contemporary song composition and spontaneous folk-drama sketches. And the ancient marvel of their land – and the perspective that it imposes – still inspire the imagination to create story and song.

Thus, in their treatment of both traditional and contemporary subjects, we witness a cross-fertilization of the indigenous and the borrowed literary traditions, and a cross-cultural blend of the Inuit and Euro-American. Contemporary writing reflects the influence of a highly developed oral tradition that goes back to myth and song, an imitation of western models, minority sensibility, a cosmopolitan consciousness, and an imaginative capacity to create new forms.

Canadian Inuit writing in English is evolving. A growing number of Inuit writers are speaking for themselves about themselves in English. They are writing with a new pride and authority in their physical and spiritual roots and with a new confidence in their own literary efforts. They have fused a reverence for the past with an eloquent vision of the future – a union and continuum sustained by language – by words indigenous to a northern land, its seasons, and weather, its varied topography, its animals, its peoples, and its history.

A reverence for the sacredness of the word has marked all Canadian Inuit literature. And young Inuit writers today continue to believe, as their forefathers before them, that in language will they find the true meaning of their ancient northern homeland.

O   **Willie Thrasher** (1949–), singer and musician, was born in Aklavik, and played drums for an Inuit rock group in Inuvik. He likes to compose songs with the sounds of his homeland in the background: drum-dancing, wolves howling, arctic winds, and the Arctic Ocean. The following passage reveals his concern about his heritage and his land.

Our Land

... we are now in a struggle to retain the land. I believe that we are not only fighting for the land, but also for the animals living on it, the trees, the barren lands. We are fighting for the wind, the moon, sun and stars to keep on shining down. Only the Inuit can stand up, and they will help each other no matter what happens, and we'll keep on trying to save as much as we can. No matter where you work, no matter what you do, there's someone always there beside you, helping you. Inuit are a race of people that has gone through a lot for the past 100 years. We once had a great life. Like the old men say, this is our country. They were born on it, they feed on it, they die on it. They're gone now, and it's our job to keep on fighting for this land.

Just remember one thing: many times the clouds drop tears on the ground, then a flower grows. Many times the ice comes back, then we have to go on our dog teams to go hunting. It used to be a beautiful life. The moon shined for us during the night time; the sun came in the morning, and the animals did their part, to sleep, to kill, to survive. Now the wolf does the same thing. He roams around, killing to live. So does the polar bear and the seal, and the fish around us. Now it's our turn to save them, because the animals of the North cannot do the fighting. It's we Inuit who have to stand up and save as much land as possible. Always remember this is our land, the Inuit country.

'Willie Thrasher Tells about His Music,' *Inuit Today*, 5, 1 (January 1976) 32–3

O   **Alice French** (1930–) was born on Baillie Island in the Northwest Territories. As a child, she attended All Saints' Residential School in Aklavik for seven years. She wrote about her childhood experiences in *My Name Is Masak*, an excerpt of which follows.

My Name Is Masak

In the spring of 1937 when I was seven years old my father told my brother and me that our mother had tuberculosis. We would have to go from Cambridge Bay to the hospital in Aklavik. So when the Hudson's Bay Company ship came in with supplies, my father and mother and my brother, Aynounik, and I, sailed back on it. We got measles on board and that made my mother even sicker. I didn't know how long it took us to make that trip but it seemed to last forever.

When we landed at Aklavik my mother went to the hospital and my brother and I were told we would be going to a boarding school, whatever that was. My father tried to explain that a boarding school was where children lived and went to school. He would not be able to take care of us while mother was in the hospital and we would have to stay there. I did not like the idea. My brother was only three years old and too young to understand.

Alone

How could there be so many people living in one building? I was so scared that I hung onto my father's hand. I did not like it there and I did not want my father to leave us. There were too many people. My brother was taken away by one of the supervisors. I tried not to cry in front of my father – he felt bad enough as it was.

An Eskimo girl, whose dialect I did not understand, took me to the playroom. She was talking to me in Eskimo, but it did not make sense. Thank goodness she spoke English too. She told me that we were having supper soon. I asked her if I would see my brother. She said yes, at supper time. Then she introduced me to the other girls by my Christian name – Alice. My Eskimo name was not mentioned and I did not hear my name Masak again until I went home.

Then I became aware of different languages. I asked my new friend what dialect the girls were speaking. I was told that it was the language of the Mackenzie Delta and that most of the Eskimo children were from there, except for a few from Coppermine and Cambridge Bay. There were a lot of Indian children from the upper Mackenzie. They were mostly Loucheux with some Dogribs and Slaveys.

Then a white lady came in to tell us it was supper time. Everyone got into line except me. She took my hand and told me her name was Miss Neville. I was taken to one of the lines and told that this would be my place from now on. We marched in single file to the dining-room. Suddenly, I saw my little brother. I started towards him, but I was told to stay in line. How little he looked, lost and lonesome. I felt like going over to tell him that everything was going to be all right, only I was not too sure of that myself.

After supper we went back to our side of the school. I did not even get to talk to my brother. We saw each other only at mealtimes. Sometimes we had the chance to shout at each other while playing outside but even outside the boys and girls were not allowed to mix.

Sometime later that fall Reverend H.S. Shepherd, our minister, came to the school to tell me that my mother had died. I did not believe him because I had visited her that morning. I went back to the hospital to find her but the bed she had been in was empty. How could she be there one day and not the next? I felt terribly alone. She was the only link I had with home and the life I had been used to. My father had gone back to his trap-line and we would not hear from him for a long time. It was not out of cruelty but out of necessity that he left us.

Boarding School

Inside the school we had four dormitories on the girls' side. I was in the youngest girls' dormitory for ages six to eight. The dormitories were joined by a big common washroom. There were towel hooks along both walls, wash basins, and jugs of water on a long table. Little brushes and tins of powder were on a shelf built into the middle of the table. I had to wait to see what the other girls would use the little brushes for, so I watched what they did with them as we got ready for bed.

So that was what it was – to brush your teeth with. I wondered what that was supposed to do for you. Somebody told me that it was to keep you from having holes in your teeth. They certainly did have a lot of strange ideas. Another idea was combing your hair with coal oil when you first came to the school. That was to kill the head lice. I didn't have any but we all had to suffer through the coal-oil treatment whether we had lice or not.

Our house mother's name was Annie and she had a room just off the washroom. She told me that my mother was her cousin. That did not mean that I would be favoured above the other girls, but it felt good to know that I had a relative close at hand. She got us off to bed at night and woke us up in the morning.

The staff in our school slept in rooms off the hallway. Downstairs were two big classrooms, kitchen, staff dining-room, children's dining-room, principal's office, laundry room, a furnace room and two playrooms. The lavatory used to be outside until they had one built into the side of our playroom. The whole of the basement was a storeroom for school supplies and food was kept there, like in a root cellar.

Our days started at seven in the morning. We dressed, washed, and brushed our teeth, made our beds and tidied our dorms. Then we went down to breakfast at eight o'clock.

Breakfast usually was porridge, sweetened with molasses, bread and jam, and tea to drink with sugar and milk. It never varied except on holidays. At nine we went to the classrooms. Then a break for lunch – soup, bread and powdered milk – and back to school again. Supper was the big meal of the day with fish, meat, potatoes, dessert, bread and tea. We had this at five-thirty, usually after a walk around town, or out into the country with our teacher. Bedtime was seven o'clock for the little ones, eight o'clock for the next lot and so on, until the oldest were in bed at ten and the lights were out. I expect it was the same for the boys.

While we were getting ready for bed we talked about the scary stories we would tell after the lights were out. I shivered thinking about them while I brushed my teeth. Betty, standing next to me at the sink, jabbed me in the ribs and scared me half to death.

'Hey Alice,' she said. 'Did you know that we have a ghost in our dorm? She always sits in the corner combing her hair and you can see the blue sparks flying in every direction.' I started to shake because my bed was in one of the far corners of the room.

'Which corner?' I asked in a quavery voice.

'Your corner,' she said, and went off to bed.

Then Miss Neville came in and I pleaded with her to tell us a story. As long as she was telling a story the lights would stay on and maybe the girls would go to sleep or be too tired to tell ghost stories.

'Not tonight, Alice,' said Miss Neville. 'All right, girls, time for bed. No talking after lights out, please.'

She looked around to make sure that we were all under our covers and then she turned out the light and closed the door. It sure was dark in there then. I made certain that my bedding was loose so that I could jump out of bed fast if I had to.

Then they began to tell stories. Why did they always have to be scary ones – reindeer herders taking a coffin creaking through the woods on a sleigh, men reincarnated in dogs, rattling doors and the Devil's cloven hoof-prints on the snow?

Connie, whose bed was closest to the door, was posted as lookout. Her job was to tell us if someone was coming, but she was a most unlikely choice for the job. She talked more than any of us, and often she would forget that she was supposed to be listening for the supervisor's footsteps. As a result we were caught talking and were punished. We had to stand in the corner of the room for half an hour. This got to be very cold, for all we had on was our nightdresses.

One night I was punished in another way for using my bed as a trampoline. I was showing the girls how to go into a standing position from a belly flop. As I came down the bed collapsed to the floor with a crash. Just as I disappeared from view into the bedding, the door opened and there stood Miss Melville.

'What is going on here?' she asked sternly.

There was a silence while I climbed from the ruins of my bed. She came over and grabbed my shoulder and gave me a good shaking.

'Alice, how many times have I told you not to jump on your bed?'

'Many times, Miss Melville,' I answered with my teeth rattling in my head.

'That is correct,' she said. 'For being a naughty and disobedient child you shall sleep in your bed just as it is for a week. Now all of you settle down and no more nonsense.'

I climbed into bed and found that it was quite comfortable. In the morning I work up and realized that I had slept through the night without once waking up because of the cold. By the end of the week I had grown quite attached to my bed on the floor and hated to give it up for another.

Friday night was bath night. All one hundred and twenty-five of us were issued clean bedding and clothing. This consisted of one pair of long underwear, one pair of fleece-lined bloomers, one pair of black woollen stockings, a navy blue dress and clean towels. We took this with us and all headed for the laundry room. Inside there were eight galvanized tubs ready for use. These tubs were all filled by hand and had to be emptied the same way. We bathed two to a tub. Sometimes it got so steamed up that we could not see who our partners were. Our hair was washed by the bigger girls. Following this a jug of cold water was poured over us. This was to shrink our pores so that we would not catch cold, we were politely told.

Saturday was the most pleasant day of the week. We did all our housework in the morning – sweeping and dusting and tidying our dorms. After lunch, if we had parents in town, we could go home for the afternoon. I sometimes went home with my good friend who was called Peanuts because of her size. Her house was right in Aklavik. Then we went out to the Hudson's Bay store or to visit our other friends. Sometimes we just stayed at home enjoying the family atmosphere. After the crowded school life it felt good to be by ourselves for a while. Her mother would remind us that it was almost time to leave and we would collect some dried meat, bannock, butter, and sweets to take back to school with us.

Once a week, usually on Sunday, we were given seven candies by our supervisor. We were not allowed to eat them all at once. Instead we put them in a small box with our name on it and each night before bedtime we were allowed to have one candy. Sometimes we promised a friend a candy in return for a favour, and so that day we would have to go without.

Something else that we had each day was cod-liver oil, and it sure didn't taste good. It came in five-gallon cans on the boat during the summer. Before it was dished out it was poured into a two-pound can which our supervisor held. We would file past her each morning for a tablespoon and then dash to the toilet to spit it out. When our supervisor caught on to this

we had to stay and open our mouths to show that we had
swallowed the horrid stuff. I guess that was why we were so
healthy. But by the time the five-gallon can was empty it was
so rancid you could smell it a mile away. I have never taken
cod-liver oil since.

Alice French, *My Name Is Masak* 17–30

O   **John Amagoalik** (1945–) was born at Inukjuak, Quebec, and
     grew up in Resolute Bay. A former president of the Inuit
     Tapirisat of Canada, co-chairman of the Inuit Committee for
     National Issues, and a member of the Nunavut Constitutional
     Forum, he is a prominent public figure in Inuit affairs. A vocal
     and hard-line supporter of Nunavut, he supports a tree-line
     boundary to divide the Northwest Territories. In 1977, John
     Amagoalik wrote this passionate appeal on behalf of his people.
     He is still championing their cause with the same vigour and
     conviction.

Will the Inuit Disappear from the Face of This Earth?

Will the Inuit disappear from the face of this earth? Will
we become extinct? Will our culture, our language and our
attachment to nature be remembered only in history books?
These questions bring a great sadness to me. To realize that
we Inuit are in the same category as the great whales, the bold
eagle, the husky and the polar bear brings me great fear. To
realize that our people can be classified as an endangered species is very disturbing. Is our culture like a wounded polar
bear that has gone out to sea to die alone? What can be done?
There does not seem to be one single answer to these
questions.

It may be true that the physical part of our culture has been
eroded to the point where it can never return to its full potential. But the non-physical part of our culture – our attitude
towards life, our respect for nature, our realization that others
will follow who deserve the respect and concern of present
generations – are deeply entrenched within ourselves. The
presence of our ancestors within ourselves is very strong. The
will to survive is there. This part of our culture will die a
slow death, if it ever dies at all. If we are to survive as a race,

we must have the understanding and patience of the dominant cultures of this country. We do not need the pity, the welfare, the paternalism and the colonialism which has been heaped upon us over the years.

We must teach our children their mother tongue. We must teach them what they are and where they came from. We must teach them the values which have guided our society over the thousands of years. We must teach them our philosophies which go back beyond the memory of man. We must keep the embers burning from the fires which used to burn in our villages so that we may gather around them again. It is this spirit we must keep alive so that it may guide us again in a new life in a changed world. Who is responsible for keeping this spirit alive? It is clearly the older people. We must have the leadership which they once provided us. They must realize this responsibility and accept it. If the older people will remember, the young must listen.

In a world which becomes more complicated with each passing year, we must rely on the simple, gentle ways of our people to guide us. In a world so full of greed, we must share. We must remember that, of all the things in this world, nothing belongs to us. Of what we take, we must share.

A lot of people tell me that we must forget the past, and instead, look to the future. To me it would be a mistake to completely ignore the past because the past determines the present and the present determines what will be in the future. Sometimes it is necessary to look to the past to make decisions about the future. When I talk about the future and try to describe what I would like for my children, some people sometimes say to me that I am only dreaming. What is wrong with dreaming? Sometimes dreams come true, if only one is determined enough. What kind of world would we live in if people did not have dreams? If people did not strive for what they believe in. We must have dreams. We must have ideals. We must fight for the things we believe in. We must believe in ourselves. But there are also realities we must face. We can only attempt to make the best of any given situation or circumstances. If we are not successful, we must not give up hope. We must tell ourselves that we can only try a little harder the next time.

Over the past few years, in my visits to Inuit communities,

I have had many private conversations about what is happening to our people and what the future holds for us. I have become more and more concerned about the angry words which some of our people are starting to use. I cannot really blame them for their feelings. Their feelings towards the white man are easy to understand. It is very easy to blame the white man for the predicament we find ourselves in today. But anger and hate are not the answers. We need the patience and understanding of our white brothers. If we are to expect that from them, we must offer the same in return. The Inuit, by nature, are not a violent people. This is one of our virtues which we must not lose.

It disturbs me a great deal to hear about native organizations squabbling with other native organizations. If we are to achieve anything, we must not fight among ourselves. We can agree to disagree, but we must sort out our problems together. We must be of one mind and of one voice. This is not always possible among human beings. But we must not let petty disagreements divide us.

The Inuit were once strong, independent and proud people. That is why we have survived. That strength, that independence, and that pride must surface again. We must prove to Canada that the original citizens of this country will not lie down and play dead. After all, the Inuit have been described by the United Nations as a people who refuse to disappear.

'John Amagoalik', 'Will the Inuit Disappear', *Inuit Today*, 6, 4 (May 1977) 52–4

O   **Armand Tagoona** (1926–), preacher, artist, translator, and writer, was born at Repulse Bay. In 1959 he was the second Canadian Inuk in history to be ordained deacon in the Anglican Church and has since translated much of the scriptures into Inuktitut. In 1960 he was ordained an Anglican priest. In this article Tagoona reflects on a variety of subjects.

Thoughts of Armand Tagoona

Christmas, my first recollection of the birth of Christ was when I was a small boy living in the Iglulik area. Inuit gathered for a feast in the iglu and passed out something that looked like little pieces of bread that tasted sweet. My second recollection was when Inuit gave Christmas presents of dogs. I used to get scared when they brought the dogs into the iglu to give to the person.

After that I remember Christmas in Chesterfield Inlet. Tuugaaq, Singutug's son and the adopted son of Anguti, were at a dance in the Hudson Bay Company's house. We were told not to stay up that night, but to go to sleep so that Santa Clause would give us something. Santa Clause, we were told, gives only to good boys and to those who listen. While they were still dancing we went to sleep as we believed it to be true. When we woke up in the morning, yes, indeed, we saw packages. Inside were toys for us and this made us believe more that there is a Santa Claus.

I saw many Christmases in Baker Lake, Rankin Inlet and Eskimo Point. When we were still small we thought that Jesus was born every year. I never gave much thought to why He was born every year. I also believed that on Good Friday of every year He died and rose again. Christmases that I remember now and before are not the same. It seems Christmases in the past were happier than now. Maybe it is the fact that I have also changed as well as Christmas. When we are small there is no unhappiness. When we grow to manhood we notice the things that make us happy and unhappy. It's the mind that does these things. I know one thing, when I was young there was no alcohol at Christmas, so no one got drunk. Also, everybody – men, women and children – went to church on Christmas Day. No one stayed out.

In the past there were also different games on Christmas Day. There was running, tug-of-war, dog races and many others. When night came, we had a dance. In the past, there weren't very much people together on Christmas Day. Every year more and more people are together on Christmas Day. I'm not sure that because more are gathered together it is happier than the past. Many of us still think it was a mistake to put all the people in one place. We know three people together are happier than one hundred together. Three people's lives are cleaner than one hundred people.

Life is Different Today
Some say that older people are not giving younger people advice anymore. Advice on how to live the good life if they want

212

their life to be a success. Older people are still willing to tell young people, but young people don't have time to listen anymore. In the past, older people used to talk to young people because they were ready to listen anytime and do what the older man or women advised. Young people understood that older people's advice proved to be best most of the time. Those who did otherwise were sorry afterwards that they didn't obey.

These days, not too many young people want to listen to older people. They don't want to be given advice, they do what they want. That is one of the reasons older people are not giving advice to the young any more. They would, still, if given the time and respect by the young. Today, life is, 'I'll live my life the way I want to live it, and you do the same.' Please don't misunderstand me. I'm not criticizing young people and I'm not putting them down. I know something makes them live that way and do these things. Sometimes they are not even the way they want to be themselves. Something unseen makes them do things they don't want to do.

Today, young people can't sit still anymore, but go day and night. The only time they stop is when they sleep. Again, something makes them do these things. We know that in the past the night was a time for sleeping and the day for being up. Today, this is not so.

I think that the minds of people are very tired. Too many things to think about, more than they can handle. Everything is fast – trucks, cars, Hondas, ski-doos, airplanes, canoes with powerful engines, Man can't or doesn't want to walk anymore. He wants to get there as fast as he can. When he must walk, he is too lazy. Life today is confusing.

When little ones grow to be young boys and girls they are like grown or old men. Even little ones use tobacco. Most children eat nothing but chocolate and sweets. Only once in a while they eat something that is real. Every day they ask for a dollar from their parents so they can buy more sweets. No wonder most of them have no teeth left, they rot while they are still very small. I am not putting them down, but putting down and hate whatever it is that makes them do these things. I'm not saying that all children are the same. Thank God there are many good and clean children.

As I said before, I think the minds of people are very tired.

When the mind is tired, the person easily gets mad. Man is getting madder and madder every year. That is not his desire, but he can't help it. The prices of items in the stores are getting higher every year. Food prices are up. A man doesn't have enough money to pay his debt at the Bay or enough to pay his rent. His children must go to school almost every day. The mining, exploration and pipeline plans are bothering him, his land and his animals. For these things and many other things, man is made mad. He even gets mad at others without reason. These things are happening because there are too many people in one settlement with too many ways. If this kind of life continues to grow, the future is ugly and we are travelling toward Hell. Happiness will take the place of Hell in our future, only if some come who know how.

Generation
Man cannot help but love those who are getting old, who were one time young. Everyone knows that the young get old, then life ends. We know many people who were young and very active. They were the envy of many, and now they are old and soon their lives will end. This also will come to all the young people. All this comes by itself and no mere man can stop it. I said these things because time and life are always changing. The type of life are always changing. The type of life of the past is passing away. It would be useless if we tried to live it today. The new type life is for today. We older people don't like the new type life of today. This will repeat itself from generation to generation. Our ways always seem to be the best kind of life, and the rest always the bad kind. Even though the life of our children is different from ours we should try to understand it. We shouldn't force them to live like us. If we lived in their time we would have lived as they are today. A young person once said to me, 'Older people always think we live the bad life.'

In the past, the good hunter concentrated on being a real man and the good sewer on being a real woman. Today this is not so. In the past, the man looked for a wife who could sew well and the woman for a man who could hunt well. Today this is not so. Men today, when they look for a wife, look for someone to love, someone they like and are thrilled by.

214

It doesn't make any difference if she is a good sewer or not. Women are the same. It doesn't matter if the man is a good hunter or not, if a woman loves and likes him, she marries him.

One time, a young girl who didn't like her father, said to her mother, 'I will marry the one you don't want me to marry. I would have tried to stop you from marrying the one you did, if I had been there.' I say these things to prove that the present generation always dislikes the next generation. The next generation always lives different from the passing generation, because time changes.

Churches
Churches are also changing. The form of church services in the past would be boring and useless today, although they were good and useful then. Today, unless the church services are hard and forceful we don't consider it useful. This is the time for it. I remember in the past, here in Baker Lake, we used to go to church with the whole family even when we had a severe blizzard. Inside, the church was very cold so you didn't warm up once you got in. It was so cold inside you could see your breath. The walls and ceiling were full of frost. When our breath reached the ceiling the frost dropped onto the floor and onto our heads and hands. It was not bad for women, as they were allowed to wear hats or a hood. For men it was different, we were not allowed to wear hats, but all of us wore gloves. I was the organist and often it was so cold I couldn't pump the organ. Sometimes I played the organ with my gloves on. No one complained, as we had no choice.

After the service we went out into the cold again. Our bodies were still cold and often children's faces and hands, even adults, were frost bitten or frozen. Today I don't think many people would go to a cold church on a stormy day. They would complain a lot and even get mad.

Today, the churches are warm. So warm you can even take your parka off if you want to. Now, churches have organs, guitars, amplifiers and loud speakers, soft floors and other things. When people sing along with the organ and guitar we can even dance. Some do dance to the songs and music in the churches today. In the North, the authority to dance is in

King David's Psalm 149:3 'let them praise his name in the dance.' In the past, we should have danced in the cold church to keep warm.

In the past we had only 151 gospel songs in Inuktitut. We sang the same ones over and over again. Now, there are over 500 gospel songs in Inuktitut. We don't have to sing the same song over and over again. Most of these songs are translated from English to Inuktitut.

It would be much better, now, if we Inuit started making our own gospel songs that we could feel. We notice that Inuit sing much better when we sing Inuk song, Ayaa-yaa. I don't mean that we should start singing Ayaa-yaa in our churches. I mean we should have our own songs, written by Inuit themselves. A white person told me that Inuit are very poor at singing white man's melody. When they start singing in Inuktitut melody, they are very good singers.

The churches in the Arctic should start making their own songs. It would be a sign of being Inuit, not having to copy the white man's way of church services.

Long ago, Inuit used to make beautiful songs, good and wise words with a beautiful melody. Now this is stopped because it was taken over by white man's songs and melody. There are young people today who play many different musical instruments but they only copy white man's songs. As one Inuk told me, 'I don't like their songs, because they are copying white man's songs.'

I myself have heard Inuit singing white men's songs and their voices are not too good. When they change to Inuit songs their voices change and sound very beautiful. White man's songs have stops, but Inuit songs do not. If two Inuks sing together, one stops to breathe and the other continues singing, like chanting. So, my desire is to have our own songs and our own melodies to praise God.

'Thoughts of Armand Tagoona,' *Inuktitut* (winter 1978) 47–56

O **Davidialuk Alasuaq Amittu** (c. 1910–76), a celebrated Inuk artist and storyteller, was born on a small island near Povungnituk, Quebec. He told of his life and work in *La Parole changée en pierre*, an excerpt of which follows.

La Parole changée en pierre

In the heart of the winter in 1910 when the 'Avunnit' moon is full, the moon of the occasional aborting seals which is the coldest time of the year, a great restlessness reigned over Nunagiirniraq's hunting camp. On this little Hudson's Bay island to which seems to cling the coastal ice field belting arctic Quebec, three snow igloos facing the open sea towards free water, ice floes and waterfowl, emit a hot white smoke from their ventilation shafts.

The hunters left this morning to hunt the ringed seal, despite the overcast weather. The women in Aqpatuq's igloo busy themselves while Amituq's wife, who is in the process of giving birth, crouches down on a caribou skin in the Inuit way. Advised by her mother, she scrupulously followed the prescriptions of the pregnant women, getting up first, and going outside every morning to incite the fetus to a quick and healthy birth. She loosened her hair and her bootlaces in order to avoid any entanglement of the umbilical cord around the baby's neck – and then the moment approached. Those who aren't directly involved in the birth process are forced to run out so as to influence the baby to leave his little uterine house. The mother and the sisters-in-law of the labouring woman surround her and help her. Her hands are held. Her stomach is hugged tightly to facilitate the expulsion. And then the newborn baby appears, her first son. The biggest helper, the one who was placed behind her takes the baby into her right arm so that he will be right-handed. Then she takes hold of his penis to prevent its shrinking and its splitting. It is believed that in effect, a boy can transform himself into a girl and therefore become an 'Arnaruqtuq' (a deficient boy).

Outside the weather is still overcast. It is fine weather for hunting and later when the child is big, he will be a 'companion to overcast weather.' He will influence the weather in this way whenever he goes hunting. The umbilical cord is quickly tied with a braid of sinew. Then, after it is cut, and the placenta is cleaned up, the newborn's skin is wiped with birdskins. Aqpatuq is happy and proud; she is anxious to read the joy in the faces of her husband, Amittuq, and her old father, Alasuaq.

And then the old man enters; everyone draws away in a quasi-religious deference; the emotion is intense for he asked that his name be given to the infant. Their lives will be but one now; he can disappear. All his experience, all his knowledge and power, all his strength and his longevity are going to be communicated to the newborn just as he once received them in his grandfather's namesake and this stems all the way back to the very beginning. Everyone will now address the newborn as though he were an elder. Little Alasuaq becomes the father of his own mother, the father-in-law of his father, etc.; he will be respected and loved. So, protected by an adult taboo and a proven affection he could endure through all the dangers which are encountered by a child in his first few years. As the living symbol of the Inuit tradition, he will participate from this point on in the maintenance of cultural order and to the continuation of the group if often threatened by physical hardship, by man's madness, by force of the spirits.

They will give him an extra protection, another of his grandfather's names: Davidialuk (the Great David), which he received many decades ago from Qallunaaq ('big eyebrow,' White ...) with Uqammaq's long beard [Reverend Edmund Peck], the man with the magic word which brought to the Inuit the great Book of the White Man containing their beliefs and without a doubt, the secrets of their power. Until then they saw the arrival of the Whites as the great migrating species, who with each summer passed in the open sea off the Inuit coasts in their strange boats and left again just as mysteriously in autumn.

These white men who fascinated the Inuit for generations because of the precious goods they possessed: metal and firearms. These whitemen whom they also dreaded, they who were allied with the Indians from the south and who sent them sometimes to decimate Inuit bands. These Whitemen so powerful in their boats or their establishments but so weak when they were lost or grounded on Inuit land that they (Inuit) therefore did not hesitate to massacre them in order to lay hold of their possessions. At Kuuvik, the place of Alasuaq's origin, a crew of whitemen who survived a shipwreck were killed not too long ago.

Before the arrival of Uqammaq, they had learned to mistrust

the Whiteman because of their greediness for the products from the Inuit country – the furs, ivory, and the women as well. Then things were getting better, and a few of the Inuit from the coast were now going regularly to visit the mission at the time of the annual voyages to the trading post at Kuujjuaraapik (Big Whale River), 500 km to the south ...

The sun only showed itself a few hours above the horizon on that winter day. Darkness had already invaded the camp when Amittuq and Aupaluktaaluk, his brother-in-law, returned from the hunt, each one pulling the seal that he killed.

Upon entering the igloo, the happy father had difficulty in hiding his joy for finally having a son. A future hunter could assist him one day, then replace him as the provider of game, who could also through the lives of the children that he will procreate in his turn, perpetuate that of his ascendants.

Amittuq still has present in his mind the tragic separation from his first wife, when with the whole group, they were carried away by drifting ice, pushed by a violent east wind.

It was three years ago in the beginning of spring, when they returned with their six-dog teams from the trading post at the Kuujjuaraapik (Big Whale River), at the tree line. There, they had their pelts exchanged for various imported products and on the way, they had cut a significant provision of wood which they needed in order to build the qajaq. His old father Talirunili died on the way, near Inujjuaq, and it was his mother, Aullaq that they now went to see for important decisions. She was surrounded by four of her children and their families, which constituted the core of the group. Putagulq, her eldest son, whose wife Paaluk carried their little Juu Talirurnilik [the artist Joe Talirunili], hardly one year old, on her back; Arnasualuk also and her sister Angutausugiq. There was also a friend of the family, Surniq, Alasuaraaluk's brother, and Nuvalingaq with his brother, Qumaq. Miggamiq, as well as all the others ... they were about forty. The sleds advanced slowly on the ice field. They were approaching Kuugaaluk and already they could see the camp tents from afar. Amittuq's young wife, Iqqumiaq, who had walked ahead a little, had already reached the place, when, behind her, the ice floe suddenly detached itself washing away her husband and his party into the open sea. They were never to see each other again.

After the moment of panic following the break-up of the ice, they organized, under the direction of Aullaq, the lives of the survivors and all through the spring, they drifted a hundred km into the open sea. But the small island was beginning to melt; it was extremely urgent that they plan boat launchings. The men decided to build the qajaq with the wood brought from the south, but that meant the abandonment of the old men, the nurses, and a few children. Amittuq was strongly opposed to this idea, and took advantage of another solution: they would build a collective 'umiaq'; everyone considers this task carefully. They unhitched the sleds in order to make the frame and the women put together a waterproof blanket made from the seal skins from those killed while enroute. They raised a mast and let out a sail made of skin and embarked on another new adventure of extreme risk: the judging of navigation in the narrow channels of free water between the moving fields of ice. The islands finally appeared on the horizon. Aullaq identified them. They were the Arviliit (Ottawa Islands), a traditional high-ground for the Inuit. It is there where Lumaajuq's family lived for a very long time; this infamous mother who profitted from her son's sufferance of snowblindness of depriving him of his first polar-bear that he just killed and making him believe that it was their dog. They had been released by their friends from camp and lacked food. The selfish mother only wanted to share the bear with her daughter. But the tuuliq (big fishhawks) willfully restored the young man's sight, who in witnessing his mother's disgrace, decided to take revenge on her. He asked her to attach herself to the extreme end of the thin strap at the end of his harpoon to help him hoist up the wild animals on the shore when he hunts the belugas who were arriving in herds in the waters off the island. The mother accepted, hoping in return to receive a significant share, but instead of harpooning a young beluga, as was the habit in this type of hunt, he stuck the harpoon in the biggest beluga of the herd and the indignant mother was dragged into the waves where he still comes to see her attached to the beluga. When she surfaces with the animal, they can hear her cry Lumaaq, Lumaaq ...

Everyone in the boat was familiar with the legend, but it was the first time that they saw this mythical land. For a long time the Inuit have lived there, perhaps some still remain. A whaling boat was smashed to pieces there; the wreckage and the remains of a dwelling of some fortune still exist, it seems, and the shadow of this mystery which surrounds the island strengthens when they suddenly have the impression that in spite of the oarsmen's efforts, they were staying in a fixed place. They rowed all day but towards evening, they had not progressed one stroke. Aullaq then remembered having heard in his youth that when one arrives on a new land for the first time this land is disturbed, like a woman approached by strange visitors. She keeps them at a distance preventing their coming near. It was necessary to defeat her resistance by hurling a projectile at her. Amittuq did just that, by firing a gunshot in the direction of the high cliff which blocked the horizon. Immediately the spell on the boat broke and they attacked the cliff on foot among the cries of the 'pitsiulaaq' colonies (sea gulls) nesting in great numbers in this place. It was time.

They had profitted from the last minutes of calm sea waters, thanks to the ice fields which held back the waves. A storm began: the umiaq was pulled up onto the shore, turned over and they took shelter there for seven days, with nothing to feed anyone, but some scraps of meat, and skin and bones from the small game killed before the departure. The children screamed with hunger; the adults were starving, they had nothing more than skin on bones – skin which was burnt all over by the sun in the beginning of the summer, on which they subsisted both day and night. The tension was thick. Aullaq was convinced that if the storm should continue they would have no other solution than to survive by eating the weakest of the group. And that is what would have ensued.

In great haste and despite everyone's weakness, they took to the sea once more to search for a safer place and for an access to the island's interior. They moved slowly along the southern coast of Arviliit's principal island, when suddenly they saw three tents on the shore, as well as moving human bodies. All the occupants were filled with great hope. The rowers accelerated their pace and Aullaq, standing on the makeshift ladder, began to wave his arms. But far from arousing any enthusiasm, the arrival of the survivors seemed to provoke a great commotion. Women and children ran for refuge in their tents. Three men armed with their spears and their knives headed up the bank watching the slightest movements of the group, ready to defend dearly their lives and those of the others. Never have they seen in the Arviliit a boat attack in the beginning of July. They waited for no one and trembling still at the memory of the drama which had so cruelly hit their families, the three men tried to understand what was happening. Were they Allait (Cree Indians) in search of war trophies who came to attack them by surprise, like that which happened along the Hudson Bay coasts, which is believed on the basis of the accounts of the elders particularly when a boat of white men was reported missing and when the news was peddled all the way south that the crew members were massacred by the Inuit. Were they shipwrecked Qullunaat (Whitemen) wanting to be rescued? One knows therefore, the eagerness and the strength that they represented confronted by three Inuit families. Were they spirits?

During this time, in the umiaq, they thought they recognized the three men. Surmiq thought he could distinguish Kanrva-lik, his old camp friend from Kuuvik, before the drama which had staggered Saniraq's population (region situated between Cape Wolstenholme and Cape Smith). The other two perhaps were Takkataq, his son-in-law, and Quinnuajuaq, who with him ran off in the dead of the winter to the bridge of ice which separated the island from the continent. Hence, from his powerful voice Aullaq began to cry out 'Hey, we are Inuit!' 'We are not Allait. We are not Qullunaat, we drifted with the ice floe.' Then as they were right next to the shore and many were related to the three families of the island, he called off all the occupants of the boat by name. On the shore the men made visible efforts to recognize their relatives in these walking cadavres who were made thin and darkened by the sun. Finally, the fear subsided; they called those who had stayed in the tent and this brought on an outburst of joy. They were crying as they told each other of the adventures that had been experienced by both sides. And firstly, they fed the newcomers plenty of fresh or dried food. Then they took care of organizing their installation in the best way possible in the camp. They made tents with the blanket from the boat and also with the beluga whale skins. To imitate the islanders, they made a rock-base for tents in order to save the skins. Little by little, life regained its course ...

Saladin d'Anglure, *La parole changée en pierre* 14–23, translated from the French by Carolyn Oleksak

O **Joshua Obed** (1906–81), hunter, trapper, and pilot, was orphaned during the 1918 influenza epidemic that wiped out the settlement in Labrador. As a result, he went to live with his aunt in Nutak, where he became active with the Moravian mission, playing the organ, violin, and a number of brass instruments for the church band. When the mission station at Nutak was closed in 1956, Obed moved to Nain where he was employed by the provincial government as a pilot until 1971.

Descriptions of illness and epidemics were among the most vivid of Inuit recollections. Obed recalled the terrible devastation caused by the flu epidemic.

The Spanish Flu, 1918

Soon after we were left by the epidemic in which so many people died, I was the one who was left alive. Let me tell you about it, how we were left as orphans in Hebron in 1918. In 1919 I had my thirteenth birthday. There was no longer a question of celebrating the young men's day. When the young men's day came, there were no young men to celebrate – not when I turned thirteen. Ruth and her mother came to Hebron just before the epidemic struck, on a mail boat, when Webb went to the place where there was a war. They went to stay at Hebron. Soon after she arrived, the mother broke out in red pimples and died, while her husband was away at war. In the end we heard that the Germans lost the war. Just at the same time people here were dying from the epidemic. I was not depressed or anything like that, because I was just a child at the time. I was able to use a gun, and when dogs got into peoples' houses in order eat the dead, we started to shoot at them because they were eating corpses. McLean, one of our storekeepers, and I were the ones who shot dogs. My mother's house was full of dead people, the people covered the floor. Some were lying on the clothes boxes, some on the floor touching each other ... We had five dogs, some of which belonged to Timothy. It seemed as if they would not move away from the house. I think there were five of them. They did not seem to be eating corpses, that's why we never shot them.

One morning they were gone, nowhere in sight. I did not see them anywhere when I went out in the morning for a breath of air. Because they were not in the porch, I was told to go to see if they were in my mother's house, where there were dead people. I peeped in through the window to see if those five dogs were eating corpses, too, because a lot of dogs were eating dead people at that time. We thought maybe those five dogs were doing the same. But they were not inside the house, so I started to call for them near the house with the dead people and dogs. Then, faintly, I thought I heard someone crying on the floor inside the house. I must have got scared, because I ran to other people to tell them I had heard someone crying inside the house among all the dead. This was in the morning – my aunt would be away every morning. She went and she started to check the house, and then there seemed to be nothing to be heard, no sound of anyone crying inside.

... After a time, the houses with the dead people were smoked out, before anyone entered to try and remove the bodies. We worked on my mother's house first because it was so full, and then we worked on the other houses. The houses were not built like the houses that people use now. The smell of bodies burning came through very strongly because I was helping others to burn houses. I went near the entrance of a burning house, and the smell of the whole thing came to me, and that same evening I got ill and nearly died. I threw up bile, and after that I felt a little better. I was sick for a long time, not being able to get out of bed all the while. There were people still dying after my grandfather and family had gone. I was not able to help others because I was sick in bed myself for a long time. There were still many people dying.

There were many foxes around at that time. Beata and my Aunt Caroline and I went to get firewood from the house we were going to have built. My brother and I got the logs for our house from Napatok before the epidemic struck. We were going to have the house at Hebron. We hauled the logs near Hebron from Napatok. There were many of them, and it turned out that they were to be our firewood during the epidemic. Because there were so many logs for firewood, and because I have never felt depressed by it all, being a child, while Aunt Caroline and Beata were pulling me on sledges, I was sure I saw a fox just when the women walked over a dead dog. Sure enough there was a fox, just in the right position to be an ideal target. It had been fighting the dogs. Fox would even go around the village. There were many foxes then. There were always foxes around any time I went off anywhere. People were always coming back with foxes on their backs.

Our Footprints Are Everywhere 320–1

O   **Leah Idlout d'Argencourt** (1940–), interpreter, translator, and writer, was born near Pond Inlet. She was one of the editors of *Inuit Today* and an early editor of *Inuktitut*. In 1988 she was living in Ottawa, an active member of the Inuit Tapirisat of Canada.

During the 1940s and 1950s, the Canadian government tried to cut down the tuberculosis that was threatening to wipe out the Inuit population of the north. The medical expedition ship, *C.D. Howe*, was sent to the various communities and the inhabitants examined. Many victims of the disease were sent to hospitals in the south for treatment. Eleven-year-old Leah became one of this number when her X-rays on the ship detected the disease. Here she tells her story.

C.D. Howe

... It all happened so fast, I scarcely had time to think. By the time we arrived back on the ship, I knew for sure that it was true, that I was really going, although I was totally unprepared and didn't even have any baggage to take along ...

I hardly remember anything that was happening or being said to me at the time of departure, except that my dear oldest sister Rebecca (Qitsualik) was crying. Was I going away for good? I didn't feel sick. Was I going to die in the white man's hospital? It terrified me to think of these things ...

All I can remember was my father's boat that I could hardly see anymore through my foggy eyes, so many tears were flooding warmly down my cheeks. And I couldn't wipe them away, for if I did, everyone would notice me crying there. There were so many white people lined up on the upper deck, watching as the C.D. Howe moved away from the settlement. I tried hard to hold back my tears, at the same time straining to keep sight of my father's boat until I could hardly tell which one was my mom or dad.

Then the ladders folded back into place, which meant that nobody would be able to leave the ship again until it reached the next settlement ... I had no idea or picture in my mind of what it would be like to travel on the big ship for a long trip. Now nobody from the settlement was ever again going to be able to climb back on board with us. Done is done.

I was not going to jump to the salt water either in order to get back with my family. Even though I so badly wanted to stay and never go away, I was far too terrified of the deep dark blue sea water below. I had never even wanted to leave my family, not even to go to other camps. I did go alone with my father to the settlement once. At that time I was so miserable to be away from the camp and my whole family that my father never took me away again.

No more than two or three hours after I first learned that I too would be a passenger this time, the C.D. Howe gave a whistle like she always did when she was leaving the settlement. Doug Wilkinson and his wife Vivian were leaving at the same time after having spent three months with us at the camp ... Doug pulled me back under the ladders, because of the dirt that was dropping down like rain from the whistling ship. I couldn't care less if I got dirty or not, just as long as I could see my father's boat. At that moment, that was all that mattered. I was feeling so full of loss, like a baby seal without its mother ...

I didn't bring any extra clothing with me, but had only the things I was wearing: long underwear, bloomers, a dress, a duffle parka with white cover, seal skin boots with duffle socks and long, brown woolen stockings. I also had my Inuktitut New Testament and my handmade wooden dolls ...

It was very dark inside when we entered the lower level of the ship, even though there were portholes on either side. When my eyes finally adjusted to the dark, I could see beds screwed to the wall, one on top of the other like bunk beds, all in one open space. There was also one flush toilet room with a sink, a long table with benches on either side and a laundry sink to wash dishes. This was to be our place for the whole trip, for all the sick men, women and children.

I soon made friends with two young Inuit boys. One, from Arctic Bay, was about my age. The boys names were Suujuq Kadluk and Sanguja, Ituk's son. His family had lived with us once at our camp.

Attempting to settle in, we each picked our own bed. I chose the top bunk over Suujuq's bed. My bed had 'white' sheets that looked like they had never been changed. They had a strong human smell, and a dirty bed spread over top. These were the beds waiting for us – the sick passengers! There were no ladders to climb up to the top bunks, but somehow I learned a way to climb up to my bed. Climbing up wasn't so hard but climbing down was awkward because the beds were made of metal with sharp rims that threatened to cut your skin.

I remember the heater in that room that, once in awhile, made so much noise that it sounded like a man hammering and banging at the pipes. Somehow I got used to sleeping there, but it was an awful scary noise to wake up to in the middle of the night.

Soon after the ship moved away from Pond Inlet, I went back outside to get some fresh air and to see what the land looked like around us. I was amazed at what I saw! I was seeing landscapes in the Pond Inlet area, which had always been my home, that I never seen before: high cliffs, foggy, with snowwhite caps on the mountains, and so cold looking that it made you feel lonely and shiver all over. Suddenly the ship seemed so empty. All the white passengers and crew had disappeared. I started to cry again. I thought then that, if I ever return to my family and visited Pond Inlet, which had been so scary to me before, it would never be as frightening as the C.D. Howe. I felt a huge lump swelling in my throat and an emptiness in my heart. I had never felt so alone before.

There were no white people in our eating, sleeping and crying place. And I had no idea what their living area, in the white, painted upper level of the C.D. Howe, was like inside. Then one day, Doug Wilkinson came to see us, and he took me to his cabin. It was a miserable day, rough and stormy, and I had never felt so sick to my stomach before. Their cabin looked so comfortable, and clean and tidy. It even had curtains over the port holes and a sink right in their own cabin. But I got so sick from the motion of the ship that I could hardly hold it any more, and I threw up right in their clean sink. They gave me a pill and a glass of water, then took me back to my Inuit fellowmen.

Whenever there was a rough day, the ship would keep on rocking back and forth slowly for hours and hours. You could see the sea crashing over the portholes, first on one side of the ship and then on the other. Sometimes it seemed as though the C.D. Howe was going to turn right over on its side.

During the times when I was sea sick, I had to keep running back and forth to the toilet room. It seemed so far from my bed. I had to climb down and then back up again, so many times it seemed. If the toilet room was occupied and we couldn't wait, we would lean out the porthole to be sick.

As a little girl, the C.D. Howe had always seemed so huge to me compared to the motor boats we had. When she arrived in Pond Inlet, she would fill up the sea water across the whole front of the settlement. My father's motor boat usually seemed so big alone by itself, but it looked like a baby beside the ship. But now, the C.D. Howe looked so small too in the middle of the ocean.

We had no idea how long we had to travel before we reached the white man's land, and of course, I had no idea what the white man's land looked like. All I had ever seen were the colored pictures in Life magazine, full of dead bodies lying on the ground, wounded men, scenes of war with the Japanese, the families of the Queen and King George VI, the Russians, and so on ...

During the trip we were given three meals a day. They usually consisted of large portions of potatoes and boiled meat with a lot of fat that became thick and hard when it got cold. The fried eggs tasted like plastic, and the meat had its own peculiar taste too. Once in awhile we were given some fish, mostly on Fridays, but it was tasteless and odd smelling. There were no more Saturdays and Sundays for the family to get together. Back in the camp, that was always the time for my father to stay home with us, and to have Sunday services three times a day with the children. On board the ship, the only way I could time what time of the week it was, was on Fridays when we were served a fish meal.

We younger ones would set up the tables with the army-style, white, thick plates and a set of patterned tea cups that were just big enough to hold one gulp. It would get so noisy in there when we were eating with the knives and forks. They made a hard, sharp clicking sound like teeth when they hit together, and a screeching, cutting sound on the plates. They were so different from our own sharpened men's knives and ulus, or women's knives ...

At first, everyone would be so pleased to see the food brought in to us, after the long waiting hours; but it was always the same – meat and potatoes. Back at home, we were used to eating whenever we got hungry. Here on the ship, it seemed that we were always waiting and starving. For breakfast every single morning we had eggs and porridge over and over again, along with plenty of cold toast. But that was all there was, so we had no choice but to eat it. We younger kids were forced to eat by the older Inuit, although it was not too pleasing for our poor Inuit stomachs, both because of the sea sickness, and because we were not used to eating the white man's food, especially the stuff being prepared by the chefs on the C.D. Howe. Many times when the sea water was too rough, there would be fewer people to eat, only those who were strong enough to stand. We would eat what we could and then throw away the leftovers through the portholes, and the sea gulls following the ship would willingly finish them off.

Between meal times, there was nothing to eat or to chew, not even to drink. Here we were, travelling in the middle of the ocean with plenty of water all around us – even running water, all we wanted, but it was too dirty and awful tasting to drink.

Suujuq, Sanguja and I would go on deck once in awhile to run around and take a tour of the ship. It was fun to watch the ship moving forward, and at the same time to be running backwards.

Whenever we stopped at a settlement there would be an Inuit family there crying, which always meant somebody new was going away to hospital in the white men's land too ...

After the first long month on board the ship, I got so uncomfortable wearing the same clothing all the time, even to bed. One day, on a trip to the toilet room – that was so tiny, there was scarcely enough room even for the toilet – I locked myself in and examined my long underwear. There were clothing lice there of a kind that I had never seen before – something different from the ones in my hair. They were crawling slowly between the seams of my clothing, with their long white legs, big ones too. I really didn't know what to do. Crying was not going to do much good. It certainly wasn't going to scare them off and make them disappear. Instead, I spent hours locked in the only toilet room we had, slowly picking them off. I felt like flushing the whole thing down the toilet, but what was I going to wear instead? I was so uncomfortable, ichy [sic] and dirty all over, right down to my toes. At home, at least once a week, usually on Saturday, my mother used to give us a bath and change our clothing. But now I was miles and miles away from home, left alone to do everything myself. There was nothing much else I could do but pick them off one by one.

One time Suujuq and Sanguja almost had me scared to death. They told me they had met a man who was interested in making some kind of clay mask on us. Amazed, I answered, 'What? A clay-masking man? How would he do it?' They said that it was raw clay that he would put on our faces and then freeze it. They assured me that this was really true – that he wanted to have this done to us, the Eskimo kids ...

I didn't go of course ...

Once we saw a real live polar bear – it was the first time I had ever seen one. He was swimming frantically in front of the ship, trying hard to get away. He looked so scared, and I didn't blame him. Of course, when news got around that there was a polar bear, it seemed that everyone on board rushed out to watch. Lots of white people were taking pictures. I felt so sorry for him. The bear finally managed to get away on the ice and, relieved from the threat of the big ship, he ambled away.

The C.D. Howe had left Pond Inlet at the end of spring, 1951. It was not until the second or third week of October that the ship was finally approaching Quebec City.

It was really something to see the white men's land for the first time, especially after being on the water for so long. I had grown several months older on that ship without even once touching the ground. We didn't see any land at all for a long while either. Now we were entering the St. Lawrence River. It was late fall and there would already be plenty of snow at home, but there was no snow here yet. It was completely different in every way from the Arctic. The land was covered all over with amazing, beautiful green grass, and it was full of tall, green trees. We passed by hundreds and hundreds of houses, and wee-looking cars that, from a distance, looked exactly like the toy one Suujuq and I had received from one of the white passengers.

During the trip, the white people had always looked so clean, and even smelt clean. Now, when they came out to watch their land go by, they seemed to be even cleaner and more dressed up, with their southern coats of a kind that I had never seen before. The men especially looked strange in long coats that looked like women's dresses.

By the time we arrived in Quebec City, the white people's faces had become familiar to us. Now they were all happy-looking, and that made it all the more exciting to have finally arrived in the white man's land.

Part II: The Hospital

We arrived in Quebec City in the late fall of 1951. Unlike in the North, the C.D. Howe docked right close to the pier, so we didn't have to use any boat or barge to take us to the shore.

Everything that met our eyes on the shore's edge looked so unbelievable! All around us where the ship docked – the streets, sidewalks, parking lots – were concrete and so ugly-looking. Even the buildings were made out of stone and bricks. It was hard to believe that we were really seeing what was before us. Just to think that men had created all these things: the high buildings, some as high as 14 stories; buildings that seemed so long, they just went on and on; and rows of outdoor

231

lights all along the roads. It just seemed impossible that human beings had actually created such things! Probably in that very place once not too long ago there had been no buildings at all, just trees and grass.

There were already crowds of white people lined up on the pier waiting for the passengers to disembark from the C.D. Howe. It was so crowded that it was kind of scary, but we Inuit stayed close together so we wouldn't lose each other. None of us could understand either English or French. I had learned how to say 'hello' from the white passengers, but I was not about to say hello to anybody in Quebec City just then, I was scared stiff and far too shy.

The women especially looked so funny in their fancy hats, with fox pelts draped over their shoulders – pelts that the Inuit could have put to much better use as fur trim for parka hoods. And the high-heeled shoes that looked impossible to stand up on; they appeared so uncomfortable, they made my heels feel tired just looking at them.

It was clear that many of these white people had come just to see us a smiling bunch of Eskimos from the far-off North! Some of them even gave us little articles from their purses – coins, key chains, and other small things. One lady gave me a tiny dainty pen that I kept with me for a long time afterwards. As for the 'smiling Eskimos' – it is true that in the High Arctic, we often used to smile at each other when we met, instead of saying 'hello,' or 'Leah-ngai,' or 'ai!' But here it was different. We were not the 'typical' smiling Eskimos, we were far too shy and frightened ...

From the pier we went directly to the hospital, or what we Inuit called a place to be sick.

The car ride felt so smooth on the concrete road. There were so many other cars ahead of us, and on the side and behind, that I was sure we were going to crash into one of them.

We were passing by so many things so fast that we didn't really get a chance to see everything around us. But the thing I remember that really amazed me was the mannequins in the store windows in the lower level of old Quebec. They were all dressed up in such fine clothing, and yet there were scruffy-looking people passing by on the street. It wasn't so much that the people were really dirty, it was just that the mannequins were dressed so much better than they were. The driver of the car didn't seem to notice any of these things, he just kept on driving.

When we arrived at the hospital, I was received by a nurse dressed all in white from head to toe. There was even a little white cap with a wide black stripe perched on her head. First off, the nurse gave me a bath and washed my hair. Then she dressed me in fresh clothing – slacks that I had never worn before, and a T-shirt with sideways stripes. It felt so good to have a bath after three months! Then the nurse put me into a crib with the bars up. Everything about me was all in white, even my crib was painted white with white sheets and a white pillow case.

I don't remember too much of anything that happened at that time ... But I do remember that I hated being put into the crib with the bars up. I had never seen a crib before and I thought it was only a thing one found in hospitals.

Once again I felt so lonely and more lost than I had ever felt before. Being forced to stay in bed all day and all night was too much for me. At home I had always been busy helping my mother and father in the house, or playing freely outdoors whenever I wanted on the land that was peaceful and free.

The only times that I was allowed to get out of my crib and onto the floor was when I was served meals and when I had to go to the toilet very badly. Aside from that, I spent hours and hours each day and night just looking out the window, staring and wondering what was going to happen to me next. I felt so distant from the family. I knew very well, as had my parents, that the only transportation we had was the C.D. Howe, and it was not going to return to the Arctic until the following year – July 1952. Here, it was only late October of 1951.

A day or two days after I was put in the hospital, the wife of our former Hudson's Bay manager, Mrs. Barbara Hislop, walked into my room. I was very surprised and very happy to see her again. I couldn't understand how she had been able to find me, there were so many buildings and streets. She came alone too – I could hardly believe that she had come to look for me in the middle of the city, all by herself. I was so grateful to her for that, and I felt as close to her as if she were my own sister.

233

I had never felt that way before with a white person.

She brought me a baby doll, a brand new one too, with real-looking eyes and a mouth and hair. It was very different from my home-made wooden dolls at home. Mrs. Hislop could speak a little bit of the Cape Dorset dialect, so I was finally able to talk with someone again. She told me that my new clothing looked really nice on me.

I felt like crying again when she left me, but at the same time it felt so good to have someone come to see me who knew my family very well.

A long while after I had been put alone in the room with the crib, I was surprised to see some Inuit there who had been in the hospital long before our group, and there were also some of those who had come on the ship with me. They were all wearing brown hospital robes with flannelette pajamas – everyone of them dressed in the same outfit in the same colours. Of course, I, too, had to exchange my slacks and T-shirt for a hospital robe and pajamas.

The nurse placed me in a bed right beside Annie from Pangnirtung. She became like a mother to me during the so many months we were together. It was so good to be with my own fellowmen and to be able to speak with others again ...

Indian people and Inuit were all together on our ward. The beds were all in rows in one open space. The men were on the third floor above us. It was the first time I had even seen Indians. There was one particular Indian woman from Fort Chimo who spoke Inuktitut, because in that year, 1951, there were still Indians living in Fort Chimo along with the Inuit.

We had to get up at 6 o'clock every morning to wash up and brush our teeth. The hospital supplied us with combs and a toothbrush each. Then, we had our breakfast around 8 o'clock in the morning, lunch at noon and supper at 5 o'clock. Everyday between noon and 5, we had to have an afternoon nap. Sometimes we only pretended to sleep and lay there giggling at each other, but the nurse just kept watching us all the time.

The hospital food was completely different from what we had given on the ship. This time we were served a lot of fresh vegetables and fruit. Some of the vegetables tasted bad – especially wax beans, spinach and turnips – and we seemed to be served them all too many times.

I was able to visit my grandmother's brother, Maki Angutu-juaq, once in awhile, since at times we were allowed to walk around on the floor, although we were never allowed to go outside ...

I used to visit Maki until one time during the winter an epidemic of German measles broke out among the patients. As a result, the men and women were no longer allowed to visit each other. They used to write to each other, however, by tying letters to long strings and hanging them out the windows to be retrieved by the women on the floor below.

We were all stricken by the epidemic of measles, and finally I received the news that Maki Augutirjuaq had died. For a long time, I couldn't really believe that he was dead, because I had not been taken to the funeral ...

I think that I almost died too that time. I remember when the nurses stayed by my bedside day and night. Although I was exhausted and wanted only to sleep, they kept waking me up every couple of hours or so to take my temperature and to sponge my body with a rough damp cloth. A few days after I was stricken with the illness, however, they put me in a little house outside the hospital where I stayed with only one other patient, an Inuk boy from Cape Dorset. His name was Manu-mikallak, Qarjugaarjuk's son. We spent several days there before we were returned to the sanitorium at Parc Savard Hospital ...

Leah Idlout d'Argencourt, 'C. D. Howe', Part I: *Inuit Today*, 6, 5 (June 1977) 35–45; Part II: *Inuit Today*, 6, 6 (July/August 1977) 46–50

O   **Minnie Aodla Freeman** (1936–) was born on Cape Hope Island in James Bay. Several of her poems and short stories have appeared in the *Canadian Children's Annual*. Her autobiography, *Life Among the Qallunaat*, was published in 1978. She spoke at the celebration for 'A Century of Canada's Arctic Islands, 1880–1980,' held at Yellowknife.

Living in Two Hells

... The oral history I have heard since I was a child goes way back. When I say 'way back,' I mean before my time, and I am pretty old. The descriptions and stories that I heard are of funny boats that used to be seen travelling around at a distance. Because it was not known who they really were and where they came from, Inuit called them *arnasiutiit* – Women Kidnappers. They were described as being tall people, with long blonde hair, who smoked white pipes. Their boats used to be described in detail, such as that they were shaped like old worn-out boots, the front coming up inwards like a turned-up nose. They had paddles that were long. Why I remember these stories is because I used to get scared to go very far from our settlement by myself ... Oral history has always been very strong in Inuit culture. You could imagine how old this history could be. I cannot date it myself, but I know that the telling of those first *qallunaat* arriving to the Arctic were not fantasy stories, but they were old nevertheless.

However old they are, those *arnasiutiit* has a tendency to kidnap women and if anyone touched them, like shaking hands, the person who was shaking hands, the person who was touched usually died not long after the event. Anyone who saw them close enough described them covered with impetigo-like infection, all over their hands.

Those oral histories are alive today mingled with other Inuit oral histories. How long ago it began, I do not know. But I believe that they were the first *qallunaat* to arrive in the Arctic.

Though Inuit that long ago did not change much from the first arrivals, Inuit knew that a different culture was looming amongst them. They were cautious because the strangers did not communicate, also, maybe because in those days killings among strangers always happened.

Here is a story that I heard when I was growing up. I used to think that it was a fantasy. My grandfather used to predict that one day Inuit lands would be full of *qallunaat, qallunaat*-language and *qallunaat*-equipment, and that if Inuit did not show their own ways they would be covered all over the *qallunaat* ways. He was not wrong.

It is not my intention to be prejudiced or sarcastic, nor to be unaccepting to the history that has happened on these Inuit

Islands. I did not grow up to panic while sitting on cracking ice. If I do not seem to be speaking for all Inuit throughout all these Islands, then I would like to speak as a person who is involved during this history-making in Canada, to express my views how on our native side (the other side of one coin so to speak) changes have affected Inuit. Most of you, and I, too, are aware that 20 some years ago the Government of Canada did have good intentions to care for Inuit. That was the first mistake the Government made. Why do I think that it was a mistake? Because every culture has different eyes, different ways of looking at things, situations and events. Now that I have lived among *qallunaat* for the last 26 years, I understand that Inuit upon being first seen by the early *qallunaat* arrivals looked so destitute, helpless, and smiling too much. The first *qallunaat* arrivals did not understand our ways, our culture, which is intangled so much with psychological beliefs. Probably the first thing that came to their minds was to look after Inuit the way they would with welfare-needy people in the South. I also understand now that *qallunaat* culture is very based upon material possessions. Can you just picture a *qallunaat* seeing Inuit in furs, with skin tents, fur bedding and stone utensils? To some *qallunaat* that is enough for them to run back south and tell the government that there are people living very poorly. In some ways, they were a lot like my grandmother, who upon first being sold a cotton jacket down on the beach at her settlement, tried it on and took it off as fast as she put it on and said, 'How useless, the wind goes right through this' It was a mistake. It was a mistake, at least the way Inuit understood the intentions on the part of the *qallunaat*. It is also a part of this event as Canadian history. For Inuit people, my grandparents and my parents, understood that the Government of Canada committed themselves to look after the Inuit for the rest of their lives, and they still believe that.

I have heard for the last two days how much progress has been made here in the Arctic. Once again, you all have shown me (little Inuk) that I have much to learn. I think all of you in this room realize that any good change is always welcome to any kind of culture. Inuit have always looked for better ways, for useful things to aid survival. For instance, if you look at the *uluk* – the woman's knife, it went through several changes, and always to so-called progress. I could imagine that at one time it was made out of ordinary stone, and for those archeologists who are familiar with these objects from their diggings all over these Islands, I am sure they have seen the changes the *uluk* went through. But I do not think changes that happen within the culture itself hurt as bad as the changes that have occurred during the last 100 years. How many of us can go from extreme hot to cold conditions within a few minutes? There is bound to be some very painful change within our body. The changes the Inuit have gone through are similar to that example.

While Inuit have been here more than 100 years, the changes that began 100 years ago within our culture are not all bad, but as my grandmother always used to say, 'it is human nature to learn the bad things first.' Maybe it is not necessary for me to mention the lack of information Inuit have had with drastic changes. Who would have known that excessive drinking was bad? Who would know that garbage from the *qallunaat* world is not the same as garbage we had, which was all natural and therefore it did not pollute the land? Who would know not eating properly with *qallunaat* food is unhealthy? Who would know that irregular sleeping habits when one has to work and go to school in *qallunaat* style is bad? What are bad and good manners in *qallunaat* style? Inuit have all kinds of examples.

The changes are here to stay, that we realize very much. It is up to you *qallunaat* to show Inuit not only what, but also *why* some things are good and bad to adopt. If I were to reverse the situation, and Inuit had the dominant culture, would any of you decide to walk on the ice in the middle of May? Would you eat the liver of polar bear? Would you keep travelling when overtaken by a blizzard-storm? Would you take a walk to the next mountain (when you don't know that the distance is deceiving)? Would you behave differently in front of children who might be in their baby ways, *makutuk* ways (soft age) or *Inummariit* way? Would you know the cause of social behaviour at any given different situation? I, for myself, now understand a little the ways of *qallunaat*.

There are *qallunaat* ways I am readily willing to adopt and there are things I do not – or cannot understand. Quite a few years ago I finally learned to separate the two cultures. I became 2 people – my manners, speech and behaviour at any time during social scene changed – because both the *qallunaat* and the Inuit ways demand different behaviour.

Missionaries

The first arrivals of missionaries were quite scary to some Inuit. They affected a lot of fears and even killings. First of all, missionaries considered Inuit primitive and we Inuit considered their teachings very primitive. Everything was 'thou shall.' 'Thou shall' for the benefit of learning. I mean we Inuit survived these harsh lands through tests and trying new ways. There were so many things we did that the missionaries did not like. I don't know if they ever stopped to look at our old religion. For instance, they stopped our traditional trial marriages, which to Inuit were very vital in order to make successful marriages – as a result of which there were no separations or divorces or children separated from parents. They stopped Inuit men having more than one wife. Their rules from the book was so important to pass on, that they did not see the necessary reasons for some Inuit men to have a couple of wives. Missionaries saw it as a big sin, whereas Inuit practised it because of the importance of family life – to maintain the unity of family life, for often a man took a widowed woman in order to help her raise her many children. Plural marriage was practised not as a sin, but for the sake of strengthening family life in Inuit society.

I realize that at this moment I would not have learned to speak the *qallunaat* language if it was not for missionaries. I went to their schools and lived with them 10 months out of the year. But they did not allow me to speak my own language in their schools so that I began to think that there was something wrong with my language. At that time, I used to feel that I was in 2 hells – one while I was in school – the second when I went home, because my grandmother would not hear any other language spoken in her presence in our house. One of the strangest things that affected family life was where Inuit got separated through *qallunaat* religion, as when the Catholics managed to convert a brother while his sister remained Protestant ... Really its a farce when today, the church tells us that the family that prays together stays together. But there is one answer I always wanted to know as an Inuk from the Missionaries, that is, if Adam and Eve were the first people on earth and had 2 sons, Cain and Abel, how did we manage to multiply? That's the thought for today.

Hudson's Bay Company
I seem to have mixed up the chronological order. I meant to say something about the Hudson's Bay Company before the missionaries. I don't mean to insult the Hudson's Bay Company, especially when they always reminded us that HBC stands for 'Here Before Christ.'

I think I can say that Hudson's Bay Company made easier lives for Inuit since 1670. There were in my home area of James Bay long before I was born, fur trading with my ancestors. Inuit have always traded amongst themselves either for short period or long period at a time. Inuit understood the trading systems of the Hudson's Bay Company. I think one of the reasons why Inuit welcomes the Hudson's Bay Company was the fact that the Company never tried to change Inuit ways of behaving or thinking.

Yes, they changed our equipment, to better steel knives, steel saws, steel nails, steel axes and manufactured cloth. Inuit understood the furs that the Hudson's Bay Company were after. Inuit hunters had employment through the Hudson's Bay Company. It was the familiar job Inuit enjoyed. We still hear older Inuit today saying that the Hudson's Bay Company is most useful in Inuit lands. They did not interfere with the lifestyles of Inuit ... Hudson's Bay Company sold Fort Garry tea to Inuit first, before it was sold in Bytown ... pity ...

RCMP
The RCMP were known to Inuit as a very human people. In James Bay when their yearly ship arrived, they visited individual homes either to count the household inhabitants to see

240

how many of us were left or how many of us were born. Mind you, they never called us by our names, instead they always wanted to see our disc-numbers. I know now, the RCMP were doing Inuit statistics, gave our family allowances and registering births. I was involved as a translator in the 50's when the Department of Northern Affairs was taking over the welfare role of the RCMP. It was painful to watch and hear some RCMP and Welfare workers arguing and fighting over files. At the same time, it was funny to observe that one was trying to find work to do, and the other trying to stay on the job, because in those days there were no criminals, no thiefs, no drunks and at that time Inuit were still obeying their own community laws. Today the RCMP probably have the longest lasting job in the Arctic.

Scientists
There were many Inuit natural scientists who acquired their knowledge from their own observations and by purely wanting to understand their total surroundings, whether animals, snow and ice, people or land. Today, to me, it is questionable if those Inuit scientists are still around. Probably not many are, because for the last twenty years or so Inuit have not really passed on their knowledge to their children. Not by any means on purpose though. How much can you be aware of your own environment if you are working 9 to 5? Also the *qallunaat* system of education has interfered a great deal.

There are some communities now that are filming Inuit ways and interviewing knowledgable Inuit. Scientists from the south I know have been working in the arctic for a long time, but only a few have made some southerners understand Inuit culture.

Over the years scientists have always been very welcome in Inuit communities. Some have been adopted by Inuit – in fact I adopted one permanently. It has been said that the ideal family in the arctic consists of a husband and wife, four children and an anthropologist. As scientists are often willing to admit, Inuit have clothed them, fed them, taken them to wherever they wanted to go to do their studies. Often Inuit have taken chances, in matters of life and death, because they felt responsible for a particular scientist.

We Inuit have met many different kinds of scientists, in

241

terms of personality as well as what they wanted to study. We have studied them while they studied us. There are some communities now that have begun to screen scientists before they get to the community. One of the reasons for this was because in some places scientists who came to study community stayed in a hostel, hotel or in a *qallunaat* house, and got their information from the *qallunaat* who have never really been involved themselves with households, then went back south and wrote their reports based on hearsay. Inuit consider these scientists not only dishonest with the Inuit, but also dishonest to their superiors in the south.

Personally I have been involved with scientists since I was born. In fact I would not be here if it wasn't for that geologist who turned film-maker. Robert Flaherty. But that doesn't mean I have to like everything scientists do – does it? For instance, I know that scientists, when preparing to go into the field have to find financial support. My question is, when are you scientists going to start to include in your budgets funds to have the information you gather translated into *inuktitut* and send back north?

The Future
What is happening to Inuit over the next 100 years? I cannot stand here and view this celebration just for today. As an Inuk, I am involved in it at the present. Will Inuit be just as involved or more so during the next 100 years? I am not thinking only in terms of celebrations in Canada, for Canada, by Canada. I hear, I listen, I observe, I investigate, I make my own understandings to what is happening to Inuit today. Old Inuit have always believed that nothing is ever solved with bitter emotions. We of this and the next generation have a heavy load to carry. Will we remain without bitterness? The old Inuit, yes, did have a hard life, but their loads were familiar and there was no drastic changes during their lifetimes.

I am not saying that we of this generation do not welcome the changes. Give us the sense of informative direction, choices and resources to deal with *qallunaat* mistakes. Inuit never went out into the ocean without testing their kayak first, Inuit never put up their igloo without examining the location, Inuit did not go into action without weighing the total situation first. The plane arrives, the government or industry officials step out and out comes a new situation. Often, even today, no letters, no phone calls, no information. Are *qallunaat* always so unthinking, unfeeling and so rash?

I was warned not to speak of the present situation of Inuit, warned that I might be too bitter, too honest, too political. Warned that I might spoil this beautiful event. Well, we Inuit never had a chance to voice ourselves 100 years ago. If these Islands mean a lot for their 100 year since being transferred from England, the first inhabitants of the region should be given consideration.

As the present Inuit are working very hard to try and find meaningful ways to have a say over their land. I cannot prejudge these plans and make rash statements by myself. It is not fair to all those others or to me that I should anticipate their wishes. But starting today, no one should anymore be taking so lightly Inuit land claims, for that is where the fairness and equality begins for the native people of Canada. Here ends me.

Minnie Aodla Freeman, 'Living in Two Hells,' *Inuit Today* 8 (October 1980) 32–5

O   **Alootook Ipellie** (1951–), author and graphic artist, attended school in Iqaluit, Yellowknife, and Ottawa. One of the most talented and proficient of contemporary Inuit writers, Ipellie has written for a large number of Inuit periodicals including *Inuit Today, North,* and *Inuktitut.*

Frobisher Bay Childhood

When anyone asks me where I was born, I usually answer, 'Frobisher Bay,' but I never can tell them exactly where my birthplace was. I always say, 'Somewhere down the bay.'

But Frobisher Bay is the place where I grew up. My most vivid childhood memories are still strongly rooted in this town. It is the place where I suffered my set-backs and experienced my triumphs. Although they may not know it, the people I grew up with are still dear to me. They really are an extension of my own life. For this reason I will always come back to Frobisher no matter where I live on this earth. Sometimes, one's roots are sacred to a person.

I remember the first time I went to school. It was in a small red and white metal building, which was the Anglican Church at that time. I was about eight years old then, and we had only one teacher – she was a lady. It was a chilly winter day with the sun shining from the sky above. I had no idea why we were called together in the church. The first day we played a few games and it was cold inside, so we had our parkas on. Round and round we went holding hands together, until finally the game was all over. It was actually the first day of my education; the *Quallunaaq* feeling had entered my heart.

I cannot say exactly how I felt at the time, but I am quite sure I enjoyed it. I remember there was a machine inside the church that made a noise; I found out later that this sound came from a round disc inside a box with a top that opened and closed. I learned that the discs were records and that the box was a 78 r.p.m. record player with a handle on the side that you had to wind in order to make it play. This was very new to me at the time and another extraordinary addition to my knowledge of the new things the white man was bringing to our little town.

Many of the essentials for living came in by freight ships when the ice broke up in late July. The sight of these great vessels entering the world where we lived made thrills go through our hearts. If a ship came while we slept, the elders wasted no time telling us the news.

'Wake up boys, there is a big umiak anchored in the bay.' We got up, rushed out the door, and looked at the enormous vessel that was already unloading its cargo into the barges.

Our ship that came to Frobisher was the Hudson's Bay Company ship, bringing the year's goods to the stores. When it arrived, most of the Inuit in town went to help unload the barges. This was during high tide and everyone worked as a unit, just like a circus setting up the big tents and other things to get ready for the opening night. There was laughter among the people, a sign of happiness which never seemed to stop as long as the ship stayed. The way they worked together was truly beautiful; they reminded me of a large family. No matter how old or young they were, they were there carrying things, big or small, both day and night.

At low tide, when there wasn't much work to do, the Hudson's Bay Company staff members brought out hot tea and pilot biscuits for everyone. We were hungry by then and as soon as the paper cups were handed out, we scrambled to reach into the large teapot as if it was our last chance. It was a thrill to be among these people; my own Inuit brothers and sisters. I looked at them as truly wonderful human beings, enjoying their day together. But soon there would be a time to end all this when the ship left to go to other settlements in the North. It was time now to get paid.

This was a day of joy, when everyone lined up to receive their money. It was usually only a dollar for each day and night that they helped in the unloading of the cargo. Even a few bills satisfied them, although they had worked hard for at least a whole week. There were no feelings of being underpaid or cheated; they merely took what they were given. And the very same day, most of them were completely broke again. They loved to spend money on goods of all kinds. Fascination was in their eyes when they saw certain things for the first time, and they thought to themselves, 'I must buy this thing – it is so beautiful and different.'

In those days I remember that the United States had an Air Force base in Frobisher Bay. We, as Inuit kids, would go over to their base to wait outside their kitchen in hopes of being offered something to eat. We often succeeded and the smell of their food was like nothing that we had ever smelled before.

There came a time when at least once a day I would start to dream of having tons and tons of *Quallunaaq* food right in our little hut. Even if all of the food could not go in, I would think of becoming a genius at storing food and somehow get it all in there.

One day, when a group of us were just outside the Hudson's Bay store in the base area, a number of guys came out of the store and got in their jeep. As the jeep started up one of them threw us what looked like paper money. We scrambled for it like hungry pups ... only to find out that it was play money made for the game of monopoly. We looked up at the guys on their jeep and they were laughing their heads off. We nearly cried in disappointment.

I can remember one day I picked a fight with one of the students at lunch hour. The boy was one of those who was always causing trouble with other children and teachers. I distinctly had the feeling that I could beat him easily that day. I was feeling very strong and all my friends cheered me on. It was as if we were fighting for the heavy-weight boxing championship of the world. All the kids made a 'ring' around the two of us and we crashed into each other without a bit of hesitation, fists flying and muscles bulging from our arms! We grabbed each other's parkas and wrestled to the ground and up again. We swung our arm like sledge-hammers towards the opponent's head and made noises like only fighters made! I heard the crowd around us shouting words of encouragement and it was clear that the majority were rooting for me. It was important that I did not suffer a defeat in front of my friends. I fought hard but in the end, I received a bleeding nose and cried. Luck was not with me that day and it was good that my old friends were still my old friends. I never fought again after that.

There was a community hall in Apex Hill, which is about three miles from Frobisher Bay, and I remember they used to have a free movie for everyone on Sunday nights. Those of us who did not have very much money to throw around could not pass up the chance to see a full length movie free. So we would walk to Apex and back to see the shows that were often filled with action.

When the first movies came to our land, a whole new world was introduced to the Inuit. Our eyes would open up in fascination when the lights went out to start a movie. When the first frame appeared on the screen, we started to live in a world of fantasy.

The walks back home were as entertaining as the shows. Everyone got a big kick out of what they saw and amused themselves by reminiscing about the action-filled parts of the movie. Some of us would re-enact the roles of the movie stars and we had fun entertaining each other.

When we got back to Frobisher after the movie we'd find a deck of cards and start playing. My group of buddies played cards at least once a week like 'hard-nosed' gamblers. We would take our places and decide who was to deal the cards first and then go on to the serious business of winning as many games as we could. There was no cheating, and we played until one of us won everything the other players had.

What we were playing for were pictures of Hollywood stars.

Probably every kid in town had a movie idol in those days and pictures of these movie stars were considered as valuable as any good wristwatch or bicycle. So we never missed an opportunity to look through any magazines and newspapers that we could find around town. If we happened to find one good picture of John Wayne or Tony Curtis, it was as if we had found a gold nugget worth at least a couple of hundred dollars. Photographs of stars from western movies were without a doubt the most sought after because they were worth the most at the card table.

Next came the sword-clanking stars like Kirk Douglas or Steve Reeves. And there were the strongmen – like Tarzan, Hercules and Sampson. They were big heroes when I was an Inuit child. The photographs of clowns like Jerry Lewis, Bob Hope and the Three Stooges were also popular. So were Laurel and Hardy, and that timid knee-shaking character, Don Knotts.

The quality and the size of the pictures were very important. A good photo of John Wayne was worth two poor ones of the same star. Colour pictures were worth a few times more than black and white – no matter what condition they were in. The pictures of the stars in newspapers were considered good bargains but they were not as crisp as the magazine pictures and did not last long. Most of us could not get photographs from magazines so we had to resort to movie advertisements in the newspaper and newspapers were very scarce in our town in those days.

I can remember many times when my pockets would bulge with magazine photographs after a successful day of playing cards. They were valuable to me, so I could not afford to leave them around at home where they would not last for two minutes. I took great care not to crumple them. If I did, they would not be worth much when we started playing cards. So they were a bit of trouble to me because I could not move around the way I wanted to, and sitting down was always a problem. If I sat down many times during the day, I would find out that some of the faces of the movie stars were completely wiped out because of all the rubbing they were going through. A picture without a recognizable face was worth not a penny at the card table.

Clipping out photographs of movie stars was 'big business' for us as Inuit children. A good collector would naturally be considered the one to beat at the card games that would last for several hours. If he happened to be little greedy about his collection we had all the more pleasure when we won his precious pictures.

These are a few memories of my childhood in Frobisher Bay. Life in the Arctic is changing fast and Frobisher has changed along with its people. If Frobisher has a distinct character today, it is that it has become 'home' to many Inuit from other communities in the North. On any given day in Frobisher you might meet an Inuk who had come from a town as far away as Port Burwell in the east or from Tuktoyaktuk in the west. There were Inuit from Northern Quebec, from the High Arctic, from the Central Arctic or the Keewatin. Today there is no surprise in meeting an Inuk from Alaska or even from Greenland, on the streets of Frobisher Bay. Who knows, maybe one day we will begin to see whole families coming in from Siberia to live in Frobisher Bay!

Alootook Ipellie, 'Frobisher Bay Childhood' *The Beaver*, 310.4 (spring 1980) 4, 6, 8

Damn Those Invaders

The satiric element, clearly evident in Alootook Ipellie's short story, follows the Inuit tradition of using satire as a powerful social sanction.

The abundant flowers were in full bloom on Jeesusi Island and plenty of ripe berries were on its grounds to be picked at will. Hundreds of tiny birds had gathered together to prepare for the long migration to the South. They dotted the sky as they passed overhead, moving toward what seemed to be an endless mass of water. They were on their way to the mainland, and on to the warmth of the southern sun. They were the followers of the great light that produces and protects all life on earth. They would be gone for the duration of the long Arctic winter.

Jeesusi Island was a natural habitat for many species of Arctic

animals, and for those who travelled up from the South for the summer months every year. It had not yet been conquered by progres-
sive-minded men, except for Inuksiaq, a teenaged Inuk who was a
friend to many of the animals. Inuksiaq's family had a camp on the
island where they went to live from the start of every summer until
the end of summer.

Inuksiaq often took long walks on the island alone, and enjoyed
the beauty of the surrounding environment. The crisp fresh air filled
every available space on the land and the silence pressed against
his eardrums. It was interrupted only periodically by the sound of
animals and the wind. The behaviour of the great land was still the
same as God had planned it. Peace was at hand.

On his free time, Inuksiaq one day went up to the highest point
of Jeesusi Island and sat there for a good part of an hour looking over
the island and the sea that lay beyond. A flock of ducks and geese
passed by every once in a while, bringing with them their young who
had gone through so much in the few short months since their
birth, learning the art of survival, and the traditions their elders
passed on to them.

Inuksiaq was very protective of the environment around him: the
great beautiful land which his people rightfully owned, and the delicate animals that he loved with all his heart and who had become
his friends. He was old enough to have learned the many habits of
the vast Inuit lands and to respect those habits whenever possible.

Inuksiaq's family was a part of a small band of Inuit who had decided to go back to the land and to live in the traditional way which
they had abandoned years before. But now they had had enough of
the 20th century lifestyle and the materialistic ways the settlers followed as if they were part of their religion. The world of the settlers
was destroying the Inuit bit by bit with their new beliefs and moral
values. All this was happening even though many of the older Inuit
could not understand a word of the settlers' language. Undoubtedly,
the colorful material things attracted the Inuit and they could not
resist having them.

But Inuksiaq's family and a handful of Inuit had sense enough to
look away from this colorful world and turn to the Inuit values
which were once again priceless to them. These values were based
on living in harmony with nature, producing nothing but peace
within their souls. To them the forces of nature were a challenge
to their strength and produced a wonderful satisfaction within their

hearts. They were rubbing shoulders with the land and its enormous energy. It was a way of life they knew well and enjoyed. Nothing or no one was ever going to take it away from them if they could help it.

Inuksiaq was enjoying the last day of summer. The sun was high in the sky and hardly a cloud could be seen. A warm breeze was coming up from the south making the temperature perfect for discarding the parka.

Inuksiaq was resting his back on a rock when Tuktuaapik quietly moved up behind him. Inuksiaq was startled by the noise. He quickly got up and turned to see what it was, then smiled when he found out.

Tuktuaapik was a bull caribou whom Inuksiaq had received as one of his best animal friends. The two greeted one another and laughed. Tuktuaapik bent his legs to rest on the ground, his enormous antlers spread across above his head. He appeared tired and started to say:

'What a day it has been. When I got up this morning a beautiful sunrise greeted my eyes. The air was cool and the water out there was something to behold. It was like a giant mirror lying on the ground. I certainly was looking forward to the day because we haven't had nicer weather all this week. I was one happy fellow when our herd started out for our usual feeding grounds. But when we arrived, the day started to go down hill ... even with the wonderful weather we're having.'

'What happened?' asked Inuksiaq.

'Well, I'll tell ya,' Tuktuaapik continued. 'We ran into two geologists roaming on our favourite feeding place, and so most of the members of our herd haven't had a decent meal to eat all day. The young have been crying their heads off with hunger placed within their stomachs. I'm afraid we will have to keep away from those mineral-hungry geo's for some time to come. They have put a camp right in the middle of our kitchen. We just don't have any room with them there. What can you do to help us out, Inuksiaq?'

Inuksiaq hesitated for a moment and then said sympathetically:

'All I can say is that we Inuit are just as much concerned about them geologists and the oil people as you are. When we first started noticing the advancing raid on our land by these complex-minded people, we immediately sent our protests to the government of Can-

ada, since it was government people who had agreed to give out
the permits to the mineral and gas companies without us knowing
it. The power-minded elected representatives of our country are a
sneaky lot who seem to hold no sympathy for the rights of the inhabitants of the North. I wish I didn't have to say that about them,
but the facts are there before us to see.

These invaders have succeeded in exploiting almost every corner
of the world using their sensitive magnifiers and their computer-
operated machinery.

'Our precious land is the last match in their box and they are
attempting to ignite it as quickly as they can. When the last speck
of fire has lost its heat, the invaders will leave and ask us to pick up
the ashes. The whole situation is damn frustrating. Our wonderful
homeland is becoming a battleground and we aim to fight to the
last.'

Tuktuaapik then said, 'You know what is so heartbreaking about
today? It is the first time in the history of our caribou herd on Jeesusi
Island that our land has been trespassed. This day, I'm afraid, is the
beginning of our end. It's a sad day for me, and even more so for
the young ones. Our group is an honest herd because we have never
before infringed on the rights of others, and we will keep it that
way as long as we live.

'But when our whole life and everything we own is threatened,
it strikes you in the middle of your heart. Our very freedom is put
on the edge of a cliff, hanging only from a piece of rock three inches
thick. It's a scary feeling. And yet there seems nothing we can do
to save ourselves from this real threat of extinction if those geologists
keep bothering us the way they are doing today. My feeling of pride
for the caribou herd on this island is deeply rooted in me and I
must fight for them with the hope that we will eventually survive.
Do you understand what I am saying, Inuksiaq?'

'I couldn't understand you better,' Inuksiaq replied. 'The situation
your herd is in is a reflection of our own. I understand you perfectly.
Those geologists who have just settled on your land are there looking for riches, and for other reasons too complicated for you to fully
understand. This earth is running out of energy-producing resources,
and all these mining and oil companies are scrambling to find it on
our land. Some of them have already found large amounts of mineral
deposits and natural gas finds have been made in our waters. These

finds have triggered a tremendous excitement in the hearts of the invaders and they are about to trample us to death, inspite of our objections.'

Tuktuaapik was silent for a whole minute while he looked over the island that was his whole life. He looked at his herd resting beside a lake about five miles to the west. There were more than a thousand of them and he wondered how soon they would start to reduce in their number. The young ones were hungry for the first time in their lives. He wondered too about the other animals that inhabited the island, and about those who visited it every spring and summer. What will happen to them if this island is not preserved? Will they all die too, along with us? Or will they somehow survive the destruction that lies in wait for us?

What about Inuksiaq and his people? They are humans like the invaders, but their rights too are being ignored. They are as vulnerable as we are, and have suffered so much already. Their culture is being buried as the energy-hungry companies dig hurriedly across this vast land. Time is running out for them too. Something has got to be started now to stop the impending disaster that lurks before us all.

Tuktuaapik stood up and turned to Inuksiaq. 'I have to go and join the herd down there,' he said. 'I am needed to help them find what food there is left on the land. I am sure we will meet again soon. Give my regards to your family. I am sure they know the kind of danger they are in. It's becoming a scary world to live in. But remember, we are still here to fight on. There is still a lot of room for optimism, and for our pride too. We will survive through the suffering we are about to experience. Just you wait and see.'

Inuksiaq watched Tuktuaapik descending in the direction of his herd until he could hardly see him anymore. He watched him join the herd beside the lake, and he could see that Tuktuaapik was telling them something. Then he watched him lead the herd to where he hoped he would find some food to eat. The young ones were hungry.

'Damn those invaders!' he yelled. 'Damn them foolish folks if they don't heed our call for help! Damn it, don't they see that we want to live too!?'

Inuksiaq's voice echoed five times before it faded.

Alootook Ipellie, 'Damn Those Invaders,' *Inuit Today*, 5, 10 (1976) 36–41

○ **Tumasi Quissa** (1948–), singer, composer, and carver, was born at a camp near Akudlivik in arctic Quebec. A popular recording artist, he wrote the words and music for this song.

Come to Our Place Since You Got a Seal

Come to our place, we will eat, we will eat, we will eat.
If I eat alone, I will not eat well.
I remember when we use to be hungry and wanted
  bannock.
Wild meat was always scarce, always, always, always.
I remember seal hunting, searching for our catch, not ever
finding our search for wild meat

Come to our place, come.
Come to our place, we will eat, we will eat, we will eat.
If I eat alone, I will not eat well.

Sheldon O'Connel, 'Music of the Inuit,' *The Beaver*, 310:2 (autumn 1979) 13

○ **William Kalleo** (1947–) was born in a small spring/fall scaling camp near Nain, Labrador. Interpreter, translator, and editor, he worked for the Inuit Cultural Institute travelling across the Northwest Territories. He was in 1988 a land claims negotiator for the Labrador Inuit Association.

The Known Mystery of Seals

Hunting seals,
Hunting different seals,
Different ways of hunting different seals.
There is a joy in knowing the mystery of hunting seals.

The weighty harp seal with its inflated neck pouch
fills wonder into my virgin eyes.
The mighty square-flipper,
its crowning majesty of whiskers,
so different, so weird.
The little jar seal,
pea-brained and frivolous,

the source of my comic joy
Now, the adult jar seal,
stingy and miserly,
I am helpless against it,
and look askance.

Inuktitut, 50 (May 1982) 70, translated by Rose Pamack

○   **Susie Tiktalik** (c. 1880–1980) could remember back to a time
before there were any white people in the north. She recorded
these recollections of her mother and grandmother on tape.

Susie Tiktalik – From Her Life Story

I don't know how old I am. I know I'm from long ago, and I'm
old, but I don't know really when I was born or how old I
am. The first born of my mother and father's children was left
to die. At that time, when people didn't want any children,
they just left them to die. They didn't hurt them or do anything, they just left them. I was my mother and father's second
child, and even I was a baby girl, they saved me.

   This is a story about when people started moving in the fall.
They would build snowhouses – many people came together
from other places to make camps at night. When you went
out, you could see the snowhouse lights, just like stars there
were so many people. One fall a man named Kuyuk came with
his family to see his sister who was at the same camp with
us. There were many people there. One person got sick and
died, and his family was in sorrow. For no reason they wanted
to kill anybody just because their relative died. This Kuyuk
was grabbed by a man who had lost his relative. He got hold
of him and tried to kill him, trying to stab him with a knife.
But Niakualuk just pulled the man away by his head, backwards – she was a strong woman. Kuyuk was so scared he
sweat even it was cold weather, because he knew this man
was trying to kill him and Niakualuk saved him. She was
Kuptan's mother.

   This is another story about Banks Island, about the people
at Naugaluk. People used to come from places to stay and
gather at one big snowhouse to do some shaman work. This
was before they went out hunting on the ice. I've seen them

do some medicine work. They even made a seal come up through the ground with water splashing up. Then they played spearing it. There would be all kinds of action; I used to watch them myself. Everyday they would do more shaman spell because they didn't want anything to happen to them while they were out hunting on the ice.

They would cook some meat and walk backward with the cooked meat and throw the meat over their heads. After this they went from snowhouse to snowhouse, getting little pieces of meat from each house on a plate or in a little bag just like children at Hallowe'en. It makes me think of old times when I see children at Hallowe'en.

One time the men woke up just before going out hunting. The men blocked our snowhouse door. We could hear from our snowhouse porch some kind of noise, just like a moaning sound, struggling noise like a big man killing somebody. When they quieted down, we all took a look outside. There we saw blood all over the place. There was nothing to be seen, but we saw blood. And no body. The shamen made all kinds of sickness. They did this when they got together from different places, some from Eastern Arctic or from Western Arctic.

The people used to hunt on the ice, and when a person killed a seal, they would go rushing to cut up the seal. People took what they could get out of the seal or ugyuk. They just cut up the skin and all as soon as they pulled up the seal. The person who did not get any part of the seal would go from snowhouse to snowhouse to get a piece to cook for himself. They would even go the place where they cut up the seal to pick up blood of the seal. Some people got less – the ones who were weak or scared. They pushed each other in order to get a piece of meat. At that time even a butter knife would have been a good knife.

In those days, they had to kill a person and take his liver out to make him become a shaman. They killed this man and took the liver out of him, but all the shamen could not bring him back to life again. They tried and tried, night and day, but were not successful. The man got stiff while lying dead. My grandmother was there who was not a real medicine woman. They got her and told her to bring this man alive again. She told the people she could not do it without the help of the spirit from the sky. When my grandmother started on that man, she called out toward the heaven. She sang a song to the man, and then she breathed into the man, and slowly that man started breathing real frosty breaths.

This story is true because I saw it myself. I didn't like to miss anything, I was always getting in front of everybody.

My grandmother called toward the heaven and got the spirit from the cloud, not from this earth. Finally the man that was dead arose, and he was so stiff when he got up! The spirit had come to make this man rise. Even the shamen made a great shout because this man came alive. This man could not turn into a shaman, that's why he died. He did not become a shaman, but my grandmother let him rise from the dead. The other shamen said this man would become a shaman, but my grandmother told them not to try to make another shaman again. One of them got mad at her because she made that man alive again. She told them she was not a medicine woman, that she just used a spirit from the clouds up in the sky. After the man rose, he was kind of staggering around. He became sick for a while, but my grandmother kept working with him. The people really rejoiced after that. After that, they kept right on playing games at the big gathering place.

My parents went to Tahekyuak for the summer. I was so lonesome for my parents my husband Kauluak took me to them from Nalugayuk. They were many women at that place. They started playing men and women gambling. They would bet anything they had, like ulu and other things. There was this one woman from Kaluktotiak named Alagi. She and my mother were the smart alecs. They played a gambling game that hung up a stick around with two holes. My mum and this Alagi gambled with each other more than any other men or women. Others played for fun, but Alagi would put down her ulu and play till she lost, but my mum would always win what she put down for gambling. They quarrelled with each other. This Alagi wanted to win her ulu back but she couldn't. Every day they would gamble.

One time Alagi started another game – wrestling. They went to where there were no rocks. They wrestled all day till they were tired out, but Alagi lost again. Again the next day they started. This time my mum pretended to fall twice until she was sure Alagi thought she was stronger. Then after she fell down, my mum just threw Alagi down like she was nothing.

There is another game, a jump game. Alagi said to Niguyuk, my mum, 'Come and get going and jump,' but my mum just answered, 'I won't try anybody.' Alagi tried, but then my mum jumped beyond her like nothing. Alagi lost her ulu again, but then she started playing skip rope. Alagi put her best dish down, made of some kind of real nice stone, but she kept losing everything she gambled with. Those two women, Alagi and my mum, would exchange husbands every now and then. Maybe that's why they were jealous of one another. Alagi said to mum to go to Kaluktotiak, where they came from. This Alagi like me very much because I was named Tiktalik, like her husband that was stabbed with a knife.

When winter came we traveled to Kaluktotiak, where Alagi said we should go. My mum and all her relatives went to Kaluktotiak. When they got there, the women of Kaluktotiak used to come to get her, but my mum's relatives told her not to go to the place where they gathered but my mum wouldn't listen. When they got there, one old woman came to her. My mum thought she was too old for her, but this old woman wanted to try her. My mum pretended to fall every time that old woman grabbed her. Then Alagi grabbed her. She was sure she was going to hurt her, but my mum threw her around till she was tired. All the women of Kaluktotiak took turns to wrestle with my mum, but every one of them lost. She took all kinds of women, young and old, but she was not about to give up for anything. The women of Kaluktotiak got tired and went home.

Before my mum died, all kinds of medicine men and women tried their best to make her better but could not make her well. The Kaluktotiak shamen put a bad spell on her to make her sick. Finally she died. When she died, my grandmother started saying to people that it was her own fault because in her lifetime she was so smart to everybody.

She could not be told anything but just went her own way, never listened even I tried my best to talk to her. My mum had a loon spirit, you know them big loons, that's why she was a smartie woman. Nobody ever beat her in her lifetime.

'Susie Tiktalik – From Her Life Story,' trans. David Kaglik, *Inuvialuit*, 6, 3 spring 1982) 15–17

○   **Zebedee Nungak** (1951–) was born south of Povungnituk on
the Hudson Bay coast. One of the 'bright young Eskimos' who
were sent to school in Ottawa, Zebedee worked for the federal
government as interpreter and translator. He helped found the
Northern Quebec Inuit Association that negotiated the 1975
James Bay Agreement with the province of Quebec. He was
manager of Saputik, the corporation which holds Inuit lands in
ownership in Quebec. As co-chairman of the Inuit Committee
on National Issues he was in 1988 actively involved in constitutional negotiations seeking to have the rights of aboriginal
peoples entrenched in the Canadian constitution. His essay below reveals that an important part of the Inuit imagination is
still ironic and mockingly humorous.

Equality before the Honey Bucket

At times, the government displays a superb sense of clumsy,
bumbling, unknowingness toward the northern communities.
Every location possess its own rich set of bureaucratic ignorance and idiocy stories. Such is the tradition since the government of Quebec stumbled onto the scene in Northern
Quebec. It has half coasted and half imposed itself into governing its own 'grande nord,' never quite sure of itself all the
while.

Granted, the problems of efficient government are permanently complicated by insufficient funding, the difficulties of
supply, and limited construction season, among other things.
Given these, any governing authority deserves the benefit of
the doubt for a decade or two as it sensitizes itself to the environment and people it has set out to serve.

It is offered here that the government has had its decade or
two. Presently, there should be no more excuse for the government not to have its act and its 'northern wisdom' together
in its orientation to this region. (One often wonders whether
it does, in fact, *have* an act or a northern wisdom.) Enough
time and interaction has elapsed. Yet still, we are required to
deal with classic cases of ignorance, lack of vision and profes-
sionalism within the ranks of government. Stories of these
could easily be compiled into a thick, amusing book.

Nothing more needs to be said of the government's grand

design to francize the names of Inuit-occupied geography, or of its deployment of riot police during the Bill 101 protest. These issues evolved into lessons on the absurdities of heavy handedness where none was necessary. Other memorable examples come to mind: The first set of northern housing units built by government in the village of Tasiujaq were left unfinished. People lived in these unfinished houses for years. Then there was the time the newly forming village of Akulivik was sent a shipment of electric stoves, when in fact electricity did not yet exist there. And so it goes ...

When resources are mismanaged and squandered this way, it becomes easier to figure why materials are in chronic short supply to the municipalities. Maybe easier to figure, but still hard to understand. Not enough money, they usually say.

Four years ago, the Municipality of Kangirsuk was offered a sewage truck, out of the blue, by the government in the annual scramble for equipment allocations. This strange offer was turned down by the local Council for two reasons: First, no houses or buildings were equipped at the time with septic tanks, and none were expected for several more years. Everybody used 'honey buckets.' Secondly, more urgent priorities existed for the community.

Then also, allocations for municipal needs in the region are notorious for their extreme scarcity. This has given birth to an annual ritual of municipalities known as MINNIRALAUTINIQ, which can be translated roughly as 'an-unruly-division-of-scarcities-every-which-way.'

1983 turned out to be a windfall year for the villages. Thanks to an infusion of federal catch-up funds, more houses and schools are being built. All new units and renovations are equipped with spanking new septic tanks, flush toilets at the ready. Being one of the recipients of this windfall, Kangirsuk now needs a sewage truck. Doubts about allocation of materials late into the shipping season left the Municipality no time to apply for this equipment in the normal process, 'through the channels,' as they say. A frantic, last-minute appeal to Municipal Affairs for such a vehicle did not produce results. No more money, they said.

So now, all people in Kangirsuk are equal before the honey bucket for another year. This vital piece of equipment maintains its status as the common denominator of native and non-native, important guest and lowly resident. So goes another episode in the continuing saga of brilliant and far-sighted government planning.

Zebedee Nungak, 'Equality before the Honey Bucket,' *Taqralik* (October 1983) 6–7

O **Mark Kalluak** (1942–) was an editor of the *Keewatin Echo* and other early Inuit journals. He has been an active promoter of Inuit culture collecting Inuit legends and stories. He collected, edited, and translated the legends which were published in 1974 as *How Kabloonat Became and Other Inuit Legends*. In 1988 he was mayor of Eskimo Point and language coordinator for the Inuit Cultural Institute. Active in language development for many years he wrote about his wish to learn syllabics as a child.

I Want to Learn Syllabics

I know I don't stand alone when I say I never learned syllabics in school ... Like many others, I learned it from the back of prayer books and Bibles, and I believe people who claim learning syllabics is one of the simplest systems there is. When I was sent to the hospital at the age of four I thought I was being transported to another world and my parents would never find me. Perhaps because of my desire to communicate with my parents, I had one object in mind – to learn to write. Maybe that is why I learned to write syllabics so early.

Kenn Harper, 'Writing in Inuktitut,' *Inuktitut*, 53 (September 1983) 27–8

O **Samuel Metcalfe** (1939–), born in Hebron, Labrador, received his early education from the Moravian missionaries and later studied at Memorial University. He was the first mayor of Nain, Labrador. He writes, reads, and speaks English and Inuktitut fluently and knows both the syllabic and Roman orthographies of Inuktitut. He has written many short stories, one of which is reprinted here. In 1988 he was program officer in the Native Citizens' Directorate for the Secretary of State.

Wooding

After mother died, things were pretty quiet and lonely around the house. There were three of us children in the family, born about a year apart; I was between two sisters. We lived in the village of Hebron on the Labrador coast, where there were about one hundred people. Dad worked for the HBC during the week while a babysitter took care of us. On weekends, dad had to go seal hunting or cut firewood, especially in the winter, by dog team. The wood was so scarce and hard to get that we used seal fat with it to try and make it last longer.

When my mother was still living, I remember we all went with dad to cut trees for firewood for two or three weeks when he took his holidays in the winter. On a fine day we would take all day just to get to a place where there were trees, about thirty or forty miles from the village. On these wood cutting trips we would put up the tent, and after settling in dad would be out all day cutting wood while mom kept busy looking after us, or cooking and singing songs, or telling us stories. When we played outside, she would be sewing clothes or making sealskin boots, mitts and parkas for all of us. Sometimes she'd go out fishing on the lake through the ice or go hunting for ptarmigan. It seemed we always had lots to eat and never went hungry, and we always had the best and warmest clothes.

It was peaceful at camp and all was so still you could hear the silence. There was a mixture of sounds such as the rustling of leaves blowing in the wind, the fire crackling in the tent stove, birds singing songs to each other, wolves howling, soft footsteps in the cold snow and chop-chop in the distance from dad's axe. We'd even hear the ice cracking at night from our tent. It was so quiet the place was always noisy. The sound travelled a long way without being interrupted.

When mom went out on the lake to cut a fishing hole with her ice chisel you could see her lift the chisel and strike the ice again before you heard the sound. It never made a rough or a sharp bang like it would if you were close to it; it sounded more like a muffled twang. When the sound reached you it kept on going until you couldn't hear it anymore, or it came back to you in an even more muffled tone when it echoed back from a distant cliff. We would often go out on the lake when the night was clear and cold just to listen to the sound travel through the ice when we struck it with a stick. The ice made different sounds which travelled at different speeds according to its thickness.

Sometimes I would go with dad when he went cutting trees.

I used to be very proud and felt much older than my age (I was about five or six) because mom would pack a lunch bag for me which I would carry in my own little sealskin knapsack she made for me, and I would use a small pair of snowshoes made just for me by dad. We would be gone all day from the tent, cutting trees and piling them up on the lake, taking a rest, shooting ptarmigan when we came upon them, chipping gum off the trees and eating when we got hungry. Late in the evening, we would start walking back to the tent. I would carry the gun and two or three partridges on my back. Sometimes dad would let me take the lead and he would follow close behind me. It seemed that during these brief walks he always took time to talk to me. While he was chopping trees down he'd hardly look at me, let alone have time to talk. He used to point out some prominent landmarks ahead of us and told me to head straight for a certain mark. When we got there we would stop and he'd ask me to turn around and study the place where we had come from. He always told me that it was not good enough just knowing where you were going. You had to know where you were coming from, which was why it was important to get a good idea of the lay of the land behind you. That way you'd never get lost because you could always go back somewhere and find out where you are. I think that's one of the reasons why I get lost in a city very easily; there is no time to stop to look back. You can only see straight ahead of you; there are too many buildings blocking your view. You can relax, take your time, find peace and comfort in the wide open spaces.

There were times when we'd stop and put on a fire to boil water for a cup of hot tea. Of course I'd be a 'good boy' and try to help dad in starting the fire. But he'd always tell me to start my own little fire. He wouldn't just sit down and instruct me how to do it. He would ask me to do as he did, step by step. When we got back to the camp and the village, I'd be very proud in telling everybody that I did all these things all by myself without any help.

There are many things that my father, grandfather and uncle taught me that I can never forget because of their approach and manner – the very way they presented themselves. For instance, I still feel incomplete or not fully dressed unless I have a good quality penknife in my pocket. Grandfather, uncle and I were on a caribou hunting trip one time and my grandfather was wrestling with a crippled caribou. The caribou was shot in the leg and grandfather didn't want to waste another bullet to kill it. He asked me for my pocket knife which I had forgotten at home. So he got my uncle's knife and killed the caribou just by piercing the soft spot on its head. My grandfather didn't speak to me very much during the rest of the trip. I just let it go by without much concern.

We got home a few days later and after we had put everything away he said to me, 'Come out to the porch with me and make sure you have your pocket knife.' When we got out he asked for my knife, opened it and pierced it into the frozen caribou, gave it a twist and pulled it back out, minus the blade. He threw away the rest of the knife and went back into the house grumbling away to himself, but I felt as though he was talking directly to me. 'I asked for a pocket knife and all I get is a piece of tin. And what a way to go hunting with no knife in your pocket! You might as well wear pocketless pants or have no pants on at all.' How I felt is hard to describe but it's something I'll never forget and will always appreciate. It has come in handy many, many times since.

Sam Metcalfe, 'Wooding,' *Inuktitut*, 56 (summer 1984) 46–50

O   **John Amagoalik**'s last speech at the Federal Provincial Conference of First Ministers on Aboriginal Constitutional Matters on 9 March 1984 is a passionate plea for the Inuit cause.

Amagoalik's Closing Remarks, 1984

Everybody keeps saying, everybody around the table, everybody in this room keeps saying that we have failed. Yes, there has been failure, but we haven't failed you have failed.
– Applause
I am sorry, but the people of Canada have to know who has failed. British Columbia, you have failed. Alberta, you have failed.
– Applause
Saskatchewan, you have failed. Newfoundland, Yukon Territory you have failed. We haven't failed.

You have failed to agree that aboriginal peoples have the democratic and human right to self-government. You have self-government. You elect your Member of Parliament. You elect your provincial government, you benefit from resource development on your lands. In the Arctic we elect our representative to the territorial government. As a matter of fact, my MLA is sitting right next to me, but we don't have responsible government, we don't have responsible government. We don't have the right to benefit from resource development, from our lands and our resources.

Now, I said you have failed and we have not and the reason why I say that is because we will continue on our land claims negotiations, we will continue that. We will continue to have discussions with the government of Canada on Nunavut. We will continue to have discussions with the province of Quebec for greater autonomy for the Kativik Regional Government. We will begin discussions with the Newfoundland government and the federal government on the land claims and self-government for the Inuit of Labrador. So we don't want people – we don't want the people of Canada to have the impression that we are leaving this conference having failed totally and beat, because that is not the case. The world continues tomorrow and we will continue these negotiations and discussions that I have identified.

Federal Provincial Conference of First Ministers on Aboriginal Constitutional Matters, Verbatim transcript, 8–9 March, 1984

O **Pitseolak Ashoona** (1907–83), graphic artist, was born on Nottingham Island, Northwest Territories. Considered one of the best of the Cape Dorset artists, she told the story of her life in *Pitseolak: Pictures out of My Life* (1971), the first of the Inuit oral biographies. Here, Pitseolak tells Dorothy Eber about her courtship and marriage to Ashoona in 1922.

Pitseolak Ashoona's Courtship and Marriage

When Ashoona came to the camp I didn't know why he came. I didn't know he came for me. I thought he'd just come for a visit – until he started to take me to the sled. I got scared. I was crying and Ashoona was pushing and sometimes picking me up to try to put me on the *komatik* ['sleigh']. Anyone trying to get married would often have to carry the girl! At that time the young girls used to be really afraid of the men – frightened to go to bed with them. The first time I was sleeping beside my husband his breath was so heavy, his skin so hard. But after I got used to my husband I was really happy; we had a good life together. The first time we went to Netsilik [a large, distant lake] we were all alone for a year and Ashoona delivered my son Kumwartok. With my mother to help. When my husband died at Netsilik even though I had relatives, it was as if my whole family had died – I had no one anymore. Ottochie, my youngest son, was in the *amoutik*. He was the only one who didn't learn how to hunt from his father. Ashoona taught his sons to hunt before he died. After Ashoona died at Netsilik, when the geese were coming south and flying overhead down here past Cape Dorset, I used to think, 'These geese have been with Ashoona back in Netsilik. They've been at Ashoona's grave.' When it was really dark and I could hear the geese overhead, I'd go outside and I'd yell, 'Goodbye, goodbye!'

Dorothy Eber, 'Eskimo Tales,' *Natural History*, LXXXVI, 8 (October 1985) 128

O **Mary Simon** (1947–) was born in Kangiqsualujjuaq in northern Quebec. She began her working career as a producer/announcer of Inuktitut radio and television programs for CBC Northern Service. Later she worked for the Inuit Tapirisat of Canada and *Inuit Today*. She was politically active in the Makivik Corporation of Quebec and was in 1988 the president of the Inuit Circumpolar Conference. Miss Simon presented the following address at the Arctic Polar Conference (Eben Hopson Chair) held at McGill University, Montreal, 19–21 September 1985.

The Role of Inuit in International Affairs

... The main thrust of my presentation today is that Inuit have a legitimate, extensive and varied role to fulfill in international matters. This role has yet to be adequately recognized. In light of the increasing impact of the actions of the international community on Inuit rights, our culture and northern homeland, we have a compelling responsibility to become increasingly involved.

When Inuit speak of promoting Inuit rights at the international level, we are primarily referring to our aboriginal rights, based on past and present use and occupancy of vast circumpolar land and marine areas. These areas transcend the boundaries of Greenland, Canada, Alaska (United States), and also the Soviet Union.

Inuit aboriginal rights must include specific rights to protect, manage and benefit from our northern environment and its renewable and non-renewable resources. Appropriate institutions relating to these purposes are required to ensure Inuit involvement in decision-making and enable concrete exercise of the Inuit right of self-government.

It is important to emphasize that Inuit aboriginal rights are not confined to land areas and land-fast sea ice. Within our regions, we possess extensive interests and use large portions of the arctic marine environment. Further, matters such as pollution prevention and control and management of marine biological resources go well beyond the coastal zone or land-fast ice areas.

In addition to aboriginal rights, 'Inuit rights' must also refer to those fundamental economic, social, cultural and political rights which the world community has enshrined in international conventions. These include such rights as the right to self-determination (which we believe includes the right to self-government); the right of a people not to be deprived of its own means of subsistence; the right to an adequate standard of living; and the right of persons to enjoy their own culture. In our view, these international rights in effect confirm our aboriginal rights.

It is our position that the recognition and free exercise of all our rights will help to improve the quality of life in Inuit communities, ensure our survival as a distinct people and enable us to promote the environmental integrity of our homeland.

In discussing the role of Inuit in international matters with you today, I will briefly cover the following ...

I. INTERNATIONAL ISSUES FACING INUIT AND
CIRCUMPOLAR REGIONS

Resource development, military, and marine boundary issues
are quickly raising the level of awareness and importance of
circumpolar regions to various countries, particularly such
superpowers as the Soviet Union and the United States. With
the aid of new and improved technologies, activities which
may dramatically affect Canada's North and the Inuit way of
life are occurring at an accelerating pace.

Issues with far-reaching implications which Inuit must face
include the following:

1) *The Polar Sea Issue and Assertions of Canadian Sovereignty.* The recent voyage through the Northwest Passage
of the u.s. ice-breaker, the Polar Sea, has highlighted the
need for Canada to take additional measures to protect
Inuit and other Canadian rights and interests in the Arctic.
Inuit have urged Prime Minister Mulroney to unequivo-
cally recognize Inuit offshore aboriginal rights and claim
the arctic archipelago as Canadian 'historic waters.' Inuit
use of northern waters and land-fast ice can help to jus-
tify Canada's claim that the Northwest Passage is 'historic' rather than merely 'internal waters.' This would give
Canada greater international legal authority to control
future military and commercial uses by other countries
of the Northwest Passage. (For example, there would not
automatically be a right of innocent passage for foreign
military and other vessels.)

Although Canada is taking significant steps to assert
its sovereignty by drawing straight base lines, building an
ice-breaker capable of year-round arctic surveillance, and
increasing military operations in the North, Inuit still
have major concerns. None of these measures provide for
proper environmental management in the Arctic. Comprehensive ocean management is urgently required with
the increasing marine vessel traffic in our northern
regions. While civil and criminal laws will be extended
in the Arctic, it still remains to be seen whether Canada
will meaningfully recognize Inuit offshore rights. This
must be done in a manner which fully endorses the right

267

of Inuit to participate in marine and other environmental management. Inuit positions have stated that advisory powers alone are not sufficient and that Inuit must have a meaningful role in decision-making.

2) *Upcoming Changes in Canada's Defence System.* Canada and the United States are presently proceeding with the modernization of the Distant Early Warning (DEW) line, which will become known as the North Warning System. The new network of 47 radar stations within Canada will be completed within 8 years, at a cost of close to one billion dollars. It is likely that many Inuit may be interested in obtaining employment and service contracts related to this northern venture and they should be accorded preference as local residents.

Inuit have always supported the strengthening of Canada and our country must have a proper defense system in the North. However, this does not mean that the Canadian government should participate in President Reagan's proposed Strategic Defense Initiative, known as 'Star Wars.' Canada should not support and take part in initiatives which involve nuclear weapons and which are likely to further escalate the nuclear arms race. Recently, Prime Minister Mulroney rejected Canadian government participation in Star Wars, although he endorsed private sector involvement. Mr. Mulroney did add that Canada, as a nation, should dedicate itself to world peace and that it has a more valid role to play in arms control at the United Nations.

In keeping with the intention in ICC's Charter to promote world peace, Inuit and other Canadians should continue to urge the Prime Minister not to participate directly or indirectly in Star Wars and to declare the Canadian Arctic as a nuclear-free zone. Currently, Inuit have cause for serious concern regarding the passage of nuclear submarines in arctic waters and the use of the seabed by foreign nations for military purposes. Since there are highly complex legal and political issues related to defence in the North, it would be useful for Canada to develop an arctic foreign policy. I firmly believe that Inuit and other Canadians would support and participate in such a vital initiative.

3) *Hydrocarbon and Other Resource Development.* With the increase in oil and gas and other resource development and the future possibility of deep seabed mining, there is a growing interest and demand for year-round shipping routes. Such increased navigation and ocean development activities pose real potential hazards to the marine environment and Inuit interests. Consequently, a comprehensive ocean management policy and transportation policy are sorely needed. These and other arctic policies (both foreign and domestic) will require coordination, so that they may remain consistent with overall arctic policy objectives, which must be determined.

4) *International Water Diversion Schemes.* Drought, pollution and conflicts over water use pose a threat to Canada's fresh-water resources. To meet growing shortages of water in the United States, former Quebec Premier Robert Bourassa has proposed a $100 billion mega-project to convert James Bay into a freshwater reservoir and divert the river water collected to the United States, through the Great Lakes.

As the value of freshwater continues to climb, increased attention will likely be focussed on northern rivers and lakes for possible diversion schemes. A national and international water policy should be formulated which encourages more efficient water use and improved water management. Northern freshwater resources must remain available for local and regional Inuit use.

5) *Anti-Harvesting Lobbies Affecting the North.* Continued efforts must be made to counter anti-sealing, anti-whaling and anti-trapping lobbies in various countries. While all these campaigns are not necessarily directed towards aboriginal harvesting activities in circumpolar regions, northern subsistence economies are being severely affected by the decrease in market demand for pelts and by-products. To support aboriginal hunters and trappers, Inuit organizations in all circumpolar regions will have to further coordinate efforts in seeking greater

international understanding and support for Inuit subsistence activities.

II. THE NEED FOR A COMPREHENSIVE ARCTIC POLICY

If these and other international issues affecting the North are to be properly addressed, it is essential to develop a comprehensive foreign and domestic arctic policy. Such a policy must accommodate Inuit interests, including those in Labrador and Northern Quebec. Inuit economic and cultural values and concerns should be integrated in all aspects of such policy, as appropriate.

For example, under the *U.N. Convention on the Law of the Sea* (not yet in force), Canada has justifiably agreed to the sharing of revenues with disadvantaged countries, in regard to resource exploitation of the continental shelf beyond 200 nautical miles. Yet, despite the existence of Inuit aboriginal rights in and to marine areas, no similar principle of revenue-sharing has been adopted by Canada in regard to Inuit offshore claims. These types of inconsistencies in domestic and foreign policy should surely be resolved as soon as possible.

An articulated policy could help promote international understanding and cooperation. It could be used to encourage coordination of policy-making and decision-making in the international community, particularly among those countries with arctic jurisdictions and interests. Moreover, the significance of the Arctic and its resources to both present and future generations of northern peoples could then be seriously taken into account.

Building a 100,000-shaft horsepower polar icebreaker for year-round navigation, alone, will not resolve conflicts among resource users or protect the delicate arctic environment. We need practical and comprehensive policies and planning which will manage vessel traffic, so as to protect ships and the northern environment. The effect of ships' tracks through the ice on Inuit harvesting activities and on wildlife resources must also be fully taken into account.

In addition, it is important that Inuit favour those policies and practices which foster peaceful co-existence and use of appropriate and safe technologies in circumpolar regions.

III. THE NATURE OF THE INUIT ROLE IN INTERNATIONAL AFFAIRS

A growing number of issues affecting Inuit rights and interests are increasingly being regulated at the international level. Examples include ocean dumping, acid rain, Law of the Sea, arms control, fish, whales, migratory birds, endangered species and resource development in marine areas. In these and other instances, national or regional initiatives alone are not adequate to protect Inuit communities, our way of life and our northern regions.

In order to devise and implement a comprehensive arctic policy, promote Inuit rights and protect the future of our circumpolar regions, we as Inuit must increase our knowledge and involvement in international affairs. In regard to such matters, action by Inuit could possibly take a number of forms, which might include the following:

1) through close liaison with our national governments, Inuit can encourage the signing and ratifying of international conventions which are consistent with the recognition and protection of Inuit rights and Inuit arctic policy. In the case of international agreements directly affecting Inuit and the circumpolar regions, it is important that Inuit be involved in at least the policy-making and implementation stages;

2) for purposes related to arctic policy, close contact and collaboration with international organizations involved with arctic issues would help to broaden the base of support. It is important to ensure that the World Conservation Strategy and other strategies proposed by international organizations fully take into account Inuit rights and concerns;

3) in the case of serious breaches of Inuit rights, recourse may need to be made to specially designated committees of the United Nations or other international bodies. For example, the Working Group on Indigenous Populations, the Human Rights, among others, potentially offer means of assistance within the United Nations depending on the circumstances; and

4) in order to foster complete and accurate information about Inuit and the North, lobbying within different countries will likely be necessary.

In promoting understanding, cooperation and support for Inuit rights at the international level, the Inuit Circumpolar Conference has a significant role to play together with other Inuit organizations in the various regions. In this regard, the non-governmental organization (NGO) status of the ICC can provide Inuit with greater means and opportunities to advance their positions and interests. Virtually all of the forms of action I have described can be facilitated by the ICC with its NGO status. Further, cultural, social and other human rights are often more carefully addressed by NGOs than by international governmental organizations.

CONCLUSION

I believe we can conclude that there must be a significantly expanded role for Inuit at the international level.

As Inuit, we have a responsibility to our people and communities to secure greater international recognition and protection of Inuit rights. At the same time, Inuit from all circumpolar countries must contribute to the integrity of the world environment and world peace, by advocating coherent life-sustaining, cooperative policies and initiatives. For example, we can offer our assistance and support to ensure a broad interpretation and application of Article 234 of the *U.N. Convention on the Law of the Sea*. This Article specifically deals with environmental protection of ice-covered areas. We can also urge Canada to steer a diplomatic course away from nuclear uses in the North and excessive militarization.

There is little doubt that there are difficult choices and challenges ahead for Inuit and all others who seriously care about the North. However, I firmly believe that with a great deal of effort and by working together, we can make the essential difference.

O   **Mary Carpenter Lyons** (1943–) was born on her father's schooner, *The North Star*, while crossing the Beaufort Sea. She attended Rutgers University and graduated with certificates in psychology and education. She has taught in Plainfield, New Jersey, and in Tuktoyaktuk. She was working in 1987 on a language project with the Committee for the Original People's Entitlement (COPE) in the western Arctic. Her poem 'Nunavut? – Denendeh? = Northwesterritories' is especially relevant at this time.

Nunavut? – Denendeh? = Northwesterritories

O arched northland of tensed wonders
Your ice-eyed beauty
Captures the strong hearted
With the privilege
of nesting in your hearth

O tenderland, uniquely north
Your fate is much discussed
By distant men who sit
And watch your primal lovers
Slowly dying

Who sit and build
invisible, governing walls
Suborning your children without consent
You hum disgust
But your crowning skies forgive
Granting oppressors safe journey south

O mighty land strike now
Show your true heart
Bear fruit again and mother us

Granny capital has heard your pleas
From men who sincerely dishonour you
Deceiving your innocent fire-watchers
How long will you allow it?
The tenders despair

O greatland, you are leached by white lies
Lip-serviced, not loved.

O   **Martha Flaherty** (1950–), nurse, model, translator, interpreter, journalist, was born at Inukjuak, in arctic Quebec. The grand-daughter of Robert Flaherty, the noted Canadian documentary filmmaker, she grew up in Grise Fiord. In 1988 she was living in Ottawa and working as writer/editor for the *Nunavut Newsletter* and hostess for the CBC television program *Taqarvut.*

I Fought to Keep My Hair

As a child, I remember when we were about to move somewhere, I knew we were being moved, because my father said, 'We are going to move. We'll see our relatives and besides there's more wildlife up there. I was told we won't be hungry anymore.' He waited for my mother's reaction but there was none. 'I was told we could come back here to Inukjuaq when we want to,' he continued.

Although I was only five I remember being completely spellbound and confused as I was surrounded by adults roaming around and talking secretly about something. I was suspicious that something was going on.

We were being relocated to Grise Fiord by a ship, the C.D. Howe, and the relocation left me with many bad experiences I could not forget for many years. I was afraid of qallunaats (white people) for years. Around the age of 20, I finally over-came my fear but still had an uneasy feeling towards them.

For as long as I can remember, Inuit believed that the white people were very helpful. Because these sayings were driven into my soft mind, I really believed we were going to get some help. Instead I went through hell with doctors and nurses.

Not to name any of them, they wore white clothes, carried needles, stethoscopes, tongue depressors, cotton balls and scissors. Of course, that is not to mention what they smelled like. That is scary enough for any kid. It is the scissors, I remember the most. With needles and other equipment, I wasn't going to lose anything. But with scissors I found out they wanted something from me. They wanted my hair – to give me a brush cut. Who wants a brush cut when she knows she's a girl? Especially coming from an Inuit family whose belief it is that a woman is to have long hair. Not me, and I fought. That's why I had a terrible time with white people.

On the ship, the medical people found a parent looking for

lice in her child's hair. Of course, the doctor, as we all knew by then, would not leave Inuit alone and made a big thing out of this. He decided, with no consent or agreement from the parents, to give all the children (boys and girls) a brush cut whether they liked it or not. By that time I knew Inuit adults would have no say in any decision made by qallunaats even though they had their own wishes. I learned that we weren't going to have any hair. But I was determined to fight to keep my hair and I did. I was the only kid on the ship with long hair. The Frenchmen used to take my picture because of my long hair and each paid me 25¢. Kids would ask me how come I always had money. I would tell them, 'because I have long hair. If you fought you'd have money, too.'

Because my parents could not do anything about my being chased by a man with scissors, I crawled under the bed. He actually crawled under to get me. I kicked him and kicked him to get out. Then I locked myself and my mother in the washroom. We were both crying. After that it was like a dream. Even now I still dream of being attacked by a bunch of people who are tying me up. That person who chased me with scissors will always be imprinted in my mind. In my mind, I'll always want to get him back, although I have been told by elders, 'When someone mistreats you or abuses you, never fight back.' I know Inummarit words are strong, valuable and important and I won't forget. I know it's wrong to lie or fight back in our culture.

Since I've learned a bit about the qallunaat way of living I can now take advantage of it. Lie or not to lie – it is up to you. Example, when someone commits murder, if he does not have enough evidence against him, he's innocent until he's proven guilty. When I was young, I thought you had no choice except to tell the truth.

I was afraid of white people throughout our whole trip, so when we got to Grise Fiord I thought I wasn't going to be scared anymore. But there were new fears. There was new land and new things to learn to survive – a new fear. People were scared when they were left behind with nothing.

It was like landing on the moon. The environment in Grise Fiord was very different from Inukjuaq. In Grise Fiord it gets dark very early. There was no vegetation, no sign of animals, and of course, no stores. There was no wood for housing nor enough willows for qarnak and no fresh water nearby except salt water or icebergs. You had to look around for a fresh iceberg that wasn't salty – and sometimes you'd look for a long time.

The mountains were so high that they looked like they would fall on top of me and crush me into pieces. Those mean-looking mountains told me there was nothing else to be scared of except them. They made me feel so small and out of place that I knew I would have to be friendly with them. Things that scared me all my life were nothing compared to the fall and winter weather in Grise Fiord.

When we first moved there, Inuit were hungry because there was no wildlife and the ice conditions were different. It didn't freeze as early because the wind was very strong. I kept asking myself, 'Where are all those qallunaat that are supposed to be so helpful?'

When I think back to those times I sometimes think dogs or animals are treated better in some cases. The (qallunaat) seem to talk a lot about humanity and yet they don't practice it where it is really needed. At least dogs are fed and looked after, although they are a lot more adaptable to the environment. Humans have less adaptability, but they are smarter.

We believe the weather, because it is so harsh up there, had a significant effect on my father's health. He died at the age of 64 from lung problems. We can believe the doctor's diagnosis of his sickness, but elders say he froze his lungs. No wonder – he used to hunt in $-40°$ to $-60°$ weather in the dark for days at times without eating. My mom said he would take off in early morning by dog team. He drank water because we didn't even have tea. He had no choice except to hunt for us. Sometimes he came home with fewer dogs. The only people who might have some food were the RCMP. But you had to have some skins to buy food. For the first few years, there were hardly any skins to sell, especially in winter. I remember one particular time with my mother carrying a baby on her back. She and I fetched food from the RCMP's garbage a few miles away because we had no food. We came home with only empty cans and a little bit of leftovers.

These weren't the only problems. My sister was lost for years somewhere down south. She was being treated for tuberculosis (T.B.) My parents did not know where she was or how she was doing. She was sent to Inukjuaq, supposedly to her parents. (When Inuit children were born, the government used to give them numbers indicating where you were born. Each person had his or her own numbers.) My sister was sent to Inukjuaq by mistake because she had no last name. After that she was sent to Resolute Bay. She did not know where her parents were. After a year she finally arrived home as a complete stranger with a new language – English. This incident had a big affect on my parents. I don't blame them; if I didn't know where my child was I would probably become insane. My parents were physically and emotionally exhausted from not knowing where their child was and from having to try to survive in a new environment. The government did this damage to the people by relocating them, but they will not do anything about it, not even apologize. They don't talk about it; it's hidden. They only talk about the 'good things' they are about to do in the Arctic. The damage they did to Inuit is evident and it is permanent.

I don't think I even had a childhood between the ages of 7 to 12 because I had to hunt with my father for food, in very cold weather, with absolutely no daylight. I had to corral seals for my father. I also had to look after 17 dogs and sometimes the dogs would be taller than I was. Sometimes my father had to help me to go to the washroom because I was too young to dress myself in the – 50° weather. But I had no choice except to hunt because I was the oldest. Sometimes I used to cry knowing how cold it was going to be, but then my father would just say, 'Do you want us to starve?'

When I was not hunting with my father I had to help my mother sew. At the age of 10 I was able to sew complete footwear. Some skins were hard to sew, but if I made a mistake or made bad stitches, my mother would take them apart, and that's when I sewed with tears. By the age of 12 I was making my own kamiks, sealskin boots, and parkas. These days people don't even have time to look at beautiful Inuit clothes. When I tell people that I used to hunt and make Inuit clothes, they laugh with disbelief. I guess you would, too, if you saw me sitting in a fancy office with high heeled shoes and fashionable clothes.

Today, I think about that move – when the sea was very rough and the ship was rocking back and forth, its pole almost touching the water.

The sea looked so mean that you didn't want to look down. When it was that rough, we had to wear life jackets, and that was scary. And when the waves were worse, our food and dishes used to fly all over. Kids were crying and adults became very quiet. Because people were crying and dogs were howling, I learned that it's not just me who gets scared. Adults get scared, too. We had to hang on or else we'd be dumped into the sea.

Martha Flaherty, 'I Fought to Keep My Hair' *Nunavut*, 5, 6 (June 1986) 4–6

O **Aksaajuuq Etuangat** (1901–) worked with the Department of Health and Welfare in the early 1950s. In 1988 he was living in Pangnirtung where he carved in ivory and soapstone. He remembers the days when whaling was an important industry around Pangnirtung.

The Whalers of Pangnirtung

... I remember two *qallunaat* who were whalers; one was the boss and the other was a barrel maker. Those were wooden barrels he made. He would put straps around them and get them ready to be filled with blubber. One barrel would be filled with seal blubber, another with square flipper fat, the rest with big seal blubber, blue whale blubber, walrus blubber and so on. The blubber would be used for oil and everything would be well organized. On the whaling days, they would go after blubber from all kinds of sea animals, just blubber and more blubber. They would not buy the blubber we brought in for money, but would trade for white man's food.

Those whalers would stop their work for a while, usually at the end of July, but would soon get going again. August was a very tiring time when there was blubber to be cut.

Then, when it was time to get ready to go whaling again, the Inuit would be given the same amount of food for their pay. The men would also go hunting caribou for clothing. They would return with skins and would be given the same amount of food again. Some hunters would be out all summer and would finally return home only when it first started to snow in the fall.

Just before the sea froze up, the whalers would turn to seal hunting. I recall there were four whaling boats, Peterheads as some called them. Those boats had harpoons on the front and were used for whaling. They had a very long rope attached to them and they always had extra rope to use if needed. Some boats had big firearms which were used on animals. If the boat didn't have those firearms, they would use the harpoons.

As soon as the ice started to freeze over, they would put the hunting equipment away in a building on shore to keep it safe until next season. When the sea was too rough for the hunters in the fall, they would go hungry for animals for a while. The whalers used to go to the islands to hunt and often had a hard time on their way because of the sea water freezing up and rough water. Usually on Saturdays the people would be given white man's food, but they would still be hungry for real food.

The whaling equipment could not be bought or sold by anyone. The Inuit hunters would just be issued spears and firearms to use during whaling days. (All the whaling boats would carry firearms.) Some of the equipment would be in need of repair before the hunters could use it. Some of the firearms were muzzle-loaders. Whenever a hunter needed a firearm, he would be issued one to use. The strongest firearm I recall was the one that used .44 ammunition.

When I was a child, if the whalers were short of men I was asked to fill in and help them. I actually took part in killing the blue whales even though I was only in my early teens. Every spring, in the month of June, while the floe edge was still a long way from land, the whaling boats would be taken down to the water on big sleds pulled by lots of dogs. The kind of boats I'm talking about had a roof over them, although some were open boats. Once the seal hunting began, the boats would stay out for weeks. Every week a boat would come around the other boats to pick up the catch and take it back to camp, and the other hunters would carry on hunting more seals to fill their boats. The boats would stay in the water until the ice was all gone, which is usually in July. Eventually, each boat would be carrying something: one would be filled with seal meat, another with blubber, etc. Everything was well organized. The *qallunaat* ... would take the skins and blubber and the meat would be given to the women for food.

The women would also go seal hunting when there were lots of seals in the springtime. Every spring, they would plan to go hunting while their husbands were whaling. They would be using their husband's harpoons, etc. The men who were still in camp with the women would also help. They would pull the *qamutiks* and women would ride on them. Lots of seals would be killed without using guns. The women would stay beside the seal holes until the seals came up for air; they would kill a lot of seals that way. The men who were still in camp would skin them and take the blubber off the skins.

Regardless of the things that the ships had brought with them, the women would be given cloth free of charge to make dresses. The men would go mainly for the things that they might need for their kayaks or some of the boats. They would take them even though they were all and not fit to be used anymore. And whenever oil or blubber would go bad (yellowish in colour) the men would boil it and when it blackened they would then paint the boats with it, and this thing that we called soot would help to give the boats their colour ...

'The Whalers of Pangnirtung: Recollections of Aksaajuuq Etuangat' *Recollections of Inuit Elders* 31–2

O **Leah Arnaujaq** lived in Repulse Bay. She recalled the events of the early years of the twentieth century when Hudson Bay was another favourite whaling hunting ground.

In the Days of the Whalers

The men and women were whaling again. The older men and women would go up onto a hill to watch what the whaling boats were doing. When the men were chasing a whale, all the women were told to lie down flat on their backs, all day if necessary. Only when the whale was killed were they told they could sit up again. While we waited for the men to come ashore there were many activities to keep us busy. the older women would make hair pins out of white sealskin and grass, and have them ready for when the whalers came back on shore. Sometimes the elders would play games with the children. They would tie a leg of one child to that of another and the pairs of children would try to knock each other down; even the grown-ups used to join in.

In the meantime the women who had sons had to fill pails with fresh water. Then the whaling boats came in, rowed by the children and the older adults, and towing the blue whales. While rowing, they got really hot and sweaty so the women who had sons picked up their water buckets and waded out into the water to meet the boats.

When they all got ashore they cut up the *muktuk* of the whale and everyone tried to get lots of it to take home. The women would put the *muktuk* in their *kiniks*, which is the front apron of their *amautiks*. They would hold the apron up to make a pouch.

'In the Days of the Whalers: Stories of Leah Arnaujaq,' *Recollections of Inuit Elders* 11–12

O   **Peter Ernerk** (1947–) was born at Lyon Inlet and went to school in Chesterfield Inlet, Yellowknife, Churchill, and Ottawa. A former broadcaster for the CBC and translator for the government of the Northwest Territories he was a member of the Legislative Assembly, NWT, from 1975 to 1979 and was re-elected in 1988. He was in 1988 president of the Keewatin Inuit Land Claims, a member of the board of directors for the Tungavik Federation of Nunavut. He has written extensively for a number of Inuit journals.

The Inuit as Hunters and Managers

We, the Inuit of the Arctic, live the life of subsistence hunters, fishermen and trappers.

We have, and always will, depend on animals for survival. From the earliest age possible every Inuk child is taught about this inherent characteristic of our lifestyle. For many centuries we have depended upon our renewable resources for survival. We will continue to do so for many centuries to come. We are the greatest managers of our renewable resources within our Circumpolar homelands. For example, we do not kill female narwhal with calves and we have never wiped out any species of animals.

Both North America and Europe support large populations which have been conditioned to think that meat comes from the grocery stores, clothes come from the textile mills and leather shoes come from Italy. Through the urbanization of man and the sophistication of society these people have acquired this false perspective. They no longer appreciate the origins of such basic necessities.

For years the Inuit have enjoyed an unmolested lifestyle of nomadic hunting. Suddenly it is necessary to defend our lifestyle and to fight for our very survival against the Europeans who brought us into the fur industry in the first place.

It has never been within the dictates of our culture to export our ideas or our ways of life, but today it seems to me that we must provide educational 'enlightenment' to southern Canadians and Western Society. As we do not have the funds, manpower or energy to accomplish this, we must depend on news media to provide the necessary exposure. Most of us who live in the Circumpolar community (in Greenland, Alaska and Canada) expect to continue to live here for the rest of our lives. We will continue to hunt caribou, seals, walrus, beluga and narwhal for livelihood purposes.

This is the lifestyle we choose and we have no intention of adapting to a welfare society (as recommended by some animal lovers and animal rights activists). According to Stephen Best of the International Wildlife Coalition and Ontario Humane Society in Toronto, Ontario, we native people should become 'full Canadians'. As we natives are the *original* Canadians (residing here long before Mr. Best's ancestors) I felt it more appropriate to extend a similar invitation to him. 'Welcome to Canada' Mr. Best and should you desire to stay, come and talk to me and my people about our traditions and culture. We'd be more than happy to discuss our future plans with you on issues such as the environment, renewable resources and conservation.

I for one am very tired of the fact that people such as Stephen Best, Patrick Moore, Brigitte Bardot, Stanley Johnson (Member of the European Parliament in Strassbourg, France) and others are never around to listen to the native people when we discuss our conservation management plans for the future. Perhaps they could learn something from us.

During the recent Inuit Circumpolar Conference in Kotzebue, Alaska (held 28 July – 3 August 1986) a resolution was unanimously passed giving full support for the efforts of Indigenous Survival International. I.S.I. is an aboriginal organization with representatives from Alaska, Canada and Greenland. It was formed to offer reasoned and positive action for the protection of indigenous hunting rights. I.S.I. lobbies successfully in the international arena to meet the forces of various groups whose policies violate the rights of all aboriginal peoples to maintain their traditional way of life. The I.C.C. resolution further condemns the actions of animal rights and protection groups wherever and whenever they move to reduce or destroy the right of Inuit and other aboriginal peoples to harvest resources for their cultural, economic and spiritual survival.

Inuit in Nunavut (eastern Northwest Territories) have already negotiated a Wildlife Agreement with the Government of Canada. It confirms that the Inuit have a right to discuss and negotiate any proposals or plans made by international governments which may affect the Inuit in regards to renewable resource management. We should have a final say in any scientific studies or recommendations.

Finally, we native people will not apologize to anyone in the international community for being aboriginal people. We will never apologize to anyone for being subsistence hunters, fishermen and trappers.

We are again facing a new form of colonialism in Canada, one which is both frustrating and uncaring from the indigenous people's perspective.

Peter Ernerk, 'The Inuit as Hunters and Managers,' *The Beaver*, 67:1 (February/March 1987) 62

O   **Angus Anderson** (1963–) was born in St Anthony, Newfoundland, and educated in Nain, Labrador. In 1988 he was employed as a reporter for the *Kinatuinamutilengayuk*, the coastal bilingual monthly paper of the Okalakatiget Society, in Nain. Anderson enjoys writing poetry. 'The Tree' was written for this book.

The Tree

As I watch a giant tree,
   I try to imagine how long it took to grow.

This tree has been through everything,
    it's been through storms like me and you.

This tree has survived the thunder storms,
    Without a single scratch or burn.
This tree has survived the hottest heat waves
    in which no man would ever return.

The colours have changed throughout the seasons,
    as a human would with mood.
Some branches have fallen off.
    but in time they were renewed.

It's lovely how the morning sun shines,
    especially through the branches.
This giant lovely tree has stood here,
    and it didn't have to take any chances.

If humans can be peaceful as this tree,
    maybe this world would know the meaning of peace.
But as we learn of other cultures and races,
    our troubles just seem to increase.

This tree is a perfect example
    of living in peace and harmony.
If only we understood the growth of this tree,
    then people, I'm sure would live in harmony.

O   **Liz Semigok** (1948–) was born in Hebron, Labrador, and
attended school in Hopedale and Makkovik, Labrador. She has
worked in a fishing plant in Nain. Since 1980, she has worked
for the Labrador Inuit Association and in 1988 she was secretary for the Torngassok Cultural Centre in Nain. She writes
poems in Inuktitut and then translates them into English.

My Little House

My little house, stinky little house,
tiny little house.

Cold little house, partly frozen,
When it warms up, it gives off
a lot of heat.
Tiny little house, my own little house.

The chamber-pot of my little house,
so small.
Hardly big enough to sit on, so
small.
All the little windows, so small.
Even the little person inside,
so small.

My little house, small little house,
drafty little house.
The little drafts, even though
they're small.
blow so very hard.
Even the little person inside shivers.
The little person with the little house,
tiny little me.

My Cooking Pot

My boiler, tarnished and no longer new,
its lid buckled and bent,
its bottom layered in charred soot.
Grateful am I when it boils something.

My pot, used, grimed, worn,
no shining, gleaming clean,
is cooking a rock-cod.
Now that it's boiling, it's steaming!
And on the side, a hole.

O **Tagak Curley** (1944–) was born in Coral Harbour. He was a
founding member and first president of the Inuit Tapirisat of
Canada. He was elected to the Legislative Assembly of the
Northwest Territories in 1979 for Keewatin South, and has been
a colourful, outspoken, but increasingly respected member. In

1987 he was minister for economic development and tourism for the government of the Northwest Territories.

Who Would Want to Live Here?

Our land has never been conquered. If it was, we would be wiped out of our culture. The minute we step out of our community we are in our historical environment. But not down south. Indian people have to cope with that. They were deprived of their wildlife, their land. But we have something that helped our people. Our environment is harsh. Who would want to live here?

Takag Curley, 'The Independent Inuit,' *Maclean's* 14 July 1986, 24

Nellie Cournoyea (1940–) was born in the Mackenzie Delta at Aklavik, Northwest Territories. She has worked as a station manager for CBC radio in Inuvik and as a land rights worker for the Inuit Tapirisat of Canada and the Committee for Original People's Entitlement. She has spoken out strongly against the anti-seal and anti-trapping movements. In 1985 she was appointed to the Nunavut Constitutional Forum.

Everybody Likes the Inuit

When someone says, 'I want to practise my own culture,' it doesn't mean going back to freezing in igloos and hunting with bows and arrows. It means regaining the control we had over our lives before ...

They glamorize and romanticize the Inuit ... and give us status the others don't have. Canadians like to talk about us eating frozen meat and living in the cold. It gives Canada something that other countries don't have. Everybody likes the Inuit.

Nellie Cournoyea, 'The Independent Inuit,' *Maclean's*, 14 July 1986, 25

Glossary / Historical Terms

Included are Inuktitut words with their varying spellings that occur in the text. This brief glossary is followed by descriptions of some of the institutions and historical terms that are mentioned.

aja-aja-ja (many variants) syllables sung as a refrain to the beat and tempo of the melody

amoutik (amaut, amautik) woman's parka

angakok (angakoq, angatkoq, angatkut, angekok) a person, a shaman, who was a priest, physician, and prophet

atigi (attigi) undershirt (fur)

fulmar an Arctic sea-bird

iglu (igloo) ice house

Inuk a person

inukshuk landmark

Inuit the people

Inumaruit (Inummarit, Inummariit) the real or genuine or true people

Inuvialuit the name the Inuit of the western Arctic give themselves

kadluna (Qallunaaq, Qallunaat, Qullunaat, Qullunaaq, Quallunaaq, Qallunaats) non-Inuit, literally people with heavy or bushy eyebrows

kamik shoes

kamotik (komatik, qamutik) sledge

k'annerk mouth

kayak (kajak, qajaq) boat

kikkaq (kikkak) a bone on which there is meat left to chew (a choice morsel)

kinik front apron

moolo, *see* ulu
muktuk skin of the whale
oogyuk, *see* ugjuk
oolu, *see* ulu
qagge (qajaq) the great snow hut which used to be set up in every village for the song festivals
Qallunaat, Qallunaq, *see* kadluna
torngak (Torngaq, Tunggak, Tungyak, Torngak) the major spirit of the Labrador Innus
ugjuk (udjuk, ugyuk) a bearded seal or square flipper
ulu (uluk, oolu, moolo) woman's knife
umiak (umiaq) big boat
Uqammaq Eskimo name for the Reverend Edmund Peck, meaning the one who speaks well

HISTORICAL TERMS

Arctic Co-operatives The Inuit hunters of the George River area of northern Quebec first tried to market their products co-operatively in 1959. In 1988 a network of such co-operatives stretches across the Arctic.
COPE Committee for the Original People's Entitlement, Inuvik, NWT, a regional affiliate of the Inuit Tapirisat of Canada
Denendeh, *see* Nunavut
Eskimo disc numbers Numbers introduced by the federal government in 1941 to enable non-Inuit to identify the Inuit, since they found the Inuit family naming system too complex. The disc system also had problems and was discontinued in 1971.
ICI Inuit Cultural Institute, Eskimo Point
ICC Inuit Circumpolar Conference, as international organization representing Inuit of Canada, Alaska, and Greenland
ITC Inuit Tapirisat of Canada, founded 1971, the national voice of Inuit living in sixty-six communities within the Northwest Territories, northern Quebec, and Labrador
Labrador Inuit Association Regional affiliate of the ITC
Makivik Corporation A regional affiliate of ITC with broad-ranging economic activities
Nunavut Our Land, name given to the eastern territory in the division of the Northwest Territories which, subject to a referendum among the 51,000 territory residents and agreement of the federal,

288

provincial, and territorial governments, should exist by 1991. The name of the western territory is Denendeh.

Project Surname A program launched by the government of the Northwest Territories in 1970 to persuade all Eskimo adults to adopt a surname or family name

Bibliography

Complete citations for all printed sources of the literature included in this book and cited in brief are given here. In addition I have included entries for the specialized periodicals, some of which were published only a few years, giving the sponsoring body and dates of publication. Citations of archival sources are for the most part given in full in the text.

Allen, Victor. 'The Snow Goose and the Mosquito – A Question of Development. *North*, xv, 1 (January/February 1968) 28–31

Amagoalik, John. 'Will the Inuit Disappear from the Face of This Earth?' *Inuit Today*, 6, 4 (May 1977) 52–4

Anoee, Eric. 'My Writings.' *Inuttituut* (winter 1977) 5–51

Arnakalak, Kowmageak. 'Northern Lights.' *Inuit Today*, 4, 7 (July/August 1975) 47

'Ask and ... You Shall Receive ... ' *Eskimo*, 20 (March 1951) 9

Ayaruaq, John. 'The Story of John Ayaruaq.' *North*, 16, 2 (1969) 1–5

Baikie, Margaret. *Labrador Memories: Reflections at Mulligan*. Happy Valley, Labrador: *Them Days* n.d.

Balikci, Asen. *The Netsilik Eskimo*. New York: The Natural History Press, American Museum of Natural History 1970

Bilby, Julian W. *Among Unknown Eskimo; An Account of 12 Years Intimate Relations with the Primitive Eskimo of Ice-bound Baffin Land, with a Description of Their Ways of Living, Hunting, Customs and Beliefs*. London: Seeley Service 1923

Blake, E. Vale. *Arctic Experiences: Containing Captain George E. Tyson's Wonderful Drift on the Ice-floe, a History of the Polaris Expedition*. New York: Harper and Brothers 1874

Blodgett, Jean. *The Coming and Going of the Shaman: Eskimo Shamanism and Art.* Winnipeg: The Winnipeg Art Gallery 1978

Boas, Franz. 'Second Report on the Eskimo of Baffin Land and Hudson Bay: From Notes Collected by Captain George Comer, Captain James S. Mutch and Rev. E.J. Peck' *Bulletin of the American Museum of Natural History,* 15, pt. 2. New York 1907

– *The Central Eskimo.* Lincoln: University of Nebraska Press 1964. A reprint of the Bureau of American Ethnology, Sixth Annual Report, Washington, D.C. 1888

– and Henry Rink. 'Eskimo Tales and Songs.' *Journal of American Folk-Lore,* 2 (1889) 123–31; 7 (1894) 45–50; 10 (1897) 109–15

Brody, Hugh. *The People's Land: Eskimos and Whites in the Eastern Arctic.* Middlesex, Eng.: Penguin Books 1975

Burgess, Helen. 'Tookoolito of Cumberland Sound.' *North,* 15 (January/February 1968) 40–3

Campbell, Lydia. 'Sketches of Labrador Life by a Labrador Woman.' *Evening Herald* (St John's), 3, 4, 6, 7, 12, 13, 18, 20, 24 December; 6 February 1895

Canadian Arctic Expedition, 1913–18. *Report*
xiii: *Eskimo Folklore.* Part A: Diamond Jenness, *Myths and Traditions from Northern Alaska, the Mackenzie Delta and Coronation Gulf.* Ottawa 1924
xiv: Helen H. Roberts and Diamond Jenness. *Songs of the Copper Eskimos.* Ottawa 1925

Carpenter, Edmund, ed. *Anerca.* Toronto: J. M. Dent 1959

– 'Eskimo Poetry: Word Magic.' *Explorations,* 4 (February 1955) 101–11

– *Eskimo Realities.* New York: Holt, Rinehart and Winston 1973

– *The Story of Comock the Eskimo: As Told to Robert Flaherty.* Connecticut: Fawcett Publications 1972

Cartwright, George. *A Journal of Transactions and Events during a Residence of Nearly Sixteen Years on the Coast of Labrador.* 3 vols. Newark: Allin and Ridge 1792

Cavanaugh, Beverley. 'Imagery and Structure in Eskimo Song Texts.' *Canadian Folk Music,* 1 (1973) 3–16

Colombo, John Robert. *Poems of the Inuit.* Ottawa: Oberon Press 1981

Courtauld, Augustine. *From the Ends of the Earth* London: University of Oxford Press 1958

Cowan, Susan, ed. *We Don't Live in Snow Houses Now: Reflections of Arctic Bay*. Ottawa: Canadian Arctic Producers 1976

'The Crow and the Two Eider Ducks.' *Eskimo*, 26 (June 1955) 16–17

Crowe, Keith. *A History of the Original Peoples of Northern Can ada*. Montreal: Arctic Institute of North America 1974

d'Argencourt, Leah Idlout. 'C.D. Howe.' Part I: *Inuit Today*, 6, 5 (June 1977) 30–45; Part II: *Inuit Today*, 6, 6 (July/August 1977) 46–51, 89

Davey, J.W. *The Fall of Torngak or the Moravian Mission on the Coast of Labrador*. London: S.W. Partridge & Co. 1905

de Coccola, Raymond, and Paul King. *Ayorama*. Toronto: Oxford University Press 1956

Dictionary of Canadian Biography. Edited by G.W. Brown et al. 10 vols. to date. Toronto: University of Toronto Press 1966–

Dorothy. 'Old Woman's Song.' *Keewatin Echo*, 67 (1974) 6

Eber, Dorothy Harley. 'Eskimo Tales.' *Natural History* LXXXVI 8 (October 1985) 126–9

Ernerk, Peter. 'The Inuit as Hunters and Managers.' *The Beaver* 67:1 (February/March 1987) 62

Eskimo. Periodical published by Roman Catholic Diocese of Churchill – Hudson Bay. 1946–

Etudes/Inuit/Studies. Published in English and French by the Inuksiutiit Kataimajiit Association, Quebec City, 1977–

Finnegan, Ruth. *Oral Poetry: Its Nature, Significance and Social Context*. Cambridge: Cambridge University Press 1977

Flaherty, Martha. 'I Fought to Keep My Hair.' *Nunavut* 5, 6 (June 1986) 4–6

Forbush, William Byron. *Pomiuk: A Waif of Labrador*. Boston: The Pilgrim Press n.d.

Freeman, Milton, ed. *Report of the Inuit Land Use and Occupancy Project*. Ottawa: Department of Indian and Northern Affairs 1976

Freeman, Minnie Aodla. *Life among the Qallunaat*. Edmonton: Hurtig Publishers 1978

– 'Living in Two Hells.' *Inuit Today*, 8 (October 1980) 1976

French, Alice. *My Name Is Masak*. Winnipeg: Peguis Publishers 1976

Freuchen, Dagmar, ed. *Peter Freuchen's Book of the Eskimos*. Cleveland and New York: The World Publishing Co. 1961

Gedalof, Robin. *Paper Stays Put: A Collection of Inuit Writing*. Edmonton: Hurtig Publishers 1980

– *An Annotated Bibliography of Canadian Inuit Literature.* Ottawa: Indian and Northern Affairs Canada 1979
Gilberg, Rolf. 'Uisâkavsak, "The Big Liar."' *Folk*, 11–12 (1969/70) 83–95
Gosling, W.G. *Labrador: Its Discovery, Exploration, and Development.* London: Alston Rivers 1910
Goudie, Elizabeth. *Woman of Labrador.* Edited by David Zimmerly. Toronto: pma Books 1973
Grenfell, Wilfred T. et al. *Labrador: The Country and the People.* New York: Macmillan 1909
Hall, Charles Francis. *Life with the Esquimaux.* Edmonton: M.G. Hurtig 1970
Handbook of North American Indians. Edited by W.C. Sturtevant et al. Washington: Smithsonian Institution 1978– . Vol. 5: *Arctic.* Edited by David Damas. 1984
Hantzsch, Bernhard. *My Life Among the Eskimos: The Baffinland Journals of Bernhard Adolph Hantzsch, 1909–1911.* Translated and edited by L.H. Neatby. Saskatoon: University of Saskatchewan 1977
Harper, Kenn. *Give Me My Father's Body.* Frobisher Bay: Blacklead Books 1986
– 'The Moravian Mission at Cumberland Sound.' *The Beaver* 312:1 (summer 1981) 43–7
– 'Writing in Inuktitut: An Historical Perspective.' *Inuktitut*, 53 (September 1983) 3–35
Hawkes, E.W. *The Labrador Eskimo.* Geological Survey. Canadian Memoir 91, Anthropological Series no. 14. Ottawa: Government Printing Bureau 1916
Hendrik, Hans. *Memoirs of Hans Hendrik, the Arctic Traveller, Serving under Kane, Hayes, Hall and Nares, 1853–1876.* Translated by H. Rink and edited by George Stephens. London 1878
Hiller, J.K. 'The Moravians in Labrador.' *The Polar Record*, 15, 99 (1971) 839–54
'History of a Case of Cannibalism in Baffin Island.' *Eskimo*, 78 (summer 1968) 9–18
Houston, James. *Songs of the Dream People.* Don Mills: Longman 1972
Hutton, S.K. *Among the Eskimos of Labrador.* London: Seeley Service 1912
Les Inuit dissidents. Povungnituk: Inuit Tungavingat Nunamini n.d.

Inuit Today. Begun as *Inuit Monthly.* Published in English and syllabics by the Inuit Tapirisat. 1971–83

'Inuit Who Aided Explorers.' *Nunatsiaq News,* 27 July, 17 and 24 August 1984

Inuktitut. Formerly *Inuttituut.* Periodical published quarterly in English, French, and syllabics by Indian and Northern Affairs Canada. 1959–

Ipellie, Alootook. 'Frobisher Bay Childhood.' *The Beaver,* 310.4 (spring 1980) 4, 6, 8

– 'Damn Those Invaders.' *Inuit Today,* v, 10 (October 1976) 36–41

Irqugaqtuq, Bernard. 'The Song of the Aircraft.' *Eskimo,* 6 (fall/winter 1974) 11–12

Jannasch, Hans Windekilde. 'Reunion with Mikak.' *Canadian Geographical Journal,* lvii (1958) 84–5

Jenness, Diamond. See Canadian Arctic Expedition, *Report*

Kalleo, William. 'The Known Mystery of Seals.' *Inuktitut,* 50 (May 1982) 70

Kalluak, Mark, ed. *How Kabloonat Became and Other Inuit Legends.* Yellowknife: Program Development Division, Government of the Northwest Territories 1974

Keewatin Echo. Periodical published in English and syllabics by Adult Education, Churchill, Man.; later moved to Eskimo Point and edited by Mark Kalluak. 1968–75

Klutschak, Heinrich. *Overland to Starvation Cove: With the Inuit in Search of Franklin 1878–1880.* Translated and edited by William Barr. Toronto: University of Toronto Press 1987

Kohlmeister, Benjamin, and George Kmoch. *Journal of a Voyage from Okkak, on the Coast of Labrador, to Ungava Bay, Westward of Cape Chudleigh.* London: W.M. McDowall 1814

Kroeber, A.L. 'Animal Tales of the Eskimo.' *Journal of American Folk-Lore,* 12, 44 (1899) 17–23

– 'Tales of the Smith Sound Eskimo.' *Journal of American Folk-Lore,* 12, 46 (1899) 166–82

Lauritzen, Philip. *Oil and Amulets Inuit: A People United at the Top of the World.* St John's: Breakwater Books 1983

Leechman, Peter. *Eskimo Summer.* Toronto: Museum Press 1950

Lewis, Richard, ed. *I Breathe a New Song: Poems of the Eskimo.* New York: Simon and Schuster 1971

Loomis, Chauncey C. *Weird and Tragic Shores: The Story of Charles Francis Hall, Explorer.* New York: Knopf 1971

Lopez, Barry. *Arctic Dreams*. New York: Charles Scribner's Sons 1986

Loskiel, George Henry. *History of the Mission of the United Brethren among the Indians in North America*. Translated by Christian Ignatius La Trobe. London: Brethren's Society for Furtherance of the Gospel 1794

Lowenstein, Tom. *Eskimo Poems from Canada and Greenland, from Material Originally Collected by Knud Rasmussen*. London: Anchor Press 1973

Lubbock, Basil. *The Arctic Whalers*. Glasgow: Brown, Son and Ferguson 1937

McDonald, Alexander. *A Narrative of some Passages in the History of Eenoolooapik, a Young Esquimaux*. Edinburgh: Fraser and Co. and J. Hogg 1841

MacGahan, J.A. *Under the Northern Lights*. London: Sampson, Low Marstone, Searle and Rivington 1876

McGrath, Robin. *Canadian Inuit Literature: The Development of a Tradition*. Ottawa: National Museum of Man, Mercury Series 1984

Markoosie. *Harpoon of the Hunter*. Montreal: McGill-Queen's University Press 1970

– 'Wings of Mercy.' *Inuttituut*, (summer 1972) 29–38; (autumn 1972) 19–22; (winter 1972) 32–6; (spring 1973) 34–8; (autumn 1973) 33–6

Mary-Rousselière, Guy, ed. *Beyond the High Hills: A Book of Eskimo Poems*. Cleveland: World Publishers 1961

– 'Gone Leaving No Forwarding Address, the Tununerusirmiut.' *Eskimo*, 24 (fall/winter 1982–3) 3–15

– *Qitdlarssuaq – l'histoire d'un migration polaire*. Montréal: Les Presses de l'université de Montréal 1980

– 'Yvonne Writes to Her Son.' *Eskimo*, 20 (March 1951) 6

Meech, Susan Billings, comp. *A Supplement to the Descendants of Peter Spicer*. Groton, Conn. 1923

Metayer, Maurice, ed. *Tales from the Igloo*. Edmonton: Hurtig Publishers 1972

Metcalfe, Sam. 'Wooding.' *Inuktitut*, 56 (summer 1984) 44–8

Missions in Labrador from Their Commencement to the Present Time. Dublin: Religious Tract and Book Society for Ireland 1831

The Moravians in Labrador. Edinburgh: William Oliphant and Son 1835

Murray, T.B. *Kalli, the Esquimaux Christian: A Memoir*. 2nd ed. London: Society for Promoting Christian Knowledge n.d.

Nansen Fridtjof. *Farthest North*. New York: Harper & Brothers 1898

Naumealuk, Jimmy Patsauq. 'Wondering in Silence.' *Inukshuk*, 16 (22 May 1974) 11

'Naya Pelagy Writes ...' *Eskimo*, 24 (March 1952) 13–15

Neatby, Leslie H. 'Hantzsch of Baffin Island.' *The Beaver*, 306:3 (winter 1975) 5–13

− 'Joe and Hannah.' *The Beaver*, 290 (autumn 1959) 16–21

North/Nord. Begun as *Northern Affairs Bulletin*. Published in English and French by Indian and Northern Affairs Canada. 1954–85

Nuligak. *I, Nuligak*. Edited and translated by Maurice Metayer. Markham: Peter Martin Associates 1966

Nungak, Zebedee. 'Equality before the Honey Bucket.' *Taqralik* (October 1983) 6–7

− and Eugene Arima. *Eskimo Stories from Povungnituk, Quebec*. National Museums of Canada, Bulletin 235, Anthropological Series 90. Ottawa 1969

O'Connel, Sheldon. 'Music of the Inuit.' *The Beaver*, 310.2 (autumn 1979) 12–15

Okpik, Abe. 'What Does It Mean to Be an Eskimo.' *North*, ix, 2 (March/April 1962) 26–8

'Origin of the Sadlermiut.' From 'Three Iglulik Legends.' *Eskimo*, 38 (December 1975) 22–4

Our Footprints Are Everywhere. Nain: Labrador Inuit Association 1977

Panipakuttuk, Joe. 'The Reminiscences of Joe Panipakuttuk.' *North*, xvi (January/February 1969) 10–17

Patterson, Palmer. *Inuit Peoples of Canada*. Toronto: Grolier 1982

Periodical Accounts Relating to the Foreign Missions of the Church of the United Brethren, Established among the Heathen. London: vol. ii: 1797, vol. iv: 1806, vol. v: 1811, vol. ix: 1823; 2nd century, vol. ii: 1893

Peterson, Robert. 'The Last Eskimo Immigration into Greenland.' *Folk*, 4 (1962) 95–110

Pitseolak. *Pitseolak: Pictures out of My Life*. Edited by Dorothy Eber. Montreal 1971

Pitseolak, Peter. *People from Our Side: A Life Story with Photographs by Peter Pitseolak and Oral Biography by Dorothy Eber*. Edmonton: Hurtig Publishers 1975

− *Peter Pitseolak's Escape from Death*. Edited by Dorothy Eber. Toronto: McClelland and Stewart 1977

Rasmussen, Knud. *Across Arctic America: Narrative of the Fifth*

Thule Expedition from Melville Bay to Cape Morris Jesup. London and New York: G.P. Putnam's Sons 1927
- *The People of the Polar North.* Philadelphia: J.B. Lippincott Company 1908
- *Report of the Fifth Thule Expedition, 1921–24.* Copenhagen: Gyldendalske Boghandel, Nordisk Forlag 1929–42
  Volumes consulted were:
  VII, 1 *Intellectual Culture of the Iglulik Eskimos.* 1929
  VII, 2–3 *Intellectual Culture of the Caribou Eskimos.* 1930
  VIII, 1–2 *Intellectual Culture of the Netsilik Eskimos.* 1931
  IX *Intellectual Culture of the Copper Eskimos.* 1932
  X, 1–2 *The Mackenzie Eskimos.* Edited by H. Osterman after Knud Rasmussen's posthumous notes. 1942
Recollections of Inuit Elders, Inuit Autobiography Series, 2 (January 1986). Eskimo Point, NWT: Inuit Cultural Institute 1986
'The Revenge of the Orphan Boy.' Translated by Leah Idlout d'Argencourt. *North,* 14, 4 (July/August 1976) 57–8
Rich, Edwin Gile. *Hans the Eskimo.* Boston: Houghton Mifflin Co. 1934
Rink, Heinrich Johannes. *Tales and Traditions of the Eskimo.* Edinburgh: William Blackwood and Sons 1875
Roberts, Helen H., and Diamond Jenness. *Songs of the Copper Eskimo. See* Canadian Arctic Expedition, *Report*
Ross, W. Gillies. *Arctic Whalers, Icy Seas.* Toronto: Irwin Publishing 1985
Rowley, Graham. 'Bernard Hantzsch: The Probable Cause of His Death in Baffin Island in 1911.' *Polar Record,* 18 (September 1977) 593–6
Rowley, Susan. 'Population Movements in the Canadian Arctic.' *Études/Inuit/Studies,* 9 (1985) 3–21
Saladin d'Anglure, Bernard. *La Parole changée en pierre. Vie et oeuvre de Davidialuk Alasuaq, artiste Inuit du Québec Arctique.* Québec: Gouvernement du Québec 1978
Schulte, Father Paul. *The Flying Priest over the Arctic.* New York: Harper and Brothers n.d.
Scott Polar Research Institute, Cambridge, Eng. MS 1202/1–5 #3. Joseph Ebierbing's Book (mfm reel 58)
Smiler, Isa. 'Inukjuak.' *Inuktitut* (summer/fall 1977) 45–92
Smith, D. Murray. *Arctic Expeditions from British and Foreign Shores from the Earliest Times to the Expedition of 1875–76.* Southampton: Charles H. Calvert 1877

298

Stefansson, Vilhjalmur. *Hunters of the Great North*. London: G.G. Harrap 1923

– *The Friendly Arctic: The Story of Five Years in Polar Regions*. New York: Macmillan 1921

– *My Life with the Eskimo*. New York: Collier Books 1962

Stories from Pangnirtung. Edmonton: Hurtig Publishers 1976

'Susie Tiktalik – From Her Life Story.' Translated by David Kaglik. *Inuvialiut*, 6, 3 (spring 1982) 15–17

Tagoona, Armand. *Shadows*. Ottawa: Oberon Press 1975

– 'Thoughts of Armand Tagoona.' *Inuktitut* (winter 1978) 46–56

Taylor, J. Garth. 'An Eskimo Abroad, 1880: His Diary and Death.' *Canadian Geographic*, 101, 5 (October/November 1981) 38–43

– 'The Two Worlds of Mikak, Part I.' *The Beaver*, 314:3 (winter 1983) 4–13; Part II. *The Beaver*, 314:4 (spring 1984) 18–25

Them Days. Published in English and some Roman orthography syllabics by the Labrador Heritage Society and the Old Timers' League, 1975–

'Thomas Umaok, Reverend.' *The Arctic News*, 6–60 (June 1960) 4–13

Turner, Gordon P. 'The Breath of Arctic Men: The Eskimo North in Poetry from Within and Without.' *Queen's Quarterly*, 83 (spring 1976) 13–35

Unknown Ungava: The Home of the Heathen Esquimaux. London: Colonial and Continental Church Society n.d.

Utatnaq, Alexis Pamiuq. 'Blood Thirsty Enemies.' *Keewatin Echo*, 71 (1974) 8

Wallace, Mene. 'Why Arctic Explorer Peary's Neglected Eskimo Boy Wants to Shoot Him.' *San Francisco Examiner* (magazine supplement) 9 May 1909

Wallaschuk, Richard. *Primitive Music*. London: Longmans Green and Co. 1893

Whittaker, Charles Edward. *Arctic Eskimo; A Record of Fifty Years' Experience and Observation among the Eskimo*. London: Seeley, Service 1937

Wiebe, Rudy. 'Songs of the Canadian Eskimo.' *Canadian Literature* 52 (spring 1972) 57–69

'Willie Thrasher Tells about His Music.' *Inuit Today*, 5, 1 (January 1976) 28–33

Zavatti, Silvio. 'La Poesia degli Eschimesi.' *Nuova Antologia*, 489 (September 1962) 99–106

Acknowledgments

I am indebted to many people and institutions for their assistance in the preparation of this book. I am grateful to The Gladys and Merrill Muttart Foundation which provided a research grant. Although I can mention only a few here, many librarians and libraries were helpful to me: in England, especially the Moravian Archives, London, and the Scott Polar Research Institute, Cambridge; in Canada, the Eskimo Museum, Churchill; the Inuit Cultural Institute, Eskimo Point; the Eastern Arctic Teacher Training Program Library, Iqaluit; the Anglican Church of Canada Archives, Toronto; and the Archives Deschâtelets, Ottawa; and in the United States, the New London County Historical Society, New London, Connecticut; and the Dartmouth College Library, Hanover, New Hampshire.

I also owe a debt of gratitude to a number of people whose unfailing support has sustained me, particularly Dr Robin McGrath and Mr David Webster, formerly of Indian Affairs, who has seen me through many a crisis. I should also like to thank my patient editor, Mary McDougall Maude, as well as Gerry Hallowell of the University of Toronto Press, who has believed in me through the years. And I pay special tribute to all the Inuit who gave me their time and permission to use their work.

Grateful acknowledgment is extended to the following for permission to use material quoted. Every reasonable precaution has been taken to trace the owners of copyright material and to make due acknowledgment; any error or omission will be rectified gladly in future editions. Printed sources are cited in brief in the text with full citations given in the bibliography; archival sources are cited in full in the text. Text pages on which quoted material appears are given here within parentheses.

Eskimo and the Diocese of Churchill–Hudson Bay, Churchill: permission to reprint 'Origin of the Sadlermiut' (12–14); 'The Crow and the Two Eider Ducks' (20–1); 'Sister Pélagy's Letter' (132–3); 'Madeleine's Letter of Request' (134); 'Atuat's Grim Tale of Cannibalism' (141–7); Bernard Inqugaqtuq, 'The Song of the Aircraft' (163–4)

'Origin of the Sun and the Moon' (14–16): reprinted by permission of *Etudes/Inuit/Studies*

North/Nord and the Minister of Supply and Services Canada: permission to reproduce 'Revenge of the Orphan Boy' (17–19); 'John Ayaruaq's Autobiography' (138–9); Luke Issaluk, 'I See Your Face' (148); Joe Panipakuttuk, 'The Historic Voyage of the St. Roch' (155–62)

Itireitok, 'A Sea Chant' (36): reprinted by permission of Raymond de Coccola and Paul King

Canadian Museum of Civilization, Ottawa: permission to reprint Uloqsak and Ikpakhuaq, 'The Origin of the Clouds' (33); 'An Incantation for Good Weather' (40–1); 'The Joy of the Dance' (41); 'Ohnainewk's Diary' (130)

'Mother and Child' (38–9): reprinted by permission of Edmund Carpenter

Evelyn Stefansson Nef: permission to reprint 'The People of the Cariboo Antler' (40); 'Tannaumirk's Reactions to Stefansson, 1910' (92)

'A Healing Chant' (48): reprinted by kind permission of the Intercontinental Church Society, formerly known as Colonial and Continental Church Society

Rose Pamack's translations of 'Tikisiak' (49) and 'Winter's Exodus' (50): by permission of translator

'Creation' (51): reprinted by permission of James Houston

Hurtig Publishers, Edmonton: permission to reprint material from C.F. Hall, *Life with the Esquimaux* (67, 68)

New London County Historical Society, New London, Connecticut: permission to quote material from their collection relating to Ipirvik and Taqulittuq (68, 69–70, 71–2)

'Uisakassak's Impressions of New York, 1898' (79): reprinted by permission of Rolf Gilberg, National Museum of Denmark

'Ada Blackjack Johnson's Diary' (93–9): reprinted by permission of Dartmouth College Library, Hanover, New Hampshire

'Abraham's Diary' (109–10): reprinted by permission of J. Garth Taylor

'Lydia Campbell's Autobiography' (112–15): by permission of Them Days Archive, Happy Valley–Goose Bay, Labrador

'Opartok's Diary' (127–30): by permission of the Archives Deschâtelets, Ottawa

Thomas Umaok, 'Interview' (134–7): reprinted by permission of *Arctic News* and the Anglican Church of Canada, Diocese of the Arctic

Victor Allen, 'The Snow Goose and the Mosquito – A Question of Development' (137–8): reproduced by permission of the author and the Minister of Supply and Services Canada

Abe Okpik, 'What Does It Mean to Be an Eskimo' (140–1): reproduced by permission of the author and the Minister of Supply and Services Canada

The Minister of Supply and Services Canada: permission to reproduce Markoosie, 'Wings of Mercy' (148–55); Jimmy Patsauq Naumealuk, 'Wondering in Silence' (164); Dorothy, 'Old Woman's Song' (165); Isa Smiler, 'Inukjuak' (171–6); Eric Anoee, 'My Writings' (176–80); 'Thoughts of Armand Tagoona' (211–16); Mark Kalluak, 'I Want to Learn Syllabics' (260)

Alexis Pamiuq Utatnaq, 'Blood Thirsty Enemies' (165–6): reprinted by permission of the author

Dorothy Harley Eber: for permission to reprint Peter Pitseolak, 'The Sinking of the Nascopie' (166–70); 'Pitseolak Ashoona's Courtship and Marriage' (254–5)

Inuit Today and the Inuit Tapirisat of Canada: for permission to reprint Kowmageak Arnakalak, 'Northern Lights' (171); Willie Thrasher, 'Our Land' (203); John Amagoalik, 'Will the Inuit Disappear from the Face of this Earth' (209–11); Leah Idlout d'Argencourt, 'C.D. Howe' (225–35); Minnie Aodla Freeman, 'Living in Two Hells' (235–43)

Paulosie Kasudluak, 'Nothing Marvellous' (180–2): reprinted by permission of the Winnipeg Art Gallery

Bessie Andreason, 'No Way Out' (189–98): reprinted by permission of Elsie Nuttall, Tuktoyaktuk

Alice French, 'My Name is Masak' (203–9): reprinted by permission of Peguis Publishers

303

Joshua Obed, 'The Spanish Flu, 1918' (223–5): reprinted by permission of the Labrador Inuit Association

Alootook Ipellie, 'Frobisher Bay Childhood' (243–8); 'Damn Those Invaders' (248–52): reprinted by permission of the author

Tumasi Quissa, 'Come to Our Place Since You Got a Seal' (253): reprinted by permission of the author

William Kalleo, 'The Known Mystery of Seals' (253–4): reproduced by permission of the author and the Minister of Supply and Services Canada

Zebedee Nungak, 'Equality before the Honey Bucket' (258–60): reprinted by permission of the author

Samuel Metcalfe, 'Wooding' (260–3): reprinted by permission of the author and Indian and Northern Affairs Canada

John Amagoalik, 'Amagoalik's Closing Remarks, 1984' (263–4): by permission of the author

Mary Simon, 'The Role of the Inuit in International Affairs' (265–72): by permission of the author

Mary Carpenter Lyons, 'Nunavut? – Denendeh? = Northwesterritories' (273): by permission of the author

Martha Flaherty, 'I Fought to Keep My Hair' (274–8): reprinted by permission of the author

Peter Ernerk, 'The Inuit as Hunters and Managers' (281–3): reprinted by permission of the author

Angus Anderson, 'The Tree' (283–4): by permission of the author

Liz Semigok, 'My Little House' (284–5); 'My Cooking Pot' (285): by permission of the author

I also would like to acknowledge my debt to others who drew material to my attention. Tim Borlase, program co-ordinator, Labrador East Integrated School Board, sent me 'Tikisiak' (49–50). Chauncey Loomis drew my attention to the official testimony given by Ipirvik and Takulittuq to the u.s. government. Miss Judy McGrath sent me a typescript of 'Lydia's Campbell's Diary' (112–15). Dr Robin McGrath provided me with Felix Nuyaviak, 'Mangilaluk Adrift on the Ice' (183–9) and Bessie Andreason, 'No Way Out' (189–98). David Webster, Indian and Northern Affairs Canada, sent me the typescript of the Federal Provincial Conference of First Ministers on Aboriginal Constitutional Matters, 8–9 March 1984 (263–4).

Picture credits

Attuiock: from *Etudes/Inuit/Studies*, originally published in A.M. Lysaght, *Joseph Banks in Newfoundland and Labrador* (1766; London 1971)

Orpingalik: from Knud Rasmussen, *Intellectual Culture of the Netsilik Eskimos* (Copenhagen 1931)

Minik Wallace: from Kenn Harper, *Give Me My Father's Body* (Frobisher Bay 1986)

Inuktitut: **Erik Anoee conducting a Bible class, Learning to write, Rose Pamack, Armand Tagoona, Leah Idlout d'Argencourt, Martha Flaherty, Zebedee Nungak**

Ipirvik: from a photograph by G.W. Pach, published in C.F. Hall, *Narrative of the Second Arctic Expedition ...*, ed. J.E. Nourse (Washington 1879)

Taqulittuq: from a photograph by T.W. Smillie, Scott Polar Research Institute, Cambridge

Inuluapik: from Alexander McDonald, *A Narrative of Some Passages in the History of EEnoolooapik, a Young Esquimaux* (Edinburgh 1841)

Mikak: after a portrait by John Russell, 1769, reproduced in *The Beaver*

Kallihirua: from Scott Polar Research Institute, Cambridge

Hans Hendrik and family: on the Nares expedition, 1875–76, Northwest Territories Archives, N82-002:0008

Ada Blackjack Johnson: from Datmouth College Library, Hanover, New Hampshire

Shoo-Fly: Photo by A.P. Low, National Archives of Canada PA 53548

Aua: from Comer collection, Mystic Seaport Museum, cat. no. 63.1767.179

Abraham's household: from a lithograph by W.A. Meyn, published in *Canadian Geographic*, October/November 1981

Dorothy Harley Eber: **Pitseolak Ashoona, Peter Pitseolak**

Nortext: **Eric Anoee** photo by Wm Belsey, **Mark Kalluak, Sam Metcalfe,**

Index

(Titles of excerpts appear in bold-face type.)

310